SMALL TOWN SKATEPARKS

CLINT CARRICK

headpress

A HEADPRESS BOOK
First published by Headpress, Oxford, UK, in 2021
headoffice@headpress.com

SMALL TOWN SKATEPARKS

ISBN   978-1-909394-77-3 (paperback)
ISBN   978-1-909394-78-0 (ebook)
NO-ISBN (hardback)

HEADPRESS. POP AND UNPOP CULTURE.

Exclusive NO-ISBN special edition hardbacks and other
items of interest are available at HEADPRESS.COM

headpress

Contents

Spencer, WV

SOMEWHERE IN CENTRAL WEST VIRGINIA. THE MIDDAY SKY IS grim, and the road within this tunnel of dense Appalachian forest is darker still, an unnatural dimness through which my car squeaks and scatters packs of dead leaves. This is the part of the state that fits the impression I had already formed of it: lonely trailers and lawns covered in tires, trash, chickens, and chained-up dogs; steep mountainsides trailing drifts of mist; a bearded bald man walking shirtless down the side of the road, his hairy belly protruding before him; sturdy wooden TRUMP signs on every other lawn. These sights make me happy, for I had almost felt cheated by the hipsters and breweries in Morgantown.

New Englander on beyond-the-pale safari in Trump country, opioid country, a foreign country where people speak with a not-quite southern accent: this is how I feel driving from the interstate to Spencer, and I am self-conscious of the green plates attached to my car as I roll into town looking for the skatepark. For despite feeling foreign in my own country, like a gaijin on the streets of Osaka, I know the skatepark can offer a sense of the familiar and of belonging. No matter where you are, if you're a skateboarder the skatepark is home. You know the rules and you know how to act, and you know the people despite never having met them. So a shy Vermont boy can wander into an impoverished town in the hills of West Virginia and feel like he is about to meet his friends.

The skatepark isn't on Google Maps, so I stop at a gas station for directions. The clerk knows about the park but doesn't know where it is. I follow up with a young man putting gas into his truck.

"The skatepark?" he asks. He is surprised and nervous. He has large, tattooed arms and small eyes set deeply in his skull. His wife and a child bend their heads out of a window, curious about the stranger with an accent.

"Yeah."

He rubs his face and gives me a confusing series of turns to make. I thank him, he responds politely, and we leave in separate directions.

The roads in Spencer are narrow and steep, like paved paths derived from foot trails, and I quickly become lost amid the closely-built houses of peeling paint. As I'm turning around in a church parking lot, I see two boys walking together. One of them is carrying a longboard. I yell through the window.

"Hey, where's the skatepark?"

"The skatepark?"

"Yeah!"

"It's on Fifth Street!"

"Fifth street?"

"Yeah. Cross that bridge and go back that way."

"Thanks!"

I drive off, over the bridge and into a residential neighborhood. If they hadn't told me I would never have driven so far in this direction. Many of the porches are occupied by groups of young people smoking cigarettes and drinking from cans. They stare as I drive by. But sure enough I soon come to a playground, a basketball court, and a small, fenced-in skatepark. There's a family in the playground and an old woman with bushy white hair passed out on a picnic table beneath an awning. She lays spread-eagled with her arms hanging off the sides. I park my car, put on my skate shoes, change shirts, and walk across the grass to the gate in the chainlink fence.

"Hey, whatchya' doing!?" the boy on the playground yells as I pass.

2

"Jeremy!" his mom says. The belly in her tanktop hangs over the front of her jean shorts. "This ain't your park! Leave 'em alone! Sorry about him," she says, turning to me.

"Don't worry about it."

The skatepark in Spencer, West Virginia is comprised of two quarterpipes facing out from the back, two boxes, and a medley of small rails. That's it. Everything is worn, including the cratered pavement, formerly a basketball court. The conditions suggest years of weather and neglect, but also of love, for it is clear from the grinded paint on the rails and the lanes of faded Skatelite on the quarterpipes that the park receives heavy use.

I see the small, dilapidated park, and I smile. I'm filled with the excitement of the butterfly hunter who glimpses a rare breed high in an alpine meadow, or, more accurately, *the* breed he has been pursuing since the time he saw its colors as a child. This skatepark reminds me of the one in which I grew up. It reminds me of the place where I learned to skateboard and spent my childhood and adolescence, where I created the strongest friendships of my life, where I passed entire afternoons and evenings with my best friends, day after day during each infinite summer of my youth. This skatepark seems to be the one I remember but have since lost and traveled some thousand miles to find again.

Nostalgia is pathetic. It infects and spreads once it takes root so that its victim dwells more and more upon the symptoms. This is a book about nostalgia. It is about memory, and trying to recapture what one should never recapture, and cannot—their childhood. Or, perhaps, this is a book about moving forward.

What is the relationship a man should have with his past?

There is movement above in the contoured darkness. Rain begins to land on my bare arms.

I run forwards dragging my board beneath me and jump on after four quick steps. I push twice and head for the quarterpipe. The ground beneath isn't wood or metal but something synthetic made for skateboarding. It is warped and rotten and the gaps between its segments jar and snap. I axle-stall the coping, drop back in, and head for one of the boxes. I ollie, thinking about landing on my back two wheels and manualing across its surface, but in so doing I lower them more than I should and they catch on the box's edge. I'm tossed, contort in the air and land on the end of the box with my shoulder and hip, bounce, and clatter onto the pavement another foot below.

Ow.

Fuck.

I remember something: I'm not actually good at skateboarding. I never was, and I haven't skated in five years, either.

I get to my feet. Walk a few paces. The rain is now steady, and the drops drumming the pavement are starting to stay.

"Hey, Mister!" the kid yells from the playground. "It's *raining!*"

"Jeremy, shut up!"

I wave.

I try the line again, but this time I'm thinking about the ramp being slippery and I don't land the axle-stall. The dial turns, the rain increases to a downpour. The family gathers their things and runs to their car. I skate to the gate and walk to an awning on the other side of the chainlink fence. I watch the depressions in the park's pavement turn to puddles. I hope that the storm might pass. It doesn't, and as I stand under the little pavilion the din of the rain becomes louder and louder until there is a full-blown deluge exploding on the roof and everything around me, and I know that I'm not going to be able to skate Spencer's park anytime soon.

I finally find the skatepark I'd been looking for, and God decides to not let me skate there. It's like Indiana Jones outrunning the rolling boulders only to discover the little gold idol is locked behind a chainlink fence.

I'll have to find my skatepark further down the road.

I become soaked in the short run from the pavilion to my car. As I back up and pull away from the Spencer skatepark, the old woman with the bushy white hair is still passed out on top of the picnic table, arms and legs sprawled to the sides just as they had been when I arrived.

SMALL TOWN SKATEPARKS are where American children go to escape their families. They go to be with their friends, to be away from parents and teachers, to joke, to lean and loaf, to daydream, to indulge in being themselves, and yes, sometimes to skateboard. In this sense the skatepark is similar to the country club, where people also use sport as an excuse to flee their homes, where golf banter fills gaps between frank discussions concerning gossip, politics, and sex.

Unlike the country club, the small town skatepark is free and open to the public. Anyone who wants can skate there, and if the park is small enough not to have a fence and a gate that locks, they can visit whenever they please. The availability and typically central location—often next to schools and other downtown rec facilities like baseball fields and basketball courts—make it a natural place for young friends that lack money and their own space to congregate. So certain children in every small town drift to the skatepark on empty summer days to sunbathe in patches of dirt and slowly sip lukewarm jugs of fountain soda, the waxy paper of the cups becoming soggy over the course of an afternoon.

Though the skatepark is in the center of town, it is clearly separated from the neighboring municipal parks within the minds of the townspeople, and so are the people who go there. Kids who 'hang out at the skatepark' are very different from the kids who go downtown to play tennis or soccer (these are small towns, places where people are slotted into cliques and viewed with opinions fixed by community consensus). The skatepark is seen as undesirable by the parents of other children because it's associated with idleness and a lack of adult supervision, deviance and drug use. For the skateboarders themselves, however, the sense of taboo linked to their hangout is a source of pride and identification: by going to the skatepark they become a little dangerous, and they are not at all like the other kids in town.

The small town skatepark, in contrast to the nicer, more crowded skateparks one finds in larger towns, is marked by possessiveness—the skate rat kids who sit around on its ramps and rails feel that the park is their home and that by belonging to the park the park belongs to them. Thus, when an unknown person shows up, gets out of his rusty Saab with green plates and pushes himself onto the cracked pavement, pops an ollie and says hello, the skate rat kids pause in their conversation and glare with the eyes of silent old men sitting on Main Street in any small town in America.

The skate rat kids guard the skatepark as their clubhouse, and they also guard its stories. Ten-year-olds who can't yet ollie play the Meisters of Westeros: they alone preserve the memory of feats accomplished by former generations, of myths and legends that have been otherwise forgotten. The oral histories are passed down so many times it becomes impossible to know if these distant events actually occurred or are just fairy tales beginning with "It has been told…" Eventually, even the names of the heroes and villains disappear, and the characters become anonymous skateboarders from a long time ago. Then, only the skatepark remains as witness to their lives, and the long days in which children become adults are preserved only in the splintered wood and rusted iron of a quarter-pipe, preserved until the skatepark, too, is lost in the wash of time.

The skatepark is, for many, where adolescence transpires. It is where children bump up against one another and learn the rules and tricks of dealing with other humans. It is where they discover their first tribe and identify with a community, where their ideas are shaped and their values formed. It is the site of first friendships, first love, first heartbreak, first inquiry, and first existential examination. It is the lens through which young people view the universe, forever coloring the exploding shapes they see at the other end of the telescope.

WHILE MY FRIEND was traveling in Chile, a small town local told her: "Before you leave, you have to see the skatepark. Then you will know who I am." Likewise, to understand me you simply need to understand the skatepark where I was made. Therefore, imagine: an empty parking lot on top of a hill, a small town in northern Vermont. The parking lot serves an ice rink built in the 1960s. In the summer the rink is closed, and the building sits quietly with dark windows and discolored iron walls. When the sun begins to set, the whole structure glows in orange or pink light, and soon after, if there are no clouds, the moon rises above its front entrance as if bursting forth from the roof. Surrounding the vast parking lot of worn pavement and puddle-filled potholes and snaking cracks are a steep forested slope, rising like a wall, and a swamp that stretches flat to a distant road. In the corner of the parking lot between the hill and the swamp, across the empty space from the locked front door of the ice rink, there is a square of newer pavement that contrasts with the adjacent lake of gray and brown.

This smaller patch of pavement was laid down in 1999 when I was in the third grade. Then, when the tar was black and perfectly smooth, a group of townspeople came together and built a quarterpipe, a bank ramp, and a half-pyramid box. My father was one of the volunteers. He knew nothing about skateboarding or skateparks, but he was a carpenter with a hammer and a toolbox, and at the time he was enthusiastic about participating in a project that would help his kids. Later on, though, he became cynical about the whole thing.

The ramps are covered in untreated plywood. The metal coping juts out at the top of the quarterpipe. The transition is not rounded but formed by a series of choppy segments that tick in succession when you go up and down. There is a short ledge on top of the bank ramp covered in angle-iron for grinding though few skaters can ever ollie that high. The bank ramp and quarterpipe are next to each other at the edge of the pavement, above where the land falls away to the swamp, and the three-sided pyramid box is placed in the middle like an island.

That is all: three ramps on a small patch of pavement. Over time, though, as the black of the fresh asphalt turns to ash, and fractures form in its surface, other features appear: a cement curb stolen from the basketball court, a two-legged down rail welded by a roofer, a box, a kicker shaped like a ski jump, another quarterpipe to create symmetry. So, the skatepark evolves and devolves and grows constantly, degrading and decomposing, its components forever shifting in arrangement and position so that the skatepark, like the image within a kaleidoscope, never achieves permanence. The faces within the park, too, continually change. They become older—they thin out, jaws emerge, pimples bubble to the surface of skin; the faces become hairy and gaunt, fat, embittered or apathetic, for apathy is closely linked to insouciance, and insouciance—being carefree—is the foundation of the skatepark experience. As the skatepark's decorative faces bloom and wither, they gradually disappear, though when spring returns, and the kaleidoscope twists again, new shapes emerge, and heretofore unknown faces discover the skatepark, and the skatepark discovers them.

Keene, NH

THE SKATEPARK IN KEENE, NEW HAMPSHIRE IS A CAGE SUR-rounded by unused parking lots. I find it after turning off the re-furbished main street where the refurbishment abruptly stops, the coffee shops and ice cream stands quickly come to an end and the Keene I heard about as a kid quickly reveals itself: grass growing through asphalt, rusty train tracks, oversized BMX ramps dozing like elephants within their chicken-wire pen. It's Labor Day but I'm still wearing white shorts stained brown with splashes of coffee and black shoes stained white with paint from a summer's worth of projects. It's the official end of summer, but it's hot—humid air sits stagnant over frying pan pavement—and I start sweating as soon as I change shoes and take my board out of the Saab's trunk.

Trapped within the cage are a group of Keene State students smoking e-cigarettes in a corner and two young boys bouncing around the park on scooters. The cool skate dudes occupy an iso-lated alley dedicated to an iron-sided box, and the boys are con-tained within a larger area filled with ramps and quarterpipes. The pavement throughout the park is creased with vestigial lines and dents, clues to a previous use for the space no one any longer remembers. A cement manual pad is surrounded by a hexagonal gash that spills anthill sand like blood from a wound, pushed away in double lines by the skate wheels of previous weeks.

I start skating around with the scooter kids. Another young boy arrives on a Spider-Man bike. I haven't skated in five years and the ollies and kickflips feel familiar yet unattainable, like words you can't remember when you're drunk. I roll over the anthills and ollie onto the cement box, but my manual won't lock. I axle-stall the coping on the smallest quarterpipe but my wheels catch before I drop back in. I try to boardslide a down rail but the rail is sticky and my board won't slide over the metal. I like the line, though, and try again, and again, and several more times until I finally approach the rail with purpose. I'm unprepared for the landing and when the rail ends and I drop off in the backseat the board shoots out from beneath me, my feet fly into the air, and I drop with a fat man thud on my ass and elbows.

Ow.

"Are you OK?"

I look up. The young boy has stopped his Spider-Man bicycle and is looking down at me. The sides of his skull are buzzed short, and the hair on top is long and wispy, little-boy blond dyed blue and purple.

"Yeah, I'm fine."

"OK."

I skate away pretending I don't feel my elbows throbbing or notice the blood mixed with pebbles on top of the skin. The only thing more pathetic than a grown man trying to skateboard is a grown man trying to skateboard and failing on the wimpiest, slowest of boardslides.

Who does this old guy think he is?

I try the line again and land it, and can feel the confidence growing. I move to the isolated alley with the box. One guy is trying a noseslide pop-shove it and his friends are leaning against the fence chatting, smoking, and sometimes watching. I begin work on an ollie-manual to backside 50-50 line. I alternate with Noseslide Dude, who is young and overweight but well dressed, in black jeans and a black shirt with gel in his hair. His cologne follows him like the wake from a boat when he jumps on his board. When I finally make the line, ten minutes later, now dripping sweat from nose and chin, the skate dudes don't pause in their conversation, but Noseslide Dude gives his board a little tap against the ground.

I skate for another half hour. The purple hair kid with the Spider-Man bike keeps talking to me. I make the mistake of acknowledging him, and soon whenever I stop to catch my breath he's next to me. When I take my shirt off because of the heat he takes his shirt off too, and bikes through the park with the pale bony frame of an infant. I wonder if the kid doesn't get enough attention at home and so comes to the skatepark.

"Cool bike," I say to him. I'm standing on top of the tall quarterpipe waiting to drop in, and he's stopped on the pavement below, looking up, waiting for me to say something to him.

"No, it's stupid. I don't like it."

"You don't like it? Why not?"

"'Cause Spider-Man is dumb!"

"Then why did you get the Spider-Man bike?"

"I didn't choose it! I got it for my birthday."

"I see. But Spider-Man is cool!"

"No. Why did I have to get the bike with the *good guy*? I don't want the *good guy*... I want something evil. Like Chucky! I wanted to get a Chucky bike!"

"Haha. But don't you think Spider-Man could beat up Chucky?"

"No way! Chucky would kick Spider-Man's ass!"

The kid has a point, I think, and drop back into the skatepark.

WHEN WE WERE younger, we skated in the day when the sun was high and you were lazy on the warm pavement, but only watched in the evening, when the light became orange and shadows stretched towards the ice rink and the older crowd arrived. When they did, we sat in the grass to the side and ran commentary on the spectacle unfolding before us. Though the older skaters didn't know our names, we knew theirs, and we whispered them back and forth as they slammed on ramps or slid down rails, sweating and swearing and slapping hands. They skated differently than we did. In the heat of day, skateboarding meant pointing your board at a feature and making an attempt at a singular trick: pushing gently into the box, popping halfheartedly towards the angle-iron, grabbing your board when it didn't lock in and trying again. For the older crowd, though, skateboarding was a continuous dance in which each flick and pop was linked to the next, in which rail slides prefaced ramp tricks, and the ramp tricks were then only a precursor to flat-ground tricks, and you kept flowing on spontaneous inspiration until you slipped up and your line came to an end. This was real skateboarding. It was about speed, power, grace, creativity, style, aggression, emotion, bravery. We couldn't skate like this, and, were we to skate like we did in the daytime, congregating somewhere in the middle of the park, we would just be getting in the way, for the older skaters only lined up in the far corner and sprung forth from there, sprinting forward and jumping on their boards so that baggy shirts billowed behind them.

For the pre-pubescent, the post-pubescent are godlike, or at least extraterrestrial: they are tall, hairy, and muscular, they are fast and strong, they speak loudly and confidently in tones of pitch and manner unfamiliar to boys. In short, they are cool. For us, the older skaters who arrived in the evenings were celebrities, or, perhaps more accurately, professional athletes, for though we knew little of their lives, we were intimately aware of their habits and capabilities on a skateboard, much as baseball fans can recognize the players of their team merely by the posture of a batting stance.

We each had our favorites. Tommy liked Sam, who was cynical and so technically sound he only tried tricks once or twice before he landed them, at which point, like a pickup artist making a conquest, he never came back. Keith liked Jake, who valued style over all else and preferred to only do things if he could do them perfectly, with control and poise. This ran contrary to my own philosophy of skateboarding.

Brandon was not the best of the evening skaters, nor was he the coolest. He was not the loudest, or the most joyful; his presence within the gaggle of skaters waiting to drop was modest. This may have been why I sympathized with him and idolized him over the others. However, my fondness for Brandon was also related to how his presence changed when he stepped on his board. Brandon always went the biggest. He was reckless in his pursuit of amplitude and speed, showing disdain for dandyish, sloth-like technicality by pounding around the skatepark with his pushing foot far out in front of his nose then far out behind his tail after it propelled him forward, constantly and insatiably—desperately—urging his board to carry him faster and faster, as fast as it could! He was an ollie specialist, and when he popped his tail and jumped into the air his board stuck to his feet as his knees rose to his chest, to his chin; like this he floated over tall orange traffic cones, stacks of skateboards, fluttering strands of yellow tape. When he hit terminal velocity and launched from the quarterpipe to the bank ramp, all those in the park stopped what they were doing to see how high he went, and when he landed, flying over the pavement without a flicker of emotion beneath the flat brim of his cap pulled low over his eyes, the park would be yelling and all skateboards would be slapping against metal coping and asphalt.

Once, in the early days of the skatepark, the older crowd pushed the launch ramp to the pyramid box so that there was an Evel Knievel gap from the kicker over an empty chasm and then the flat of the pyramid to its downward transition. One by one the skaters charged the gap, ollied off the ramp and soared through the air, eyes fixed on their hopeful landing. Sometimes they came up short so that the board's back wheels snagged on the pyramid's deck and its rider was flung to the pavement—steak slamming on a butcher's block—sometimes they stomped the landing with a bang, their four wheels resounding on the plywood of the down ramp before clanging over its metal strip, and everyone would cheer. When everyone had made the gap—or given up—the launch ramp was pushed back. One by one they tried again, and the tension grew.

Soon all but two skaters had become spectators. The ramp had gone so far away from the pyramid that now someone was lying lengthwise between them. Surely, we thought, surely this was too far: staring at the chasm from the jump to the pyramid, and then over the pyramid's deck to its abrupt downward transition, it was impossible to imagine a skateboarder making the transfer. Chris went first. He ran, sprinting and dragging his tail so that it scratched against the pavement, and then hopped on the board as he simultaneously let it drop to its wheels. One frantic push, and he squared to face his fate. His board only stayed under his feet until he reached the apex of his trajectory. Then, either because he lost his nerve or sensed that something was wrong, he kicked his board away and ran his legs in panic through the air, fifteen feet above the ground, twenty feet across its face, desperately trying to stay upright and land feet first on his distant target. When he landed he tumbled like a ninja and then like a log over dirty pavement.

The previous autumn, on a bleak day when all the leaves had already fallen, and branches were bare, and a thick hoody was just enough to keep you warm, my friends and I had walked through an event in the ice rink. The ice hadn't been put in yet, so within the large paved oval between the puck-stained boards were picnic tables filled with tourists. A pimpled magician was searching for the courage to smile and bewilder between the bouncy house and the cotton candy machine. His performance was all the more embarrassing given his outfit and his shame. His name was painted in purple on a piece of cardboard lying in front of him: 'The Great

Brandini.' We laughed for so long after walking back into the dim gray afternoon that the name came to be an inside joke between us. It was only natural for one of us to one day see Brandon the Skateboarder ollie like Michael Jordan would dunk and whisper, under his breath, 'The Great Brandini', not with silliness but with reverence, and the nickname stuck forever after.

The Great Brandini now stood alone in the skatepark's far corner in the crosshairs of the splintered launch ramp. Things became quiet. He stared at the ramp, he looked down so that the brim of his hat hid his face from all those looking at him. There was the sound of wind in leaves and of traffic flowing distantly on Main Street. He bounded forward—three, four, five steps, a sprinter off the starting block, though one in baggy jeans and a T-shirt two sizes too large. He dropped his board, jumped on, pushed once, twice, and crouched low as he charged the ramp, his trucks wobbling from the speed. At the lip of the ramp, he popped, slamming on the tail and jumping, leveling the weightless board beneath his feet where it faithfully remained. When the roar of Brandini's wheels abruptly ceased, and he was flying above the friend lying beneath him, his flight seemed to slow. For he was perfectly still, crouched, his feet wide, knees pointed apart, the excess cotton of his shirts flapping. This was early 2000s style distilled to its essence by a skater who had been raised coddled in its fabric. He floated through the air in an arch, the peak of which was higher than any of us had expected, so that when the Great Brandini paused to levitate we felt we were witnessing a miracle, for the miraculous is that which occurs though no one dreamed it first in their minds. Calmly, at his leisure, Brandini began to sink from his throne in the sky down to the landing waiting for him, where he settled with hardly a murmur from his wheels or a jolt in his relaxed frame.

Years later, when I was back in my hometown with friends from college, I saw Brandon skateboarding down the road. He was using the bike lane like he had always done, pushing with powerful strokes that made him hold pace with cars. My friends didn't pause in their conversation to comment, because, for them, there was nothing remarkable about this man riding a skateboard. For me, though, the sight was something different. For the half-second he skateboarded past I turned my head to follow him. The thread of conversation transpiring in our car left my mind, replaced by some powerful awe and wonder, the power of which I had forgotten, and had forgotten was possible, for I had not experienced it since I was a child. I knew that this was not just a man living in his hometown, skateboarding to the restaurant where he worked. I knew the truth—that this man was far from normal, and that he was capable of magic.

Stockbridge, MA

THERE WERE ONCE FIVE PARALLEL TENNIS COURTS IN STOCK-bridge, Massachusetts. At some point—no one remembers exactly when anymore—the nets came down, the fence was dismantled, the posts removed, and the courts became a skatepark. Blobs of cement were poured at random to create features: a quarterpipe and a spine and a box, a kicker and a roller. The features are scattered haphazardly in one end of the long rectangle of pavement so that there is seemingly no connection between them, and, from afar, the Stockbridge skatepark seems less a place for skateboarding than a site of pagan worship, or perhaps an art installation. This sense is reinforced by the fact that the area of three of the five former tennis courts is still empty, as if the builders ran out of money or patience and said, "This is good enough, don't you think?"

When I pull up, the emptiness is devoid of skater or tennis player. It is the early afternoon in the Berkshires on an early September day. Despite the month, summer lingers, and I think about James Taylor because of the weather and the name of the town. Cars pass above on a state highway, a river of clear water glimmers in sunlight behind a wall of bushes, two soccer nets face each other across a field of overgrown grass without white painted lines. I skate by myself, indulging in the excess pavement to float far away from the ramps and pop small kickflips in the shade of trees. I spend time hitting the box, then the quarterpipe-to-spine combination, but there are jolting cracks connecting the pavement and the cement of the ramps and nothing holds my attention, so soon I lay in the grass of the soccer field and observe the migration of clouds and fall asleep in the warmth of sunlight.

On the way out of town I see a sign for the Norman Rockwell Museum and decide to visit. Inside, I observe homage after homage to the charm of the American small town: boys trespassing to swim in a river, a man repairing a power line, a barber playing the violin in the back of his closed shop. I'm familiar with these scenes, for I grew up in them, in my own small town isolated in the woods of northern New England.

I recognize the scenes, and I resent them. They are self-consciously quaint like a resort town sculpting itself for outsiders on vacation, and 'quaint' is a quality you're definitely not allowed to like. Perhaps I resent these scenes because I identify with them, which is what really bothers me. And perhaps I resent that I have a closeted inner attraction to these scenes I knew as a child and now crave as a dislocated adult. Perhaps I crave wrapping myself in peaceful complacency, to belong to a tribe, to have coffee every morning in a diner and to get my haircut when there's nothing else to do. Perhaps my reaction to Rockwell's paintings is rooted in a small town complex: despite being calibrated in a small town to exist in a small town, I yearn to live in Tokyo, Bangkok, or Paris.

As I take small steps around the original sketches and paintings that have long been familiar, I realize that much of Rockwell's work is centered around childhood. His goal was to capture—or fabricate—a charmed portrayal of small town life. The easiest way to do this was to depict youth, for the innocence of the American small town and the innocence of childhood are in harmony. Whereas life in places like New York is complicated, life in the small town is simple, and young people raised there retain their enthusiasm and joy longer without experiencing disillusionment. So the city corresponds with songs of experience and the town with songs of innocence, with idyllic lives free from pain like those shown in Rockwell's paintings. I come across his series of portraits of smiling children: close-ups on freckled cheeks and gap-toothed grins, pretty girls with red ribbons in their hair, boys with ties beneath sweaters and fuzzy muffs over their ears.

Rockwell was born in New York City but moved to Stockbridge, where he lived and painted for the majority of his life. The small town became his muse. The fact that he was an outsider was perhaps significant. People are sensitive in new surroundings, and Rockwell may have been especially perceptive to the scenes around him in this small Berkshire community. Moreover, Rockwell saw Stockbridge with the eyes of someone raised and educated in Manhattan. His cheerful visions of childhood and small town life were perhaps projections that did not correspond with reality. Of course, then as now, alcoholism existed in small towns, as did sexual abuse. There was poverty and hunger, domestic violence and disease, death and divorce. Children were cold in winter when their families couldn't afford to heat their homes. When I get to the end of the smiling portraits, I learn they there were advertisements made for Crest toothpaste.

I see a canvas of a boy sitting on a log fence. His hunched back is to the viewer. In the background, a train slides through a green valley. I wonder if Rockwell's rosy-eyed vision of the New England small town is similar to my tinted nostalgia for a childhood and adolescence spent at the skatepark. My memories of the summers in which I was either at the skatepark or desperate to get to the skatepark represent a certain ideal—the same ideal Rockwell cashed in on for his magazine covers. I have forgotten any unhappiness or anxiety I felt during those years and only remember long afternoons in sunshine, lazy afternoons of banter, uncounted hours of skateboarding with my best friends. When I was a child at the skatepark... when I was a child at the skatepark, oh, when I was a child at the skatepark!

Surely I have romanticized my past into something perfect it never was? Or, on the contrary (and the thought depresses me)—have I forgotten some of the sweetness? Do I remember less of the milk and honey that filled our waking dreams?

Regardless, I detect in tone and subject matter a strong resonance between Rockwell's paintings and my memories of a younger life at the skatepark. Both consecrate certain aspects of childhood in a small town: resolute friendship, freedom from supervision, life spent outdoors, innocent mischief, puppy love. The only difference between his paintings and my visions are the eighty years separating them, which makes me speculate: if Rockwell was around today, would his paintings be of American children dawdling at the skatepark?

Though his life briefly overlapped with that of skateboarding (he died in 1978), Rockwell never used it as a subject. This is a shame, because the small town skatepark and Norman Rockwell would have made a perfect match. Since he could not, let me produce the tableaux Rockwell would have wished to make:

Four boys sit atop a bank ramp's ledge, all of them wearing jeans and skate shoes. Their legs dangle freely. Two boys wrestle, half-laughing and half-scowling at each other; one is giving the other a titty-twister. The third boy props his elbows on his knees and holds his head up by his cheeks. He watches with disinterested eyes the vague form of a lone skateboarder. The upper half of the fourth boy is indiscernible as he is laying on his back. His forearms are crossed above his head to block the sun from his closed eyes.

Or:

Four boys sit on their skateboards in the grass on the side of the skatepark. Their shirts and the legs of their jeans are covered in dirt and spots of blood. Their shaggy hair sticks to their temples and foreheads with sweat. Their faces are flushed red. All four stare with silent amazement at the same object: an older skater, perhaps in high school, high off the ground, his scratched skateboard flipping beneath him. The body and legs of the floating skateboarder are the only parts the viewer can see. His baggy pants balloon outwards, freed from the weight of gravity.

Or:

A girl (the one with a black eye, and a smile) slides down a rail in a perfectly balanced 50–50 grind. Her arms are contorted above her, and her eyes are fixed at the spot of pavement at the rail's end. In the background, four boys watch with expressions of exaggerated disbelief.

Or:

In the foreground: a pile of jeans, shirts, and upside-down skate-boards; eight shoes and eight socks scattered at random amid a tram-pled-down clearing in high grass. In the background: a boy standing in his boxers on a rock ledge above a river, the heads of two boys poking out of the river's surface, another boy clinging to a rope as it swings him high above the water.

I walk over a grassy knoll soaked in afternoon sunlight and visit Rockwell's studio. They've kept it as it was when he worked there. I try to imagine a tall, lanky man perched before an easel with a pipe in his mouth and a floppy-brimmed hat on his head. But I know nothing of Rockwell. I can't picture what he would have looked like or what it had been like to talk to him. I retrace my steps across the hilltop lawn and go to my car. I leave Stockbridge. Soon I cross the state line and enter New York, and then I'm driv-ing over the deep blue Hudson River and New England is behind me and I think of what Sam said to Frodo: "If I take one more step, it'll be the farthest from home I've ever been." That night I sleep in a foggy dell in the Catskills, troubled by the thought of waking in a world I no longer recognize.

OUR DAYS BEGAN and ended at the skatepark, but there was a circuit of other spots we visited, too. All someone had to say was "Wanna go to ..." and the others would shrug and acquiesce. No one really cared—the point was that we were hanging out together and had the freedom to go wherever we pleased. The irony of having the liberty to choose between limited options was lost on us. There aren't many places to go to in a small town, but when you're a kid the options seem endless.

In no particular order, the other stops on our daily tour included: the elementary school, where we sat on the bench outside the music room; the gas station, and its high ledge out back; a swimming hole behind the church where we threw rocks at the fat rope hanging from a branch; the pizza shop owned by my brother's friend's father; and the skate shop, called Cherrybone.

We did in Cherrybone what skate rat kids always do in skate shops. We gawked and handled the merchandise without ever buying anything. We watched skate videos, skateboarded on the carpet or wooden floor, made a mess with pizza crusts and soda cups and in other ways pissed off Jong, who was the owner and the only person that ever worked there, as far as I remember. He opened the shop at eleven, and sometimes we would be waiting outside or would show up just as he was taking out the keys at the front door, and he would often have to shoo us out when the shop closed at six. Jong was kind and let us sit around in his shop even though we never bought anything.

Cherrybone changed locations when we were young, and then when we were in high school a chain snowboard shop opened in town and Cherrybone went out of business. It is thus married to the skatepark in my mind, for both dominated my childhood but are now extinct and few remember them. Those that do think of them less and less and with increasingly distorted recollection.

The first Cherrybone location was near the bottom of the Mountain Road, in the old building by the curve where cars were always backed up. The shop was more congested then. The building was ancient with creaky wooden floorboards we could skate on, making circles around the racks of sweaters and shirts while we raced each other. There were two identical three-stairs that led to the lower section of the shop. Here there was a couch and a TV and more space for trying kickflips and pop-shove its. The shop eventually moved up the road, and different businesses came and went in the old building with creaky wooden floorboards. None of them ever stayed.

The second Cherrybone location was in the old movie store. The smell—a unique blend of mold, water damage, and timber walls—reminded me of VHS tapes on plastic display shelves and going home without picking anything. Eventually, though, the musk came to be associated with the dim light and quiet of the skate shop. The floor was soft purple carpet covered in stains and snagged threads. The TV was placed just in front of the couch in a little alcove so that you had to put your feet on the TV stand when you sat on the couch. There was nowhere else to sit, so four or five or six people might squeeze together to watch a video with someone sitting on the back rest with their feet between two bodies on the couch. The only video we watched was *Sorry*, even though there were other tapes to choose from. We watched *Sorry* until *Really Sorry* came out, but then we went back to watching *Sorry*. There was something nice about watching the one video we knew so well, when we knew what each trick was going to be based on the progress of the song in the background.

"Ah, here it is, here it is! Watch this, watch how steezy this is, hardflip down the 12-stair, watch… Boom! How sick is that!"

We liked the quirky British guy walking around the mansion and I think we liked, also, how each part was so different in terms of style and attitude. Mike and I liked Ali Boulala—his part was spliced with shots of him puking, chugging beer, farting into a lighter, breaking skateboards and guitars. He always wore tight black jeans and a black leather jacket. Keith liked Bastien Saliban-zi, who wore baggy clothes and had a smooth style. Tommy liked Geoff Rowley because of the I Am the Walrus punk cover and Arto Saari because he skated to David Bowie.

If it rained, we sat in Cherrybone until it stopped or until it was time to go home.

Like every skate shop I've ever been to, Cherrybone had a glass case displaying trucks, wheels, bearings, and stickers (we studied and discussed the stickers more than the other items). This is where Jong sat, on a stool behind a desktop computer, clicking and scanning the screen as he talked to us. But he didn't talk much—he generally did his thing and we ours, as if we were Craigslist roommates who didn't care about getting to know one another.

The most distinct memory I have of Jong and Cherrybone is older, because it takes place in the first store.

Tommy and Keith were on Cherrybone's snowboard team, so Jong knew them better. He would always talk to them and call them by their name. To Jong I must have been just 'Tommy's and Keith's friend' and nothing more, and I never went into Cherrybone without them.

Cherrybone had a phone and was one of the spots we would go when we wanted to call to get picked up. On this particular day Tommy and I went to Cherrybone to call our parents. Tommy's mom came and got him and then it was just Jong and I alone in his quiet store. It wasn't yet five o'clock, but it was fall and so was getting dark. The bright yellow lights sparkled on the metal of the racks and lit up the shoes resting on their platforms on the wall so that shadows stretched beneath them. After the bells on the door jingled when Tommy left, there was suddenly silence, and I became uncomfortable.

"So, your mom's coming, too?" Jong asked.

"Yeah. She should be here soon."

"Cool, cool." He went back to clicking on his computer.

I paced around the store and looked at all the items I already knew were there. There was the Pink is Punk shirt Bryan and his friends were wearing. There were the black and red Osiris shoes I wanted. The World Industries hoodies with Flameboy and Wet Willy. The Blind gear with the little grim reaper in different cartoon scenarios. I rifled through the shirts not because I was interested in buying anything but because I was hyper-aware of Jong sitting on the other side of the room. His presence was the only thing I noticed—I felt like he was staring at me—so I fiddled with the merchandise to become invisible.

I walked around the store and looked at everything again.

Sometimes this happened, when I called home and it was a long time before anyone came to get me.

Please come soon, I thought.

But no one showed up.

I found my skateboard and started skating around in circles. I only pushed once and then tik-tak turned my front wheels to keep momentum going.

Tik-tak, tik-tak, tik-tik-tak, tik-tak, tik-tak, tik-tik-tak.

I went around and around in circles. Jong sat behind the glass display case clicking the mouse connected to his desktop.

I went down to the TV area and started trying kickflips. I had landed my first kickflip the previous winter on the cement floor of our unfinished basement. I didn't have skate shoes then so I did it in my snow boots, trying again and again for weeks. My brother would get on his skateboard to show me how, popping and flipping his board and landing back on. When he did it, it looked so easy! Finally one night I popped, flicked, the board barrel-rolled and landed back on its wheels, and I landed back on with my feet together in the center. I looked up at my brother, and his eyes were just as astonished as mine must have been. My mom ran down to the basement because of all the yelling, and I told her "I landed a kickflip! I landed a kickflip!"

Now, on the old wooden floorboards of Cherrybone, I started another kickflip session. I stood on the stationary board, shifted my feet back and forth until they were in the right position, with just the toes of my front foot on the edge of the board, all the way down by the back bolts; I balanced like that for a moment before I crouched low, and then, *pop*, the wooden deck popped against the floor then slapped down violently upside down with me standing on top. I righted the board and tried again.

And again.

And again.

Trying a kickflip every few seconds for minutes on end without ever getting close.

Sometimes the board flipped correctly but drifted away from my feet. Other times it stayed beneath me but didn't rotate, while others it rotated too much. On one random attempt after dozens of others, the board flipped a full rotation, landed on its wheels, and I dropped back on top of the griptape. For a brief moment I was ecstatic, and the happiness was mixed with surprise because I had actually landed a kickflip. Then the surprise increased and the happiness left because all of my weight was behind me. The board shot forward, I flew backward until I crashed ass-first to the floorboards. My skateboard slammed hard into a rack causing it to wobble then slowly tip and fall with cacophonous noise.

I held my breath.

"WILL YOU JUST GET THE FUCK OUT OF MY FUCKING STORE!" Jong yelled. "JESUS CHRIST! GET THE FUCK OUT!"

"OK."

I didn't even try to put the stand back up. I just grabbed my skateboard and walked out.

It was raining. I didn't want to stand close to the store but I couldn't go anywhere else because that was where my parents were supposed to meet me.

I waited for a gap between the cars and ran across the street.

There was a little stone wall and then a garden at the bottom of a lawn. I sat in the mulch on my skateboard so that a bush was blocking Cherrybone but so that I could still see its parking lot. I sat there watching each car as it came into view to see if it was either my mom or dad.

Five minutes later, Jong was standing on the sidewalk across the road. He yelled through the cars that drove between us.

"You wanna come back inside, man?" He said. "It's raining out here."

"No, I'm OK. My mom's about to be here."

"You sure, dude? I'm sorry for yelling."

"It's OK."

"You sure?"

"Yes."

"You gonna be alright out here?"

"Yes."

"OK, dude, see you around then."

I sat there for what seemed a very long time. When my dad's truck finally pulled into the parking lot, I ran across the street when he was turning around so that he wouldn't see where I'd been waiting.

Bloomsburg, PA

THE RAIN HITS AS I DRIVE SOUTH ON I-81 FROM BINGHAMTON: heavy, wipers-at-full-blast rain that fogs the windshield so I have to drive with the windows down and my shirt becomes soaked. The storm passes quickly, though, or I drive through it, and the pavement is dry by the time I reach the exit for Bloomsburg, Pennsylvania, and I decide to go skateboarding.

To find the Bloomsburg skatepark, turn off the highway and go down a long, straight road lined with AutoZones and Subways and Mattress Lands and turn off at the lipstick-pink brick building advertising the sale and purchase of gold and coins and bounce over train tracks in the direction of the airport. Just before a bridge that would take you over a wide river, turn right and follow the leafy trees along the bank until you reach the skatepark.

Like me, you may be impressed as you pull into the gravel parking lot and a large cement skatepark is before you. There are sections of rails and curbs at both ends and a series of quarter-pipes and kickers through the middle of the park, all of which is connected and supplemented by waxed ledges, cement bumps, and euro gaps on which the creative skater could link different transfers and combinations. There isn't much, but everything is well-proportioned, thoughtfully arranged, and well built. In short, it is a gem of a small town skatepark.

I am alone in the park as I begin to make laps. The cement is dry but the sky is all shadowy gray swarms exploding and rolling over one another, and the wind is strong so that branches bend upwards and the bright white undersides of leaves flicker like strobe lights. It feels good skateboarding. I land kickflips on flat ground, off ledges, from one transition to another. The rails are waxed to a greasy slickness so you only need to creep into boardslides to drift across the metal or bumpy cement. I ollie into a manual across the raised bed of halfpipe and roll on only two wheels until I don't see a mogul of a snake run and crash into it, tumbling over its backside while my board stays put.

I skate without stopping. A guy cruises up on a mini-dirtbike. I assume he is older, but when he skates into the park with his bike helmet under one arm I realize he's in high school. I say hello as he skates past; he gives a nod and grunts, suspicious of a stranger. I want to ask him questions about the park, and perhaps he senses this, for as soon as he stashes his helmet, he calls a friend and begins to skate around the park with his cellphone held to his ear, chatting and laughing as he does tricks I will never be able to do.

Suddenly the strong gusts of wind are filled with fat rain drops, and there is a crescendo of water pounding against cement. I'm getting close to manualing across the halfpipe, so I jump on my board for a final try. As the high school kid fires up his bike and takes off, I pop into a manual and watch my two back wheels make parallel tracks over the speckled cement between the mogul and the waved wall of the quarterpipe. I drop off the far side and raise my hands in victory.

I run to my car, shut the door, roll up the windows. Rain sounds on the roof and the hood. Water drips down over my face and the back of my neck. I open my phone, check my email, check the news, check sports, check Instagram, open Tinder and start swiping.

It's only later, 120 miles away as I'm camped in a grassy turnabout off a logging road deep in the woods of Buchanan State Park, that my phone pings and I see I matched with a beautiful woman back in Bloomsburg. She runs a clothing store and has long blonde hair. We chat. I want to ask if she would like me to drive back, or if I should even move to Bloomsburg to be with her. I want to ask if she goes to the skatepark or knows the young man who rides around town on a miniature dirt bike. She stops responding, though. I wait for a long time holding my phone. When it stays dark and silent I take out Tolkien and read by headlamp, alone in the black forest, the cries of an owl and a thousand different bugs surrounding me.

THERE WAS A horror movie playing in Williston that we knew wouldn't be coming to town, so one afternoon Mike's mom drove us forty minutes to the big theater in the shopping plaza off the highway. We decided to go early so we could skate the sidewalks around the box stores and the spots around the big parking lots.

One of these spots was an eight-stair in front of the cell phone store. All week we talked about the eight-stair as much as the movie. Like the others, I acted excited and said I would try to ollie the stair set, but in reality the idea of the concrete stairs with green metal railings and the sidewalk with big cracks between its panels, as well as the many people driving by in their cars, coming in and out of restaurants, and the shop owners who wouldn't like us skating—all of it gave me anxiety so that I was secretly looking forward to when the skate portion of our day would be finished and we would be sitting in the dark movie theater as the previews began.

When we exited Mike's minivan, the first place we skated to was the eight-stair. We stood below looking up and above looking down, and skated into the stair set, skating slow but crouching like we would ollie then putting our foot down to stop ourselves just in time. The thought of trying to ollie over all the stairs made me jittery. Blood pounded through my skull, my chest, my hands so that they trembled when I held them in front of me. My mouth became dry and I couldn't swallow, and my face must have been as pale as those of my three friends.

"Let's warm up a bit, then come back here last," Tommy said.

"Yeah," Keith said.

"Yeah, good idea."

We went and ollied on and off curbs and sessioned a brick manual pad between a parking lot and the road. Soon, though, we were sitting on our skateboards on a curb. We sat in a row and talked and watched the cars pass until it was time for the movie.

On our way to the theater, Mike made us stop at the eight-stair.

"I think I'm gonna hit it," he said.

"Let's come back and do it next time."

"No. Today's the day."

For a long time the Skate Crew had been Tommy, Keith, and I. We were in the same class, had been friends since kindergarten, and had all started skateboarding at the same time. Mike was in our class, too, but he didn't skateboard, nor did he play other sports. He was slow and uncoordinated when we played games on the playground and hung out with the other slow and uncoordinated kids—the fat kid, the goofy new kid from Florida, the short kid who liked trains. These were our classmates who didn't get invited to birthday parties or sleepovers.

In middle school, Mike started skateboarding. He started wearing jeans and grew his hair out. He started playing his dad's guitar and listening to classic rock bands, even wearing AC/DC T-shirts to school. He started hanging out at the skatepark, too. We were distant towards him at first, but eventually he became a normal fixture of the skatepark and of our clique, and he was absorbed into the Skate Crew so that when my mom asked me what I had

31

done that day, and I replied "We did this" or "We did that", the "we" implicitly meant myself, Keith, Tommy, and Mike.

Mike's middle name was Liam. Since there was another Michael in our class, the kindergarten teacher called Mike 'Michael Liam', which then became 'Michaeliam'. In high school, when he told us how he hated that people called him by his first and middle names, we were shocked to learn that he was neither Michaeliam nor Michael, but just Mike.

Because of his ripped jeans and wrinkled T-shirts, and because of his long tangled hair that he never washed, we also called him 'Dirty Michaeliam' in the days when we hung out at the skatepark. The name—DML, for short, and sometimes just 'Dirty'—became so normal we didn't think about using it, though if we had we might have realized we made it up because Mike's family had less money, and because the dynamic within our group positioned Mike, the newcomer, as the target of jokes and belittlement. We might have realized the obvious: that our name hurt Mike. But children are cruel and lack an ability for empathy, and we didn't think about this.

Then again, Mike, like me, worshipped Ali Boulala and other punk rock skaters with grungy looks. This is something we had in common and that was reflected in our styles, if not how we skated than at least in how we wanted to skate. So perhaps in those first years when Mike started skateboarding he relished his nickname and identified as that which we called him, Dirty Michaeliam.

When he stood above the eight-stair outside the phone store in Williston, he was still very much Dirty Michaeliam—ripped jeans stained green, black AC/DC shirt, frazzled hair covering all but a sliver of his face. We stood below the stair set, in the grass to the side. Mike spent a long time bent over his skateboard at the top of the run-in, staring through the gap he kept making in his curtains of hair. When we wanted to say something to one another, we only whispered.

Was he actually going to do it?

He might try, but he's never gonna land it.

Surely if we couldn't ollie the eight-stair, then neither could Michaeliam.

Or was it just that we were too afraid to try?

Suddenly, Mike pounced. His wheels roared over the cement of the sidewalk and clacked against the cracks. As soon as he ollied, his board drifted away and he flew through the air with his legs outstretched. He landed hard, landing ungracefully so that it looked like it hurt. We didn't even laugh like we usually did if someone ate shit.

"You alright, man?"

"Oh…" Mike groaned and rolled on the sidewalk. After a moment, he stood up, grabbed his board, and jogged back up the stairs.

"You're going to try it again?"

"Michaeliam, come on, man!"

"There's no way! Come on, let's go to the movie!"

But he tried again, and several more times until a knee and both his elbows were bloody. We were split between wanting to see him land it and, due to jealousy, wanting to see him fail.

He dropped in, pushed once, crouched low as he approached the huge stair set. When he ollied, his tail popped off the ground, his knees swelled upwards with his board stuck to his feet, his hair flew behind him so that now, for the first time, we could see his face. His cheeks were pale, his jawline delicate. Mike descended through the air with his eyes fixed on his landing. He extended his legs to receive the sidewalk.

Stomp.

Crack!

The tail snapped cleanly off his board. His legs split as the board went forward and his back foot remained planted on the sidewalk. Mike yelled and thudded onto his ass.

"OH!!!!"

"Shit!!"

"Damn, dude!"

"You had it!"

"That was it, man!"

Again Mike rolled and groaned. We were equal parts astonished, impressed, and relieved—Mike wouldn't do the eight-stair, and we would save face.

We grabbed our decks and started for the movie theater. But when we looked back, we saw Mike walking back up the stairs holding his broken skateboard.

"Michaeliam!"

"What are you doing!?"

"The nose is fine! I can just ollie off the nose!"

"No way! It's not the same!"

He was standing at the top of the run-in facing the stair set. He flipped his board around so that he was now using the nose as the tail, and where the new nose should have been was nothing but a jagged line of splinters just above the trucks. He jumped on the board and started pushing.

No.

There's no way.

He pushed again—he was going fast now—crouched, and ollied. We held our breath. He popped and rose into the empty space above the stairs. His hair flew back, his face became clear before him, so unlike it normally was when hidden and drooped towards the ground. He sucked the board upwards, angled it like the pros we saw in the videos, and flew through the air proud and calm. When he landed on the sidewalk, he stomped on the bolts and rode away without a reaction, though our hysterics made up for any lack of his.

Throughout my life I have often thought of Mike that day in Williston. In certain distraught and unsettled moments, presented with situations I wanted to avoid, I have thought of Mike that day in Williston, how he picked up his broken skateboard, jogged up the stairs, and did the impossible.

Morgantown, WV & Charlestown, WV

THE ROADS OF MORGANTOWN, WEST VIRGINIA ARE NARROW and steep, without curbs, so that slabs of broken pavement protrude over hillsides covered in leaves. The roads are precipitous turns that make me feel like I'm dropping into a halfpipe when I hit the blinker and turn right. When a black Ford F150 comes the other way I'm nervous I won't be able to squeeze past. I sit up and grip the steering wheel at ten and two and stare at the road with wide, frightened eyes like someone from out of town. Remarkably, these roads are the veins of a small city. The traffic flows on paths designed in the days before motor vehicles, when they uncoiled and settled in some organic fashion independent of central planning.

Handouts in a coffee shop advertise hunting gear, a football game, and an opioid addiction clinic. I have a cup of coffee then lose myself driving on the one-way streets and the goat trails of the residential neighborhoods surrounding downtown. Google Maps tells me to make different turns, and when I inevitably drive too far it reroutes and screams at me to make mysterious corrections on foreboding streets. By chance I find the road behind the DMV that leads to the secret skatepark. I drive by the tennis courts and the swimming pool and there, at the furthest end of the recreation area, are the metal ramps glaring in high afternoon sunlight. The pavement is littered with brown, dry leaves, and no one is there.

I start skating. Half of the large skatepark is dedicated to opposing quarterpipes and bank ramps with a long fun box in between, complete with down rails, launch gaps, and an excessively large spine, while the other half contains a mini-ramp that is wide but too high and, to my delight, a more open area with small rails and boxes. Leaves crinkle under my wheels as I push around the park, and the metal sheets on the ramps bang loudly when I ollie on them.

I sense again I'm not as good as I used to be. Tricks that should be easy are difficult—they feel awkward, and I rarely get close to landing them. I'm out of shape, and soon I'm dripping sweat and standing still for longer periods between runs. I haven't skateboarded for five years, and time has deformed the pieces so they no longer fit just as they should.

I moved to Japan five years before to teach English to small children and bored housewives. I brought my skateboard with me but only used it once, when my Hawaiian friend invited me down to the circular expanse of pavement in front of the harbor and we smoked weed in the back entrance of an oyster restaurant. We tried 360 flips as retirees and mothers and their toddlers gave us wide berths with looks equal parts interested and upset. When I was moving back to America, I sold my skateboard for a beer at a sayonara party because it wouldn't fit in my suitcase. That was fine with me. Skateboarding was something I had done when I was younger. I had never been particularly good at it, it was dangerous, and, without the company of my hometown or college friends, all of whom had skated, I had little motivation to keep doing it. When I returned to the US, I figured I would become a serious adult who had a job and a girlfriend.

Three years after coming home, I don't have a job or a girlfriend, and I'm skateboarding in West Virginia. My skateboard is an artifact my brother found in a storage closet when he moved into a new apartment. The deck is flat and chipped to a stub, the wheels and trucks are too heavy and too large, dating the board to the early 2000s. It is a terrible skateboard that makes ollieing over the smallest of obstacles a challenge, and my kickflips barely leave the pavement. But receiving it had reminded me about skateboarding, and it felt like I had remembered something important that I was never supposed to forget.

The kids come first—younger ones, one on a scooter and one a skateboard, then a boy that might be thirteen or fourteen. He has a squeaky voice and a childish way of talking to whoever will listen to him. He exudes a certain emotional melodrama that makes me shudder, for I recognize it from the memory of who I had been but also from knowing who I still am. Then, the older crowd—a guy pulls up in a nineties soccer mom minivan, another in a stylish old car that is completely rusted, rattling, and falling apart.

Minivan is a hipster-skateboarder with Janoski sneakers and a folded beanie and flannel despite the Indian summer weather. Jalopy is more punkish, with tattoos and a shaved head. He's wearing camo shorts and I notice that one of the inked images on his calf is that of a skateboard. This—afternoons in the small town skatepark—this is who he is. Skateboarding is a vine winding itself around the drainpipe of his soul, growing thicker and sprouting shoots as the years pass, the soft green stalk becoming brown and weathered bark so that a reckless child could climb its length without pulling it loose, plant and plastic having fused into a single pillar. He doesn't skateboard because he's professional, or even exceptional—he's better than me, but not by much. No, he skateboards because he wouldn't know who he is without this thing he's always done—he wouldn't know who he would be if he wasn't pulling up behind the DMV in his rickety brown car that made girls and mid-life crisis men turn their heads. He is intrinsically bound to skateboarding and has always known it, while I had forgotten this fact and am now remembering, rediscovering what is essential after a long sojourn in the wilderness.

Sometime after my brother had given me the forgotten skateboard, I experienced a revelation when I was in the gym. I saw someone and experienced a strong, sudden, and inexplicable sympathy, as if I knew we would be friends if we were ever to spend time together. There was nothing remarkable about this person—

he was of average height and looks, and was otherwise indistinguishable. Why, then, did I sense that he and I were somehow three stations below the frequency of the others around us, tuned in at the same number to listen to the same song that only we could hear?

I studied him from afar. What was it?

Then I noticed.

He was wearing skate shoes.

Skate shoes in the gym, just as I was, though I had stopped skateboarding, just as he had, it seemed. And I knew in an instant the significance skateboarding still held in the lives of innumerable American men and women, those twenty- and thirty-somethings bred in the skatepark and then released from it, never to return, like mutants altered in labs and secretly returned to the population. I knew in an instant the place small town skateparks held in the memories and personalities of people around the world, the imprint that splintered ramps had left on so many of my generation.

And in that instant a vision formed for a writing project.

Intrinsic to this vision was the act of recording. I imagined myself the Brothers Grimm or Asbjørnsen and Moe, who had traversed the countryside to collect and compile stories that formed the essence of local identities. I felt every single skatepark contained its own universe with its own tome of history left unwritten. Many of these histories were folk tales and foundational myths for the people who engaged in their transmission, and they would inevitably disappear if they went unrecorded.

A friend gave me a crash course on audio equipment and editing platforms. I bought a microphone and a recorder. I painted houses and saved money. At the end of August, when the afternoons on Lake Champlain were pregnant with notes of sadness, I left, emptying the things from my apartment and telling very few people I was leaving.

Now I'm in Morgantown, West Virginia, in the midst of living what had long been plan and fantasy. As Jalopy, Minivan, and I session the box behind the mini-ramp, the too-slippery waxy plastic box with scarred angle-iron and the stickers on the sides, I know it's now or never. I will either reveal to them my true intentions or I will continue to pretend that I have no ulterior motives and I will never complete my project, not for lack of desire, vision, or ability, but for lack of courage, the most shameful excuse for failure.

The source of my anxiety is an unforeseen contradiction in what I am trying to do. I want both to blend in—to show up unannounced in an unfamiliar skatepark and feel I belong there—and to separate myself as the journalist, the archivist, the recorder. This might upset some of the local skaters, who would detect mixed signals suggesting deceit and duplicity, but it is also an inherent contradiction in my artistic vision. Am I 'undercover'? Am I a journalist? Am I a local, or am I a visitor? Do I want to enmesh myself within the fabric of the skatepark in order to feel its essence, to observe the way afternoon light falls across ramps and dust, through the nearby foliage, to make shadows memorized by the subconscious of the teenager sitting in the same spot he's sat in for years? Or do I want to approach this essence from the outside—by digging and prodding as a reporter with a microphone?

Tom Wolfe avoided this dilemma by wearing a white three-piece suit. When he embedded himself in a community, the people understood that he was not one of them or pretending to be in order to gather information. It was a way of reconciling his desire to be an honest person *and* a reporter. This is perhaps different from what Hunter Thompson did, who ultimately had a falling out with the Hell's Angels because his role with them was ambiguous—was he one of them, or was he just writing about them? Increasingly, to both skate among and interview the locals seems like betrayal.

Travel implies movement and interaction with the foreign, but my desire is to hack the action in a way that allows me to move through the simultaneously familiar and unfamiliar, the known and unknown. I want to be within the foreign *not as a foreigner*. I want to camouflage myself within places I have never been before: to quietly, secretly, discreetly stare with wide eyes at the normal lives of people I do not know who live in places far away from Vermont. I want to exist, briefly, to pass single yet memorable evenings in towns and skateparks that were at once opposite and identical to the one where I grew up.

Is this too much to ask?

Opportunity comes and goes, the moment passes, and I say nothing to Jalopy or Minivan except a comment about the surface of the box that reveals me as an out-of-towner. Minivan politely extrapolates on my comment then runs forward dragging the tail of his board over the pavement and lets go, jumping on and popping a stylish crooked grind.

As the afternoon progresses the sky fills with clouds, not gradually but suddenly, huge gray swathes that materialized when I wasn't looking. The air is sticky-humid and ripe with a heavy darkness.

An older skater arrives on a shaped old school board, the kind with a flat, pointed noise and plastic bars underneath for boardslides. He is overweight, in his forties, with a beard and tattoos. His especially skinny wife stands nearby with their baby daughter in a jogging stroller. He says hi and carves around between the rails and boxes, popping over lone pieces of 2 x 4 and making high turns on the quarterpipes. Sometimes he holds his daughter in his arms as he pushes around the park, carving back and forth and whispering in her ear, gauging her reaction to the sensation more than remaining sensitive to his own, for he has known what this feels like and for her it's new.

Do you see? This is skateboarding.

"So when are you going to get her own board?" I ask, the baby back with her mother. He smiles. "Sometime soon."

"That's pretty cool, man."

"I know, it is." He beams, looking at his family at the edge of the park. The skinny mother can only see the baby in front of her.

"Do you go to WVU?" He asks.

"The college?"

"Yeah."

"No. I'm just passing through town, actually."

"Where from?"

"Vermont."

"Vermont!? What are you doing in West Virginia?"

"Haha. I'm actually doing a tour of skateparks in small towns."

"And you stopped *here*?"

"Yeah."

"Hahaha!"

He asks a dozen questions and lists the places I should have gone to in Ohio and Pittsburgh, and where I should go in West Virginia. He tells me about a church basement the pastor converted into a skatepark. You have to go and meet him in his office before you can skate. He gives me suggestions on how I should write the book, about how I should promote it online and pitch it to skate magazines. I tell him about my vision for an audio component and ask if I can interview him.

"Me? Now?"

"Sure."

"Of course!"

"Alright, hang on one second, I'll just grab my equipment."

We stand in the parking lot looking at the skatepark and do the interview.

Afterwards, we shake hands several times. I talk briefly with his wife and wave at the baby. The baby smiles at me and slaps her wrists together. I go back to the skatepark. During our interview it had started raining, and now the three remaining skaters are huddled in a crescent of dry pavement beneath an overhanging canopy. Minivan and Jalopy are smoking cigarettes—Marlboro Reds—and I feel a sharp desire to ask for one.

I sit down on my skateboard next to them.

"Well, that's it for skating, then."

"Yeeyup."

"Think it's gonna dry out?"

"Not anytime soon."

"Yeah."

We're quiet for a moment. The rain falls on the pavement and the metal of the ramps. The drops are visible as streaks against the gray sky before they make contact with the ground. Their descent seems slow, unhurried and patient, like figures in deployed parachutes.

"Well, anyone else want to do an interview?" I ask.

"Ha, is that what you were doing, then?" Minivan says.

"Yeah."

"No, I'm all set."

"Oh. Oh, yeah, I was just interviewing Jon."

"Yeah. Jon likes to talk."

"Right."

We sit there and watch the rain falling on the skatepark. No one speaks. The rain makes a soft noise against the leaves above and behind and on the metal ramps in front of us. Suddenly I feel like an unwanted outsider intruding on a sacred space. Minivan and his friends are quiet because they don't want me to overhear them—they are self-conscious of being recorded. Their skatepark is where they come to be themselves away from the judgement of the world. My presence has ruined that.

What's worse, I detect something else—the faint, earthy trace of resentment.

I had pretended to be just a skater, but there was an ulterior motive all along.

I had pretended to be one of them, but really I had been something else.

"Well, I'll get going, then," I say.

"Yep."

"Have, a good one, then."

"Yep, you too."

I walk to the rusty Saab with green plates and put my skateboard in the passenger seat. I sit for a long time listening to the rain falling against my car. The drops produce a different timber on the roof, windshield, and hood. Water flows down glass, and beyond it the skatepark is blurred and indistinct—dim squares and angles lurking in the reeds. I take out my phone and begin figuring out where I'll sleep that night.

Clint: So, where are we?

Skate Guy: We're in Morgantown, West Virginia.

C: How long has this park been around for?

SG: Around 2003 is when they built it, so it's been give or take fifteen years.

C: How would you describe this park? Is it one of the better ones around?

SG: It's really the only one around [laughs] considering you'd have to drive another hour and a half any direction to see another skatepark, so it's what we have and we live with it.

C: So everyone from northern West Virginia comes here to skate?

SG: Yes, absolutely. It's kind of slow right now, I figure the humidity is playing a part in that. Usually people come out around this time in the year around seven o'clock or so, once it starts cooling down because we're right here next to this creek which makes it even more humid than normal. Being that it's a college town, maybe there's some crazy things going on tonight that's keeping people preoccupied.

C: Have you noticed that less people are coming here over the years?

SG: No, 'cause again it's a college town so you get a fresh group of people year after year coming in.

C: Were you here in the beginning?

SG: Yes.

C: What was the movement like? Was it run by the city? Was there a push by local skaters?

SG: I wasn't living in town when that happened, but I came here right when they built it. I think most of the skating had just been street skating around the campus and everything, and more and more they were getting really tired of that. This was the city's answer to that, 'cause like, BOW park, I think both the city and the county funded it.

C: Nice. What's the craziest thing you've done at the park?

SG: [laughs] Well, I'm forty-two-years-old and I'm still riding a skateboard, so that's my accomplishment.

C: When did you start?

SG: I started in 1991.

C: Wow, that's the year I was born!

SG: Ok, yeah, I mean that's what I'm saying—a lot of the kids I see skating here, I've been skating for longer than they've been alive.

C: Did you grow up at a small skatepark?

SG: I grew up in a very small town about forty-five minutes south of here, and you couldn't even call it... It was a coal camp town, and I mean there was nothing, no sidewalks or anything. The only thing I had for skating in 1991 was a sidewalk between my house and my grandparents' house and their porch.

C: But you made it work.

SG: So I made it work, yeah. I slowly got further and further away from town until I got to the big city of Morgantown [laughs].

C: Are there some good skaters that come around?

SG: Oh, my. Well, we've had a couple demos, things like that. There used to be a shop here that drew in a lot of people. We'd always have a contest every summer. There'd be a flat-ground game of SKATE, then there'd be a best trick, overall in the whole park. I've seen some pretty crazy things go down, like this buddy of mine on the rail over the pyramid did a pole-jam to back 5-0 on the flat, pop down.

C: Wow.

SG: And I've seen some insane things on the halfpipe as far as handplants and things like that go. There are a lot of well-rounded skaters here that are both street and transition-oriented that can do it all.

C: Can you tell me a little bit about your board? You've got a special setup here.

SG: I got a shaped board now. That's the new thing, all the kids are going crazy over the shaped boards. This right here is a Schmit-sticks blank. A lot of the companies like Welcome and Mike Valley's company, they use their wood. So this is just one of the blank shapes before they get screened, it's an eight-and-a-half.

C: It's for tricks and stuff?

SG: Oh, yeah, absolutely. A lot of people would see it and they'd think it's a cruiser board which it kinda looks like, but it's just the way the nose is cut. It's just based on a popsicle eight-and-a-half shape. It's just cut down a little bit.

C: I noticed you've got a young one that you're bringing around. Is she going to be a skater when she grows up?

SG: If she likes it, yes. She'll definitely be around it, I'm definitely not going to push it on her. I don't want to be like the football dad, you know. If she likes it, that's awesome. I was cruising around with her today and she seemed to enjoy that, so yeah, hopefully.

C: Awesome. Well, thanks.

SG: Thank you.

It rains through the night and into the next day—public radio keeps warning about flash floods—as I drive south through West Virginia on I-79 until I take an exit for a winding state highway into the hills, to Spencer. I find the Spencer skatepark—an old woman is passed out on top of a picnic table—but as soon as I do it starts to rain, so that a child in the adjacent playground yells at me and asks what I'm doing there, it's raining, can't I tell? His mother admonishes him, and I leave. Two hours later, I'm in a city park outside Charlestown, the state capital, and the rain has stopped.

The skatepark in Charlestown, West Virginia sits beside a large pond surrounded by a gravel path. On cloudy weekend afternoons in September families with young children circumnavigate the pond without counting the laps as skateboarders and BMX riders bang on ramps and clang on rails above them. The skatepark is divided into two terraces of equal size, like rows in a vineyard. On the lower terrace, a pyramid sits in the small space between steep quarterpipes. There is a long, mellow double kink and a squat box perfect for nose manuals, noseslides, and grinds. On the upper terrace, there is a more dramatic pyramid, shorter in length but greater in height. The transitions are steeper, and a kink rail cascades over one of the sides. There is also a small bank ramp, but besides this the upper terrace is empty, making it the area for flat-ground tricks. Separating the upper and lower terrace is a two-and-a-half-foot stone ledge. Its face is a masonry veneer except for a section at one end where the drop is supplanted by a transition reminiscent of a wheelchair ramp.

I grab my skateboard from the passenger seat and the gallon jug from the backseat and push through the parking lot. A path feeds directly into the park, so when I turn in and maneuver around a quarterpipe the two teenagers sitting on its deck look up from their phone to see who has arrived. They don't know this person—he's a scruffy twenty-something with a mini afro and jean shorts and ripped canvas Vans covered in paint—so they stare, trying to gauge how cool he is and how good he is at skateboarding. I put the water jug in a corner and start to skate. The teenagers, it turns out, aren't shy at all.

"Where are you from?" one of them yells. He's wearing skinny jeans and a black T-shirt and has short hair like he's just gotten a haircut.

"Vermont," I say.

"Vermont? Where's that?"

"It's up north. Past Massachusetts."

"What are you doing here then?"

"I'm on a road trip to visit skateparks."

"And you wanted to stop here!?"

"Yeah!"

He laughs.

"Why would you come here?"

"Should I not have?"

"There's a million places better!"

"Well, here I am. Seems good enough."

I drop in and try ollieing over the pyramid. My back wheels catch on the deck, and I fly down to the pavement. I land on my shoulder and hip with a thump.

"You alright man?"

"Yeah. I'm good!"

I pick myself up and fetch my skateboard.

The kid is extroverted, chatty in a way that suggests a lack of filter between what he thinks and what he says. His friend wears sweatpants and has bouncy curly hair bleached at the tips and is a BMXer. He keeps trying 180s from the lower level to the upper, pedaling furiously around the park to gain speed then launching from a ramp to the upper terrace, landing backwards, trying to balance yet, inevitably, tossing his bike down to catch himself as he tips sideways. I session the pyramid and the double kink, trying to clear the deck then slide the rail's length. Haircut talks to me every chance he can, only because I'm a person standing next to him. He introduces himself as Tom.

Tom sees me try a tailslide then does one across the length of the box. I give a couple taps but cringe with embarrassment. We session the box as his friend speeds around us, pedaling hard at the small launch ramp pushed against the ledge. The afternoon is damp and dim, as if it had rained and would soon rain again.

Eventually Tom and I turn our attention to ollieing onto the upper terrace. There is another arrival to the park, a guy about my age with a hippy-stoner vibe. He has swishy cotton pants and dreadlocks (he's white) and a board that's chipped down to stubs at both the nose and tail. His girlfriend—overweight, Daisy Dukes, bra, tanktop, sandals—watches him skate from a seat on the ledge. Cotton Swishies joins our game of ollieing up the ledge and soon the three of us are yelling and cursing, pushing ourselves slowly at the wall and looping back around on the wheelchair ramp as we watch the others, too, jump not quite high enough.

"Fuuuuuck!"

"Dammit!"

"So close!"

"You gotta ease your board forward a little bit to get it over the lip!"

"Aaaah!"

"Argh!"

"Slip it over! Ease it up onto the pavement!"

Tom lands it first, of course. Swishies and I grumble. A few tries later, I pop hard and ease my board forward at the apex of the jump, sliding it up and over the lip of the stone bricks. Cotton Swishies gives me taps; Tom wasn't looking.

We move the session to the upper plateau. Tom works on a 360 flip over the hip of the steeper pyramid. Swishies and I stand on the edge of the pavement and eye the single kink. It's high off the ramp and has a dramatic pitch on the down. Swishies tells me he "used to be able to do shit like this". I give it a halfhearted effort—popping onto the flat, landing on my board but kicking out and ejecting safely without ever committing. Swishies skips the flat and tries to boardslide the down, but doesn't commit, either. He screams at himself, grabs his board, and skates back to the starting point. He tries several more times without getting closer to sliding the rail. I suddenly feel depleted and, sensing a battle with a dangerous trick, opt for flat-ground doodling on the open expanse as Swishies keeps trying and screaming. Fifteen minutes later he ollies off the pyramid's deck, slides the down, and lands back on his board with a wonderfully jerky style that makes me hold my breath. Riding away, he produces a scream little different from the ones he had made in frustration. A family walking around the pond stops to stare.

Swishies and I sit down on the ledge next to his girlfriend. They both light cigarettes, and we talk. They're visiting from Columbus. He tells me about the skateparks I should visit in Ohio, including Skatopia, where he's met skateboard tourists from around the world. One time he partied with a group of Norwegians on a skateboard vacation.

"Yeah, there's some good skateparks in Ohio, but not much else."

"Yeah?"

"Just a lot of drugs."

"Really."

"Yeah. Everyone I grew up skating with is on drugs now. No one skates anymore."

Again I notice his rotten brown teeth, the empty holes between them.

Had he been on drugs, too? Which ones? Oxies? Crack? Meth?

51

Heroin? And had skateboarding pulled him out of it? So that now he tours skateparks with his girlfriend, who is also recovering from addiction? And though she doesn't skateboard herself, does she love him and enjoy going on road trips with him, the long hours together in their old car listening to their old CDs, wrappers from gas station snacks and empty soda bottles piling up on the floor? All while their old friends they had been young with were getting high on couches in crumbling houses in Columbus? Do they have jobs? Is he a contractor, a server, a teacher?

We share a loaded silence in which I ask myself a hundred questions but wait for Swishies to say something first. He smokes his cigarette and spits. His fat saliva glob forms a bubbly white mound on the pavement.

"What's Vermont like?" he asks.

"Vermont's nice. Boring, though. Small towns. Lots of mountains. Good beer. Gets fucking cold in the winter."

"Sounds alright."

"It's not bad. Nice to get out, though."

"I feel that."

The gray ceiling seems to have dropped even lower, making the afternoon claustrophobic. The sky and the air are oppressive. I lean back and lie on the pavement. Pebbles stick into my skin, and the ground is warm. Above is only a flat, featureless canvas, not white but a uniform shade of off-black. Swishies talks quietly with his girlfriend.

I try skateboarding again. More people show up. A large group of young people hangs around the open doors of a car in the parking lot. One of them goes out of his way to introduce himself. He says his name three times before I finally understand: Elijah. Like in the Bible, he says. He has a large smile and a skateboard with bright pink grip tape. He compliments me on a noseslide.

"They're fucking hard, man," he says.

"Haha. No, they're easy."

"No, man, I can't land that shit!"

Elijah pushes himself carefully around the park, rolling slowly up and down the bottoms of the ramps. I sense a spell of melancholy setting in.

Tom comes over.

"See that trash can?" he says, nodding to a big blue plastic bin.

"Yeah."

"How sick would it be if I ollied over that thing?"

"From the flat?"

"No. From the upper deck. I'm going to pull that launch ramp over and boost over it."

"That would be pretty sick."

"Can you film so I can put it up on my Instagram?"

"I guess."

Tom gives me his phone and hurries to set up his gap. He pushes the trash can against the ledge then carries the launch ramp onto the upper deck and arranges it so it projects out over the blue barrel.

"Ready!?" he yells from across the pavement.

"Yeah! Go for it!"

"Dropping!"

He runs forward and jumps on his board, pushes twice, then pops off the ramp. He grabs melon and hangs in the air, his frame bent in easy control high above the barrel, high above the pavement, soaring forwards and floating for an extended moment. Then, just when physics seems distorted, he accelerates too quickly back to the earth, plummeting at the behest of forces more powerful than youthful ambition. He crashes and flies forward off his board, slamming on his back and rolling away.

My ankles hurt for him.

Tom, though, jumps up and asks me how cool it looked. I realize I was lucky Instagram didn't exist when I was growing up.

He tries again, and again, each time going high in the air before gravity body-slams him against the pavement and there's a thud of meat on asphalt. I film each attempt from my position on the ledge. On his fifth or sixth try Tom launches from the top deck, sails over the plastic trash barrel, and stomps the landing. He rides away quietly like he's done the trick many times before, until he's out of the shot.

"Let me see it! Let me see it!"

We watch the replay on his phone.

"Siiiiiiiick. Nick is going to love this!"

"Who's Nick?"

"Nick?" Tom's eyes cloud over and his voice changes. "He's an older guy. Skates here a lot."

"Is he any good?"

"Nick is the best skater I've ever seen. He's amazing."

"Where is he today?"

"I don't know where he is. Maybe he'll show up later," Tom says in a whisper, looking across the lawn at the parking lot.

Soon Tom is over at the crowded car with Elijah, and Swishies is pushing his girlfriend on his skateboard, and two blond boys are zooming around on scooters, oblivious to the other people in the skatepark. Their overweight parents watch defiantly from an aluminum bench. There is something keeping me there—something I have to figure out about the afternoon in the Charlestown skatepark, something I need to make sense of and cohere into a portable distillation. But now Tom is trying a kickflip down a five-stair, and Elijah's friends are skating the quarterpipes, and I am tired, and the afternoon—muggy and dim, dark and cloudy and humid, always under threat of impending rain—feels like an equation my brain is trying to solve during the last period of the school day.

Or, is my reluctance to leave caused not by a desire to glean something from the experience, but rather to not separate myself from it? To not separate myself from these people who, briefly, had become friends? Am I dragging my feet at the prospect of more time alone with myself, the person with whom I have become too familiar?

I skate over to collect my water jug and say goodbye to Swishies.

"You out, man?"

"Yeah."

"Alright, well, have a nice trip."

"You too. Safe travels back to Ohio."

"Alright, man."

His girlfriend smiles and waves, and I wave back. I say bye to Tom.

"Later, dude, add me on Insta!"

"Alright, bro. See you later."

"Later."

I leave the city and drive into the forested hills to the south. The houses become fewer and fewer, and it becomes darker. That night I pitch my tent in Kanawha State Forest. Everything is wet from rain so I can't start a fire. Instead I shower in a stall with white-tile walls coated in winged insects—fat bugs with drooping antennae that don't move when I turn on the water—and then, clean, crawl into my sleeping bag with a headlamp and Tolkien. When Gandalf and Theoden arrive at Isengard, Merry and Pippin are waiting atop barrels of ale and crates of weed from the Shire.

THERE WERE NO lights at the skatepark, but there were at the basketball court, otherwise known as 'the court' or sometimes 'the courts' even though there was only one of them. So we went down to the basketball court when it was too dark to skate and did flat-ground tricks under the tall floodlights that were swarming with moths and mosquitoes every night of the summer.

People who didn't go to the skatepark would go to the courts, too, and for this reason it was even more of a hangout than the skatepark. Its perimeter was lined with large boulders so people couldn't drive on and do doughnuts, as they had in the past. The people that came to hang out would sit on the boulders and smoke cigarettes, talk in groups, watch people skateboard or play basketball, pump loud music from minivans with their doors propped open. Cars came and went, people showed up and disappeared, there were regulars and semi-regulars and the occasional cameo to whom someone would say, "Oh, what are *you* doing here?"

The town hung a large sign that said 'NO SKATEBOARDING'. Sometimes the cops would kick us off the court, we would go and sit on the boulders until they left, then start skateboarding again when they were gone. You could see the cars that were coming when they made the turn at the elementary school, and if we made out the distinct silhouette of a Chevy Trailblazer with lights on its roof we kicked our skateboards into the bushes and sat on the rocks or picked up a basketball and started shooting hoops. "Cops," one of us would say, not in an excited or frightened way, but with a tone of mild irritation, like Mike Meyers in *Wayne's World* ("Car") and everyone would silently comply.

Real basketball players might show up early in the evening with a large group of guys and play a game, but they rarely came at night. "The surface of the court is terrible," my basketball friend said to me. "It's from all the skateboarding you guys do on it."

"Skateboarding doesn't do anything to the pavement," I replied.

"Yes it does. It ruins it."

Regardless of whether the asphalt was good or bad, a wealthy family came to town and paid for the courts to be completely resurfaced. Instead of asphalt, the courts now had a smooth green coat. The fresh cement and all the money that had been spent made the police even more strict, but it also made us even more desirous to skate. The court was now perfect for skateboarding—one push and you could glide across its entire length without making a noise. So we continued to do what we had always been doing—if there was basketball going on, we would skate the other half of the court, and if both hoops were taken up, we would skate in between them, back and forth across the center circle. Sometimes in this situation a board would shoot off into one of the games. Usually a basketball player would kick the board back with a disapproving look, but sometimes there would be swearing and screaming and the board would end up in the bushes. We only never skateboarded if there was a full-length game going on. Then we would form a team of five ourselves and call dibs on the next match.

When I was younger, the scene at the courts was frightening. Though I could hang at the skatepark among the older skaters, or at least off to the side while they skated, all of their non-skating friends showed up at the courts. These high school kids seemed impossibly older and cooler. They wore baggy pants and drove cars, smoked cigarettes and blasted music with swear words. I recognized one or two of the older crowd from the hockey team, whose every game I watched with my brother and dad during the winter. The fact that they hung out at the courts, with my skateboard idols no less, made the place even more magical. The courts was, for me, the salon of Mme de Guermantes for Proust's young narrator—it was *the* place to be, the home of the in-crowd, where everyone worth knowing would congregate, saying things and interacting in ways I did not understand but understood was very cool. I yearned to be part of it, though I never dared to stay once the lights came on and the high schoolers arrived.

Over time, however, the hour when I left grew later, and the number of people I didn't know decreased. At first me staying was due to skateboarding, as my friends and I would skateboard beside the courts salon and not take part in it, but eventually I, too, was one of the older kids sitting on the rocks. As this happened, and I became more integrated into the scene, there was an inverse reaction in which the luster decreased and the basketball court became less interesting. Perhaps the courts did in fact become less cool, for by the time I was graduating high school, the early 2000s vibe was dead, and no one hung out at the courts anymore. Then, there were only the skateboarders, who had been there since the beginning, pushing back and forth underneath the bright lights, laughing and screaming at the twists in their games of SKATE, relishing the warm evenings and the tropical air that so rarely blessed the nights in northern Vermont.

In between these two epochs, however—those in which I was too frightened to visit the courts, and then too bored by them—existed a few golden summers of overlap. I was in middle school, and maybe freshman year of high school. Then the basketball court was still the most exciting place in the world, and I was slowly being integrated into its cast of characters. During these summers I would be reluctant to leave town on vacation for fear of missing out on 'a big night at the courts', and for fear of jeopardizing my nascent position in the associated social hierarchy.

I wanted to be at the courts as much as possible. My mom would make me come home for dinner because she "didn't want me just hanging out in town all day". After dinner I would bike back down the hill as the sun was starting to descend, pedaling furiously and impatiently to make it downtown, the hub of which was the courts. I would skateboard with my friends and meet older people, most of whom would say, "Oh, you're Teddy's little brother," or "Oh, you're Tommy's friend." Eventually I would look at my watch and say, crap, I have to go meet my mom, who was waiting in a parking lot at the bottom of our hill. After years of arguing, though, the curfew finally went away, and I was allowed to bike back up the hill in the dark whenever I wanted. When I came downstairs in the morning, my mom would say something like,

"You were out late," or "What do you even do down at the courts for so long, anyway?" To which I would always reply, "Skateboarding, mom." Though in my mind skateboarding was only the prelude to the spectacle that unfolded every night at the courts.

Hannibal, MO

I STOP TO SKATE IN THE OUTSKIRTS OF ST. LOUIS, IN A BIZARRE park with too-sharp transitions and a mini-quarterpipe with gaps you can grind over. An old man pauses to watch me pumping around the bowl, and children yell out from the windows of passing cars and school buses, but otherwise I am alone skating in the afternoon heat. The heat feels good after a day of heavy rain driving through Kentucky.

While planning my trip, my mind often turned to Missouri. I had never been there, and I had no preconceived imagining of what it could be like, as is the case with places we hear about frequently like Australia, Nevada, or San Francisco. I couldn't group Missouri in with the southern states, nor with the midwest states or western states: it existed in a regional no-man's land. The only thing filling the vacuum was a certain mystery, an ambiguous mysticism linked to American folklore, the Ozarks, Mark Twain and the Mississippi River. So it seemed fitting that the first Missouri skatepark I visit be the one in Hannibal, Twain's hometown and his muse for the Great American Novel.

As Stockbridge represented the archetypal American small town for Rockwell, and so became the focus of his paintings, so Hannibal represented something larger for Twain, who at that point was well past middle age. The town became the setting for *The Adventures of Tom Sawyer* and *The Adventures of Huckleberry Finn*. In these books, Hannibal is a town filled with remarkable characters, stories, gossip, and history. It is the antithesis of communities within so-called 'flyover states', towns so lifeless and insignificant one is better off simply driving through without stopping at their skateparks. For Twain, a town like Hannibal was not empty but rich, filled with dynastic names—Percy, Fitzgerald,

Sweetser, Mayo—tall tales and unique dialects, ancient histories and rumors passed through generations. Hannibal was a universe in and of itself, a Middle Earth where Twain—white-haired, white-suited, smoking a pipe in snowy Connecticut—could retreat and pass the years caught between memory and imagination.

Like Rockwell, Twain accessed the American small town via the lens of childhood. Twain's protagonists are innocent and naive enough to be fully invested in the streets of their hometown; their entire worldview is contained within its limits, stretching from the treasure-laden caves at one end to the hills at the other, and all along the other edge, of course, is the river, the wide and domineering Mississippi. So when Tom and Huck escape to an island just upstream, it is as if they have taken a spaceship and escaped from their predetermined world to a distant wilderness. And while swapping the familiar for the unfamiliar is exciting, it also grates: soon after leaving, they become homesick and return to crash their own funerals.

Twain's small town children are similar to Rockwell's. They are unsupervised, mischievous, and endearing. They are forever outdoors, and they are the lords of their towns, deeply familiar with all of its forest paths and alleyway shortcuts. They spend every day with each other. They come from homes of modest wealth, if not of poverty, as is the case with Huck. Their misdeeds—trespassing to dive into a favorite swimming hole, skipping school, sneaking kisses from a crush—warrant chuckles and bemused head shakes from the reader and viewer. In short, they are the skatepark rats of their day, always leaving home to spend time at the outdoor hangout and, perhaps, engage in a bit of charming mischief.

Of course, I think, as the landscape turns from lush to arid north of St. Louis and orange dust clouds billow behind the wheels of tractors in empty fields—of course Twain, alive today and writing about Huckleberry Finn and Tom Sawyer, or writing fifty years from now about small town American children today, of course he would write about Huck and Tom meeting up at the skatepark. Tom in his Vans and jeans and Huck in his torn black jeans and black hoodie, Ali Boulala on the Mississippi. The two of them meeting up before skating into town to buy fountain sodas at the gas station and follow an afternoon's whims. Of course Huck would sneak out of his window in the middle of the night with his skateboard under his arm and start skating when he got far enough away. Of course the skatepark would be a refuge and a home for Huck (whose father was an abusive drunk), the place where he actually belonged, for he certainly belonged nowhere else.

Because for how many American children does the skatepark signify something similar? For how many children that I had known did the skatepark represent a refuge from troubled and broken situations at home? For how many children is the skatepark a home in a world in which they are otherwise homeless?

Twain's themes were so harmonious with Rockwell's that the painter even used Twain's stories as subject material, compiling illustrated versions of *Huckleberry Finn* and *Tom Sawyer*. Observing the illustrations, we see the bounty in Twain's vision. We can appreciate the vivid characters of a small town and the humor, drama, and conflict that arise when they interact. We see the pain of first love etched on the faces of Tom and Becky Thatcher, we see the wild eyes and curved pose of a bearded storyteller, we see the unfiltered joy in the grin of a barefooted boy in patched clothes joking with his friends. As when studying Rockwell's images, reading Twain creates a vibrant image of the American small town, albeit one that is sometimes cast in a rose-colored hue.

Twain's novel enjoys such a position in the canon more due to its engagement with a different theme—perhaps *the* fundamental theme of America—which is that of people of different races interacting with one another. Huck, as the popular reading goes, represents white America transitioning from a phase of naive prejudice to one of enlightened tolerance. His alliance and friendship with

Jim shows that racism is not natural but taught, passed to child by parent and society, and that there is hope for a multiracial America. Though Huck lives in a small town in Missouri in the early to mid-nineteenth century—a context within which severe racial biases were the norm, and the national political discourse revolved around slavery—he lives outside of society, surviving as a pariah or outcast in the wilderness. He has no parents or home, and he is a foster child and a runaway. He is not "sivilized", so therefore ingests relatively little of civilization's bigotry. For Huck, Jim transitions from a dehumanized other to a human being with complex emotions. He becomes not only his friend but also his guardian. When Jim rebukes Huck for tricking him, Huck feels guilty, as well as something he has never felt before in his young life: empathetic. Since empathy is associated with maturity and adulthood, the book therefore becomes a coming-of-age narrative, not only for Huck specifically, but more broadly and allegorically for America as a whole, which was then waking up to the sin rooted in its foundation.

This, of course, is the optimistic, modernist, white reading of Twain's text promulgated at American universities and high schools for much of the twentieth century. The postmodern reading is more critical: Jim is a caricature, he is uneducated and inarticulate, and, of course, described by that word repeated hundreds of times throughout the book. The accumulative force of the repetitions outweighs any redemption or reconciliation Twain might have been able to procure, and the book should be censored, banned forever.

My twelfth grade English teacher—a white, liberal old man with a zig-zagging spine—insisted on saying the word aloud as we read in class. It was integral to the book and its historical and cultural significance, he argued. Those unwilling to confront the word were sticking their heads in the sand and ignoring the unpleasant aspects of America's history, which was in turn forgetting them, also a crime and tragedy. This was in 2008. Perhaps teachers would not say the same thing today.

Before I left Vermont, I had a Tinder date with a woman slightly older than me. She was an adjunct instructor at a small college in upstate New York and was home visiting her parents. She was very much 'an academic', which is to say that she was excited to inform me about my prejudices. She had apparently suggested we meet for drinks so she could berate and scold me, and then to sleep with me. When we were chatting in my bed, I told her about my skatepark writing project. She snorted.

"Have fun visiting white space across America."

To which, I had finally had enough.

I was triggered.

"Skateparks aren't white space."

"Yes, they are."

"Have you ever been to a skatepark?"

"Of course."

"Besides the one you saw in an Avril Lavigne music video?"

"Hey, I love Avril Lavigne!"

"So do I."

"The only people at the skatepark are white boys who listen to Blink 182."

I did love Blink 182.

"Well, some people are like that. But some aren't. Some people that go to the skatepark aren't white. Many people, actually."

"Name one skateboarder who isn't white."

"I mean, Nyjah Huston, only the best skateboarder in the world... Daewon Song..."

"See, you don't know anyone else!"

"TK—Terry Kennedy!...Bob Burnquist? He's Brazilian, does that count? Basically every sick Brazilian skater. Every sick Mexican skater. Paul Rodriguez. He's American, actually. That guy from *Sorry...* Sebastien..."

What was his name? I could picture his part... It started with a kickflip down a Parisian three-stair, landing with his feet crossed... Ended with a big kickflip-frontboard down a handrail at a school... Baggy jean shorts... Inward heelflip with his shirt tied around his head, beneath a large pavilion in a city center, the camera pans to three white kids with their shirts tied around their head, too, and Bastien laughs...

"Bastien Salabanzi!"

"Sounds pretty white to me."

"Sounds white? He's a black European guy. Skateboarding is an international sport. I would say the majority of the world's skateboarders aren't white. Think of China! Skateboarding is huge in China."

"In America, then. It's a white sport."

"That's not true. And, furthermore, if you're so woke how can you say people that aren't white don't skateboard? Are you saying they can't? Or shouldn't, because it isn't typical? I would say you're promulgating racial stereotypes more than I am."

"I'm saying more people of color would feel comfortable going to the skatepark if they weren't so intimidated of it being a white space."

"I don't think it's like that. People of color already go to the skatepark."

"Are you sure?"

"Yes."

Was I, though?

I grew up skateboarding in Vermont. The skatepark I knew was, for the most part, exclusively white. Vermont is also the whitest state in the union, though. Surely in any other state in the country, skateparks reflected the diversity of the population as a whole?

It was something I had never considered before. But the Academic's myopic dedication to identity politics infected my vision.

Her offhand dismissal of the project and condemnation of skateboarding lodged itself in my mind and refused to leave, asserting itself again and again as I drove on secondary roads in Kentucky, Arkansas, Arizona, and Nevada. I was forced to consider her ideas and the questions they made me ask as I toured skateparks across the country, and in doing so I was led to a definitive conclusion.

America's skateparks, small town or otherwise, are not white spaces.

After leaving New England, or at least Pennsylvania, I was often the racial minority at skateparks I visited. And on several occasions I was the only white person there—for example at a large cement park outside El Paso. Most people I talked to during my trip were not white, which let me conclude that skateboarding was indeed not a 'white sport'. Perhaps the popular imagination saw skateboarding this way because of its roots in Dogtown—Surfer's California, long blond hair and punk rock; Bart Simpson, Tony Hawk, Marty McFly. Perhaps in the eighties and nineties skateboarding was more white than it is today, but anyone who spends time in an American skatepark will be able to tell that skateboarders are a diverse group, in terms of personality as well as race.

The Academic would not approve of a white man discussing issues related to race, but since I have already compromised myself in her eyes, let me continue. *Huckleberry Finn* is the story of a racist yet innocent young white person being exposed to an African-American person and consequently recognizing his internal prejudices and changing them. Huck realizes that Jim is a complex and wholly unique individual with feelings, and that those feelings can be hurt.

Jim is not 'other'; Jim is part of 'we', we together on this raft, us against Huck's dad, we together against the people of Hannibal, against the Grangerfords and Shepherdsons, against Silas and Sally Phelps. Similarly, perhaps a white child at a skatepark in a segregated small town—for example the ones in Georgia, Arkansas, and

Missouri, where there exist 'the tracks' and a white and black side of town—would meet the African-American kids his own age and spend time with them, skate with them, lounge about in the shade of the bank ramp with them and experience similar revelations. Maybe these kids would hang out at the skate shop together to watch skate videos on a recycled couch scavenged from the dump, pointing out their favorite tricks, arguing about the style of skaters with the verve and nuance of art critics leaving a gallery. If this has ever happened, which I think it has, then skateboarding has served as a bridge between neighborhoods. The skatepark has functioned as a common ground, allowing young people who would have otherwise stared at each other with malice to become friends.

Kids whose families have large homes and multiple SUVs go to the skatepark, as do kids from single-parent, impoverished homes; kids who will one day receive graduate degrees go to the skatepark, as do kids who never finish high school. The kids do not consider these discrepancies as they grow up together; for them they are the same as their friends. Every pair of jeans they buy or expression they use is to identify themselves with their crew, their skatepark crew, to blend together with their clique and to further differentiate themselves from 'them'—not another ethnic group, but all those sheep who don't skateboard and don't understand what *this* is at the skatepark. As they get older, though, they begin to notice certain differences. They notice that one of them goes to Florida every year with his family, that another lives with his stepdad, the itinerant musician and house painter. They discover that one of their families holds a membership to the country club, while another family overflows thirty-two-gallon trash barrels with empty Budweiser cans. These distinctions become apparent but are without implication until high school ends and the friendship dissolves, the Fellowship reaches Amon Hen and the Uruk Hai break them apart, sending each to wander in a different wilderness. One goes to college, one buys a snowboard and moves to

Colorado, one leaves town without a plan, one sticks around and works for his uncle's roofing company. As adults they'll look back and the links between socioeconomics and fate will be conspicuous, glaring, and undeniable. When the crew was still together, though, and they were all learning kickflips, it was an ambiguous background noise to which they never paid much attention.

The skatepark united them. When they leave the unity is broken, and they drift apart to where society would have them.

Except for that the past unites them. Having grown up in a skatepark unites them and millions of other adults and young adults who stopped skateboarding but who still wear skate shoes (the skate shoes last longer now that they don't skate), who you can meet in a bar and who will say, "Yeah, man, I used to stomp tre flips." "Yeah, man, we used to hang out at the skatepark *all fucking day.*" It unites them so that a confused twenty-seven-year-old white man from Vermont can pull into a skatepark in rural northern Missouri—the town where Mark Twain grew up, in fact—take his skateboard out from the passenger seat, skate down the paved path, and feel at home with the (white and black) people he meets.

"Hey!"

Huh?

I stop.

"Do you have a helmet?" A woman asks. She is old but slim and has the bubbly air of a teenager.

"No."

"Have you ever been here before?"

"No."

"Oh, oh, oh. Well, welcome to the Hannibal skatepark! You've got to wear a helmet here, sir, and it's three dollars to use the park."

"I have to pay to skate?"

"Yes, you do."

"Can I rent a helmet?"

"Yes, of course, we have helmets for you to rent. That will be two dollars for the helmet, so five dollars all together."

Fuck.

I didn't have any cash.

"I suppose I can't use my debit card?"

"No, sorry."

"Alright, I've got to go to an ATM. I'll be back."

I drive to the Motel 6 down the road. I check in and use the ATM then drive back to the skatepark. It's the golden hour: the green grass of the rolling lawns and the frisbee golf course are cast in brilliant light, and the few wisps of clouds suspended in the rich indigo above glow with the same soft intensity. The woman in the booth takes my money and hands me a helmet.

"So where are you coming from?"

"Vermont, actually."

"Vermont!" She straightens and looks quickly around at her desk, as if to tidy up. "Well, enjoy!"

The skatepark in Hannibal, Missouri fosters a feeling of congestion. The tall quarterpipes huddle together so intimately that it is impossible to push three times between them and so that it is sometimes hard to gain speed to pop from the top of a bank ramp to noseslide the upper segment of a steep kinked ledge. There is no flat-ground section for putzing around: any manuals or board-slides need to be done at high speeds on and off high transitions of smooth cement. In this sense it is not an East Coast park, and certainly not a New England park with chipped boxes and rusted nails sprinkled on top of rotten pavement, collecting in pot holes you try to ollie over. Which is to say, it was not the type of park I was used to, and certainly not the type in which I excelled.

I skate into the cement flats between the curved transitions. A group of kids pause in yelling at one another to look at me. One kid's on a large mountain bike, the rest are on scooters. There are maybe six of them, and the only other person in the park is a young twenty-something with a hipster beard, khakis, and bright red Converse sneakers. He's also on a scooter and interacts with the kids in a relaxed and natural way that doesn't compromise his position of maturity. He seems like a fifth grade teacher, part mentor and part peer to the scooter kids. He could hang with them and genuinely enjoy himself, but he could also step in and confront one if need be, which one of the kids could not do with his peers.

He says "Hi" and gently offers a palm in greeting. He's on a scooter, which makes me dislike him, though he seems nice.

I float around and probe the park. The transitions are too high and too steep, so I can't push around casually. I drop in from different quarterpipes and bank ramps and experiment with different lines, searching for features that lend to being linked. There are two three-sided bowls connected by a spine with full-vert pitch. I pop onto the deck to catch my breath. The mountain bike kid stops next to me and looks up. His eyes are pale and clear. He's chubby, and his sweat-drenched hair is plastered to his forehead beneath a loose helmet that hangs off the back of his skull.

"Is this your first time here?"

"Yeah."

"There's not a lot of skateboarders that come here."

"I can tell."

"Are you pro?"

"Pro!? No, man. I'm not that good!"

"You're pretty good."

"Thanks, dude. Do you skate at all?"

"No, just bike. There's this older guy that skates here, though."

"Yeah?"

"Yeah. His name is Caveman. He's the best skater in the park."

"Caveman?"

"Yeah. We call him Caveman because he looks like a caveman. He's got a beard and long hair. And he even walks like one, too, and skates like one!"

"What does a caveman skate like?"

70

"He always keeps his hands down by his sides, and doesn't move his arms at all. Like this!"

"Caveman style."

"Yep."

We look off into the park as we pause in our conversation. The scooter kids are zipping up and down, straining to make their small arcs through the air as high as possible. The park is now all in shadow, though the trees above the lawn behind us radiate sunset. The air is balmy and still—summer evening at the skatepark. Everywhere above us the blue of the sky fades from fair to the darkest hue of navy.

"I can't skate these cement parks," I say.

"Huh?"

"I'm not used to cement parks. I can't skate transition."

"I'm really good at skating transition. Well, biking on the ramps and stuff. I love going huge and landing perfect on the other side."

"You like stomping it."

"Yeah! Stomping it! Ready, watch this!" And he drops in, pedaling hard at the roller in the middle of the bowl. He bunny-hops—his body is too small for the large mountain bike—and his two wheels briefly leave the cement. He absorbs the landing, pumps through the transition, and eyes a quarterpipe in front of him.

Besides the chubby kid on the mountain bike, another kid is cheerful and eager to chat. He thinks I'm cool—he follows me around and asks me questions. One of his friends, slightly older and bigger, perhaps in middle school, does not like me. He thinks I'm an intrusion. He says nothing to me when we stand next to each other after hitting the same feature, even though he is otherwise the most extroverted of the bunch. He is condescending to the younger boys and exists both within and without their subjective world. He talks to them as one of them, follows them around and laughs at the jokes of their circle, but he can also step aside and talk calmly with Teacher Guy or with two older kids that walk by on the lawn and stop to chat through the diagonal frames of the chainlink fence, their fingers wrapped around the clefts of dry, iron wires. The way he talks changes. He speaks with more perspective and awareness than when he's with the younger scooter kids. He has more perspective than them, but he does not have as much perspective as me, and this is perhaps why he is hostile to me—my presence infringes on his position of superiority in the park. Such hostility is characteristic of middle school skatepark rats. They have enough perspective to not be children, but not enough to be as gracious as Teacher Guy, who glows with openness and positivity.

As the younger scooter boy becomes more comfortable following me around and gives me more attention, the middle school scooter boy becomes more antagonistic towards him, teasing him with a falsetto, feminine voice and deriding him when he can't land a trick. He bullies the younger boy until the younger boy lands sideways on a 180, flies backwards, slams on his back, and whiplashes his head onto the cement. His helmet makes a *crack* on impact, and the boy immediately begins to cry. The older boy drops his scooter and runs over. He kneels down and holds the younger boy's arm, and I realize they are brothers.

Evening deepens. Though the summery warmth, the green, the sleepy leaves in the twilit trees and the voices of the birds and bugs remind me of Vermont, the air is dry in a foreign way, and I know that I have crossed the Mississippi.

A tall, narrow box sits at a forty-five-degree angle between a steep bank ramp and a quarterpipe. To ollie from the ramp onto the box you have to drop in and approach with speed, and when you get to its end, you have to ollie and land perfectly on the steep curved transition below. Surviving the landing on the quarterpipe is the hardest part.

For the first set of ten tries, I ollie onto the box, lock perfectly into manual, and roll across the raised, skinny table on two wheels only to lose my nerve at the end as the drop-off approaches, kicking my board away without even trying to land on the quarter-pipe. As I jog away, I start swearing at myself.

Pussy.

Bitch.

You suck.

You're weak.

Fucking coward.

Fuck.

Fuck!

Stupid fucking shit bitch you're never going to amount to anything, you're a fucking loser!

LOSER!

Back on the board, back to the top of the drop-in. Friendly Teacher Guy is waiting for me.

"You had that one, man!"

"I know!"

"Just gotta go for it, dude!"

And he, too, becomes increasingly frenzied to get his trick, as are the scooter kids. All of us drop in on the same line, though the scooter kids deviate to try 180s and 360s off a launch ramp, the 180s failing because the kids can't land backwards, the 360s failing because the kids can't make the rotation. Then they push back to the top of the drop-in where I'm dripping sweat and growling at the transition-to-transition box my courage cannot confront. Our attempts begin to accumulate and conglomerate, energy combines and reacts and intensifies, swirling like winds within a storm. We tap and howl and drop in before the previous person has even cleared the way, each skater or scooterer focused, each circling the flow zone, that Elysian realm of divine concentration where one's physical movements and the ideal movements one envisions coalesce. And as each flirts with the flow zone, the universe shrinks so that it comprises nothing but this one corner of the skatepark with cement surfaces sunk deep in murky shadow. I am engaged and mentally invested. The next time I lock in, I think "Not this time, fucker", and pop off the end of the box. I drop halfway down the quarterpipe with my board stuck to the soles of my feet, determined to land but unsure how, and exactly what I was worried about happens. I land with my feet on my skateboard's bolts but my weight backseat, and the board shoots out from beneath me. I fly up in the air with my feet above my head and slam on the cement.

The scooter crowd groans.

Ten tries later, when I lock in manual again, I pop off the box but am off-center to the front and side this time. I snakebite—my board pinches the front left wheel and I'm tossed forwards. I land hard on my shoulder and roll.

The next one, then, would be perfect. Several tries later, I ollie onto the box, manual across, pop off and stomp the landing halfway down the quarterpipe. I pump the transition like I'm an actual skateboarder.

Teacher Guy cheers.

I cool down as I glide through the shadows of the skatepark. I've gotten what I came for, yet for some reason I'm not ready to leave. I sit on my skateboard with my back against the chainlink fence and stare mindlessly at the scooters moving in the dimness, the high golden clouds floating in purple and navy, the trees still in the dry, warm air. I realize I am reluctant to go back to my hotel.

For the first time during the trip, skateboarding has given me the feeling it used to, the feeling when I would stay at the park until it got dark and my mom would show up, angry that I was still skateboarding two hours after she had served dinner. And for the first time on the trip, and for the first time in six or seven years, I remember: skateboarding is fucking fun.

When the sweat has crusted into a salty paste on my forehead, and the damp T-shirt on my back begins to chill, I say goodbye to Teacher Guy and the Scooter Kids, skipping the older brother who doesn't like me. It's too dark to skate, and I'm too tired to pop another trick. The yearning is still there, though, just as it had been when I finally got into my mom's car, her headlights passing over the dark entrance to the ice rink, and I would already be looking forward to the next day when the sun would rise and I would again have the chance to skate.

WE WERE THIRTEEN or fourteen and sprawled out at the skatepark—two sitting on their skateboards, one stretched out on the box, one walking the down rail like it was a balance beam. It was autumn, the leaves were mostly gone, and those left clinging to the tips of branches were a deep, robust red. Each gust carried color that flipped and spun against the milky sky, leaves landing wherever the wind pushed them: in the cleft between ramps and pavement, against boxes and the cement parking blocker. You had to occasionally sweep them away with your foot if you wanted to skateboard.

It was a Saturday, and there was a school dance that night.

Dances always stirred excitement because of the unknown—who would you dance with, might you get a kiss?—and this element was now enhanced, for this would be our first high school dance. Whereas our options before had been limited to the girls in our class, now we would be mixed in with those from the three grades above us, all of whom were not only physically developed women but also, we assumed, beyond sexually experienced—they were sex goddesses.

Instead of skateboarding that day, we talked about the dance. More precisely, we talked about which upperclassmen girls we thought were hottest, and what the chances were they would dance with us.

And—just maybe—what were the chances they would want to hook up with us?

We became frenzied, imagining the hottest girls in the school coming up to us with sinister smiles, then pulling us into the cleaning closet. We rolled on the pavement and howled and slammed our fists against the leaf-strewn asphalt.

"What if..." Mike began, "What if they want to have sex with us?"

We grew quiet.

"You're supposed to use a condom, right?"

"Yeah."

"Of course you are, you idiot!"

"How do you even put one of those things on?"

"It's easy."

"You don't know."

"Sure I do! I've put one on."

"Yeah, right."

"I have!"

"Where?'

"At Aaron's house! We stole 'em from his older brother's room. He had a whole stack of 'em!"

"Is it hard?"

"Very, very easy. Self-explanatory, you'll figure it out, no problem."

"Do you think we'll actually need them for tonight?"

"Mmmm. I don't know."

"What do you guys think?"

"Well…"

"Well I'd say probably not, 'cause, like, what are the chances Alice Meyers is *actually* going to want to take one of us into the broom closet?"

"Low."

"But the chance does exist."

"Of course."

"You're right."

"Exactly. And how are you going to feel when Alice Meyers does try to bang you in the broom closet and you don't have a condom on you? You're going to feel like a complete fucktard!"

"So we should get some."

"Yes!"

We dug through our pockets for money. Together we had nine dollars and forty-seven cents.

"Is that enough for condoms?"

"I don't know!"

"Should be enough."

"So you're going to buy them, then?"

"Fuck no!"

"Well you're the one holding the money."

"I'm just organizing it. I'm the accountant here. Mike's gonna' do it."

"Why me?"

"'Cause! I'm the accountant."

"Yeah but Keith's not doing anything, either!"

"Mike, just do it."

"C'mon, Mike."

"Fine."

We skateboarded down the hill from the skatepark, passed the basketball court, playground, and elementary school, ollied on the sidewalk when cars came. When we reached Main Street we picked up our boards and walked the rest of the way to the gas station.

Tommy, Keith, and I were quiet inside by the soda machine. We made furtive glances to Mike as we filled 32oz. cups with different combinations of Coke, Mountain Dew, Sunkist, and Dr Pepper, then each paid separately with change and hurried outside.

We were in our spot on the high rock wall behind the store when Mike squeezed through the fence and the clapboard wall.

"So!?"

"Did you get 'em?"

"Sorry, guys, I wimped out."

"What!?"

"Mike!"

"C'mon!"

"Just kidding." Mike grinned and removed a little purple case from his pocket.

"*Her Pleasure!?*"

"Good choice, Mike!"

"She'll appreciate that."

"Woohoo!"

We opened the box and realized there was a problem. There were four of us but only three condoms. Mike said that since he had gone in and bought them he deserved to take one. So Tommy, Keith, and I argued about who would get the other two. We agreed that if the empty-handed person did end up getting lucky, than someone with a condom would have to donate his for the benefit of the team. However, if the individuals who had condoms were simultaneously getting lucky, then they wouldn't have to give up their condoms. So in the eventuality that all four of us got pulled into different closets, than the guy without a condom would simply be out of luck.

We did rock-paper-scissors.

Keith and Tommy threw rock, I threw scissors.

"Dammit!"

"Aha!"

"Why do I always do scissors!?"

"Cause you suck, jackass."

"But what do I say to you guys if I'm getting pulled into the broom closet? It's not like I can just say 'Give me a condom' in the middle of the dance."

"Hmmm."

"Good point."

"We need a codename."

"Yeah!"

"Something we can say wherever we are and no one will know what we're talking about."

"Perfect."

"How about... 'eagle'?"

"Give me the eagle? That's dumb."

"It needs to be cooler than that."

"How about... the shields!"

"No, shields is too close to protection. People will know what we're talking about."

"Condoms are basically sperm shields."

"Right."

"It should be something cool, but something that no one will guess about."

"OK."

We brainstormed for a while as we drank our tall fountain so-das from the wax cups that developed white crease lines as the ice inside melted. As we talked we let fat globs of bubbly spit drop from our lips and watched them fall to the pebbles twenty feet below.

"How about... 'relics'?" Tommy said.

We were quiet.

"Give me the relics."

"Do you have a relic?"

"I need the relic!"

"Crap! Where's the relic!"

"That's it!"

"Relics!"

We skateboarded to Mike's house when it got dark. His mom cooked us dinner and we watched the VHS skate video we always watched. At 8:30, we skated back into town and went to the Memorial Building. As we stood in line by the table where the French teacher sat selling tickets, I said, loud enough so that she could hear, "Hey, Tommy, you have the relic?"

"I've got the relic," he said. We all grinned.

No one needed the relics that night. Nor would anyone need them for some years to come. But we kept them in our backpacks, and sometimes when we were in school one of us would ask, "Where's your relic?" or "Do you have the relic?" And the other would pat his front pocket and say, "Relic secure". Even after we did start having sex, we would ask each other "Did you use a relic?" or explain after a senior year house party "But I didn't have any relics!" Whoever was listening wouldn't even laugh at our little inside joke because the codename had become so normalized within our vocabularies. And even to this day I sometimes see a row of condom packs hanging on their white bars in the gas station and think to myself "relics", and smile.

Farmington, MO

PROUST TALKED ABOUT THE RELATIONSHIP BETWEEN ONE'S imagination and the names of unknown places. For Proust, the train timetables alone were enough to provoke his mind to excitement, to incite visions of cliffs and black cathedral towers, waves and thunder that shook the earth. Place names were suffused with mystery, and it was the mystery that made them attractive; Proust's narrator would not have yearned to visit Balbec, Combray, or Graincourt had he known them in reality.

For me it was not the flipping names of final destinations that stoked my imagination and predilection for romance, but instead Google Maps. With the unblinking eyes of a child in the steam and clamor of a Parisian station I scrolled over faraway towns I had never seen before. I imagined they were so ordinary and unremarkable that no traveler had ever stopped to visit them. And it was exactly this banality that excited me, because, I realized, at the heart of my desire to travel was the deep desire to live more lives than the one I had been granted—to be a normal person born in Osaka, who went to high school and then became an accountant, who had one or two love affairs and then married; to be a small, anonymous man in Poland; to have been born and raised in Missouri, to become a plumber there, to play the piano and fish with my own, proper equipment. This desire was rooted in curiosity, for I felt the world was so overwhelmingly large yet I had only one life to live and knew so little because of it.

O God, Thy sea is so great, but my boat is so small.

When scanning the names of towns in states I had never been, I would search to see if they had skateparks. I would check drive times, I would click on pictures others had posted and see whether the town was situated between other towns, if there were blue strips of river or green blocks signifying state or national parks, as if the colors of place names could somehow indicate the shades one might discover there.

So, while in my motel room in the arid north of Missouri, a town sandwiched between the ribbon of the Mississippi and an encroaching green border labelled *Mark Twain National Park* catches my attention. My imagination conjures images of fat boughs sagging over the glassy surface of an imperceptibly flowing current, mist and a damp, swampy Mississippi. Tall tales, skeletons of river boat captains, rotting camps of outlaws, detritus from forgotten vendettas. The fetid and secret accretions of centuries passing within the main vein of America.

Later that afternoon, I skate out onto the worn cement of the skatepark in Farmington, Missouri. There are no ghosts or pirates and no laden boughs in sight. The thought "Oh, so *this* is what it's like", comes less with disappointment than satisfaction and even excitement: I was really here, in a place I had been wondering about.

The park is large, with quarterpipes and stair-sets around its perimeter, and several boxes, wedges, and pyramids scattered in the middle with ample space between them. The concrete is rough so it's hard to pivot or slide under-rotated 180s. Cracks in its surface and imperfections in the copings and transitions date the park to the nineties or early 2000s when skateparks were made by people who didn't skateboard. Two young teenagers are having a game of SKATE in the flats, and no one else is there.

The boys stare at me as I skate into the park.

"Hello," I say.

"Hi," one of them says.

"You from around here?" the other asks.

"No, I'm not."

"Where are you from?"

"Vermont."

"Vermont?"

"That's right."

"Oh."

"You wanna play SKATE with us?"

"Sure."

It's a hot afternoon, and our game is lethargic. The two boys seem about as good as I am. No one can land much besides their signature tricks.

"Chris! Will!"

A man is standing above us on the deck of a quarterpipe. He's come out of a pink building on the edge of the skatepark that reminds me of the changing room next to a public pool.

"Yeah?"

"It's time for class."

"OK," and then to me, "Sorry, we gotta go."

"What class is it?"

"Bible class. Wanna come?"

"No, that's alright."

"You sure? Mr B would be excited if you came. I think you'll really like him!"

"Really?"

I look into the open door of the pink building. The sunlight on the outside walls makes the interior dim, nearly obscure, but I can see teens at desks and books and backpacks in front of them. They lean across aisles and tables in a way I find intimidating.

"Come join us!" Mr B yells down to me. He's the young-and-cool type priest with wavy hair, glasses, and a polo.

I consider telling him I'm Jewish or even Muslim just to fuck with him. Instead I mumble an apology and am filled with the shame of a Christian boy skipping Bible class to putz around in the skatepark.

As I explore the corners of the wide park I think about what would have happened if I had gone into Bible class. Would the cool, hot priest have asked me questions? Would he have asked me about sex? Would I have lied, or would I have revealed my true thoughts: that life was meaningless, that man was alone, that existence was a brief candle sputtering and flickering before going cold, leaving the world no different than it had been some few minutes before?

Life was not meaningless, though. Rather, life held subjective meaning. If someone felt accomplished by working hard and refining themselves, by learning something, by making more money; if they felt thrilled and delighted at strapping planks to their feet and sliding down a mountain covered in snow, then they could do these things and their life would attain subjective value. One could find meaning in human connection, friendship or the embrace of a lover, a wholly separate and sweet-smelling human whose wide or gentle eyes—so close!—conveyed an intimate community, a bonfire of meaning in an otherwise meaningless void. Connection to other humans creates meaning, which is perhaps one draw of religion, but this is the same force at work in nationalism or a more healthy and community-oriented identification, like the connection to a local sports team.

I've always resented sports fans, nationalism, religion, and conformity to groups in general. Since middle school, I've identified as an outsider, even though I've never been one. Perhaps this was why I liked the culture around skateboarding—skateboarding hid the fact that it was a community and made its adherents believe they were non-conformists.

Since I had rejected creating meaning through belonging to a larger community, I had sought meaning and definition through romantic connection. I believed that being in love would make my life meaningful. Treating love as a means to a preconceived end, however, is a sound formula for too-quickly-risen-hopes to disintegrate like a faulty rocket ship shedding parts in Earth's atmosphere. To rely on a source you cannot control—namely, the whims of another individual—has downsides. When you are miserable, there is nothing you can do to not be miserable. You can only wallow in meaninglessness, shuffling your feet through days devoid of purpose, excited about nothing save getting drunk with halfhearted friends, sometimes fantasizing about sinking to the bottom of the lake to dissolve unobtrusively like the smoked butt of a rollie, no-filter cigarette.

But ... skateboarding?

Can skateboarding inject meaning into an otherwise meaningless life?

Throughout my trip, I have met people whose relationship with skateboarding reflected my own. They were once defined by skateboarding but had, as they aged, lost skating as a source of meaning and community. Their skateboards drifted further and further into their closets as new forces filled their lives and formed their identities. When these elements—jobs, girlfriends, political parties—disappeared, or proved themselves hollow, they were left flailing in an existential abyss. This could perhaps be described as a quarter-life crisis, an impasse when childhood had, at last, definitively come to an end and something unknown had to begin.

But what?

What would we do for the rest of our lives?

Who would we be?

Seeing no clues ahead of us, we look to the past, to the thing we've forgotten but once always knew to be true:

Jesus.

No, not Jesus.

Skateboarding!

While digging through old closets, we unearth old skateboards, the wheels and bearings coated in grime, the deck lined with cracks, the nose and tail worn to stubs.

We hold it in our hands.

It feels right.

It smells and sounds like something good.

85

The first days back are awkward. We're bad—really bad—but it's exciting.

Then something clicks, you're skating as good as before, soon better, and you make yourself a promise:

You must never stop skateboarding.

Skateboarding is who you are.

If a skateboarder stops skating, what is he?

He is nothing.

He is a man with a job he hates, who does nothing he likes: a sheep-person suffering through quiet desperation, briefly, until he dies and is forgotten.

Just as Christians hold the Bible as irrevocable, permanently right and permanently just, so I have skateboarding. In moments when I forget myself, when I am lost, I have skateboarding.

And I don't need anyone else to skateboard.

I push into an eight-stair. Push again, crouch low, and pop. As soon as I ollie, the board leaves my feet. I'm alone in the air waving my arms. I land hard and roll over the pavement. I'm relieved when I see no one was watching.

Others skaters trickle in as the sun sinks lower in the sky. Some skate and some just hang out in the corner next to their parked cars. The skatepark begins to feel very much like a small town skatepark: it is first and foremost a meeting place, and people skate there, too. The degree to which a skatepark is a small town skatepark can be measured by how conspicuously foreign a visitor feels. As I skate around by myself and a dozen young men watch from their spot in the corner, leaning on cars and sitting on bikes, smoking and laughing, I feel every bit the outsider. The question "Who's that guy?" is so loudly thought it's almost audible. Still, there is no hostility. When I back 5-0 a mini-ledge, a shirtless guy covered in tattoos smacks his board on a ramp's cement and offers a loud "Yip-yip!"

Despite the 5-0, the session isn't going well. I'm skating tentatively, without asserting my will over the board and the skatepark passing beneath it. I'm sore, I'm hot, and I'm tired. However, things start slowly coming together. I land one trick I had been trying, then another: a kickflip over the pyramid, a kickflip down a three-stair, a back-one back up it. I 50-50 on a kink ledge, I fakie 270 axle stall on the high quarterpipe, ollie nose manual on the medium box. When, after ten or fifteen minutes of trying, I stomp a big flip on the long, mellow bank ramp, I receive whoops from the hangout crowd. When I start trying a fakie big flip in the same spot (now my favorite spot), I begin to BS them into a full cab-540 flip (really just a half-cab varial at an angle with a pivot landing). After a few tries I land it. I skate away and look up at the pink building at the skatepark's edge. The walls now glow in sunset. The cool, hot priest is standing again in his spot atop the quarterpipe, cast in the same light like Moses on the Mount. Students file out of the door behind him. He smiles and gives a thumbs-up. To acknowledge the compliment, or perhaps to offer props of my own, I raise my hand and do a thumb's up in return.

THE SOUL SKATER was not always known by that name. At first, when the skatepark was new and the Older Crowd reigned, the Soul Skater was just another of its members, albeit one younger than the rest, more modest, and possessing certain other unique qualities we could not identify. Despite his age, he was still one of the better skateboarders and thus commanded the respect of the park. He skateboarded with a clean gracefulness you might associate with a neatly stacked pile of shirts—washed, folded, and ready for the closet—and for this reason he was Keith's favorite. Or perhaps because he was Keith's favorite I came to associate the Soul Skater with freshly pressed clothing, stainless white carpets, and rows of sneakers that formed a straight line.

As the Older Crowd waned and disappeared and we became the Older Crowd ourselves, the Soul Skater still showed up to the skatepark, asserting himself unannounced like a king reappearing in the court of a steward. On some quiet summer evenings when the sun was going down over the swamp, and the skatepark and the front of the ice rink were sticky in golden light, the air warm and still, and there was no one but the four of us on top of the hill lying in the dirty asphalt with skateboards as our pillows, a Jeep would arrive. Out came the Soul Skater, a name we quickly whispered to one another. He then skated into the skatepark, waving at us but wasting no time in starting to shred.

The Soul Skater skateboarded with an elegance which precluded him, in our eyes, from mortality. Mortals ollie over rails or grind ledges and flail their hands to balance themselves; they occasionally panic, or jerk their bodies in desperation. They do tricks without being aware of how silly their straight legs and bulging butts look, and when they land, they celebrate like they should be proud of what they've done. They sometimes land off balance, or don't land at all. Sometimes their wheels catch because they didn't do exactly what they wanted, and they fly forwards and hurt themselves on the cement.

The Soul Skater did not experience these things and therefore was not mortal. In our eyes, he was more divine than human, and when he skateboarded among us, we stopped what we were doing to watch because it felt like we had been blessed. He executed every trick just as he wanted; he skated fast and went big, popped tricks high above the bank ramp but never seemed to exert himself. He caught kickflips and 360 flips before landing them, he locked into crooked grinds or smith grinds without wobbling down the rail. His movements were precise and calculated and therefore some-how too sterile for my taste; there was something too textbook and inhuman about them. His style, though, was not totally with-out flavor—he moved with an easiness and confidence that comes from exceptional athleticism, conveying the impression he was calm despite the things he was doing. His skateboarding had a nu-anced cheekiness to it, a slight mischievousness as if he wanted those watching to gasp and then chuckle, then clap wildly. All of this reminds me of the way Federer plays tennis, or Neymar soc-cer—not only perfectly, but also beautifully, too.

The Soul Skater skated hard without stopping. When he showed up and started he didn't stop until both sides of his shirt were soaked through with sweat. He did a line, turned around, saw none of us were yet actually skateboarding, dropped back in and did whatever came to him, improvising for more than an hour without stopping to catch his breath. He never came with anyone and always skateboarded by himself. He did difficult tricks for no one but himself, and skated with a perfect style for no one but himself. It was only when we were older and saw him skate this way that we realized he had never been there for the scene or the crowd, but that he had been there to skateboard. And this is when we gave him the name The Soul Skater.

After I graduated from high school, and then college, I some-times went to play pickup soccer in the town fields on Wednesday and Friday nights in the summertime. Sometimes the Soul Skater was there. Just as he had shown up by himself at the skatepark, so he would arrive by himself at the fields, get out of his car and jog over in his cleats and soccer shorts, and he would seem divine, so angelic were his movements compared to those of the other players stretching before the game. And when one time I played too hard and bumped into him, and he screamed and fell to the grass, holding his knee, I felt the same guilt as the sailor who aimed his rifle at a soaring albatross, pulled the trigger for the fun of it, and realized he had killed an angel.

Mountain View, MO

SKATEBOARDING—NOT SOCCER—IS *LA JOGO BONITO*, THE beautiful game. Its beauty lies in its simplicity and consequent purity. It is a game that refines one's creativity and grace, those most particular characteristics of human beings, encouraging one to elaborate on them, to let their tendrils blossom into the most vibrant of flowers. There are no rules to follow save that one must land back on the board, and all one needs to play is a skateboard and a small square of pavement.

The skatepark in Mountain View, Missouri is a testament to this fact. It is the smallest and simplest skatepark I have ever been to. It seems the town made a patch of pavement for foursquare but, when no children came, brought in a narrow box and two squat quarterpipes and called it a skatepark. The plastic panels of the quarterpipes are peeling so you can only drop in from one to the other and then only come down one side after you axle-stall or rock-to-fakie (you won't want to drop in fakie). You can't go back up the ramp you started on because your front wheels will catch on the warped edge of a panel that has come loose from its nails.

To skate the box, you need to place your board on the very edge of the pavement, take a few steps back on the grass, run and jump onto your board. You'll have just enough time to crouch and pop, but your feet need to land where you want them because you won't have time to adjust.

There is a strip of pavement between the quarterpipes and the box you can use for flat-ground tricks, and this is ultimately what I do, jumping back and forth, popping low and slow shove-its, kickflips, heelflips, fakie flips, half-cab flips, varial flips, attempts at 360 flips and inward heelflips and backside heelflips and nollie flips. After failing repeatedly at 360 flips, I go back to kickflips, but now I can't land those, either—the board either lands upside down or drifts away from me. I swear or say nothing, put the board back in place, walk onto the grass, step and jump back on and try again.

The skatepark is surrounded by baseball fields and soccer fields. It's the day they get mowed—three guys are out on the fast, rider mowers kicking up plumes of clippings and filling the air with the buzz of engines and the green smell of the earth. Behind the skatepark is a set of train tracks. As I curse in the drone of the coming-and-going mowers a train begins to pass, one of those rusty freighters whose caboose you wait for but never see, its cars keep coming in different colors and sizes with different names painted on their bellies, and eventually you go back to what you were doing and the passing train becomes background noise. I keep trying kickflips in the mechanical clamor of the train and the crescendos of the mowers. No one else is there except the long-gone conductor and the three men mowing the fields. They must watch me with bewilderment and contempt, this grown man doing kickflips on a drop of pavement in the middle of a weekday, under a soporific sun and bloated, lethargic clouds. When they mow the lawn by the parking lot, and see a Saab with green plates and the funny word 'Vermont', their bewilderment must increase, for they have never before seen a Canadian skateboarding at their skatepark in Mountain View, Missouri.

WHEN WE GOT bored of the skatepark, we went street skating. This usually meant going down the hill to the elementary school, where you pushed off the window by the music room and dropped off a mini-curb to stall on another across the roundabout. The school had a curb people kept waxed for grinds and slides and an incline you could ollie onto, ride up, and come back down. The trick to land at this spot was 'The Trifecta': kickflip up, kickflip at the top, kickflip off back into the parking lot. Otherwise we skated at Wadd's Drop or Shaw's Drop, though the people there were fast in kicking us out, always with exasperation, or at the shopping plaza with the tall, wooden flowerbeds. We also had spots that did not immediately lend themselves to skateboarding that we could session for hours. We claimed these spots as our secrets—a large boulder on a brick path behind the hotel, a storm drain on the side of the church, the bank at the grocery store.

It wasn't really a bank ramp, just a steep and sudden decline at one of the three entrances into the grocery store's parking lot. The pavement here had cracked before anywhere else and had been redone with fresh, black tar. We saw this square of smooth asphalt as a curved little bank ramp, perfect for slash-powerslides and little flip tricks—kickflips, varial flips, shove-its, heelflips, 180s and big spins. It was a nice spot for us because its slope wasn't too steep.

The grocery store was far from downtown, for our standards, so we didn't go there very often, and when we did the trip felt special, like we were on an excursion. This out-of-the-ordinary feeling necessitated out-of-the-ordinary treats, so we would go into the store and buy the fried chicken sitting in the metal tub under the heat lamps, potato chips, a bag of blue sharks or peach gummie rings, and a soda. Then we would take our treats out to the skate spot and put them down against the building's cement foundation and skateboard, pausing or finishing the session to sit in the parking lot against the building and eat and watch the cars coming and going just in front of us.

On this particular day, it was the middle of summer, a day in June or July or August indistinguishable from those surrounding it: puffy white clouds stagnant high in the atmosphere, sun saturating all the leaves and people and cars of the earth. We were skating the bank ramp at the grocery store. As usual, cars came up the road intending to turn but then would see us and accelerate to go another fifty feet to the larger entrance. When cars were leaving, even if they were parked directly next to our skate spot, they would drive to the other exit. If a car did pass we would stand to the side and wave, excited to show that despite our long hair and skateboards we were actually harmless.

I noticed a man transferring his groceries from his cart into the back of his minivan. He was a young dad, I thought, not very old but not cool at all, either. He had a beard, short hiking shorts, a flannel, Teva sandals with the rubber soles and the colorful straps around the heel and toes. He noticed us and, when he had shut the trunk of his car, started walking over.

My heart started beating.

Uh-oh.

"No, shit," he said. We stopped skateboarding to turn and look at him. "Kids are still skateboarding here, then, huh? I used to skate this spot, too."

"Oh, yeah?"

"Yep. Back when I was a kid we used to skate here all the time, just like you guys. But we would skate out back at the loading dock. You guys ever skate there?"

"No. But my brother's done it."

"Yeah? It's a big drop, man."

"Yeah."

"Oh, man! I remember we used to session that thing hard. I kickflipped off of it once."

"Really?"

"Oh, yeah. My buddy did a 180 off it, too."

"Cool."

"I grew up here, then moved away…" The man began his life story. We all stayed quiet, but fidgeted and stopped listening. "It's so funny that kids are still skateboarding here!"

"Yeah, it's cool. "

"It's cool, dudes. Oh man, seeing you guys brings me back! We used to be just like you, hanging out in town with our skateboards…"

"Really?"

"Yeah…" The man stared at the brick wall of the building and was silent. "Hey, you kids keep skating, alright? Don't stop."

"Alright."

"Don't ever stop. I don't know what happened, man, I kind of got older and stopped skating for a little bit, then the years passed and I didn't skate at all anymore, ya know? I was good though. I was fucking good, man!"

"I believe it."

"I was! I was really good! Hey, you wouldn't mind if I tried out your board, would you?"

"Go for it."

I handed him my skateboard. He put the skateboard down and stood on it. He was much heavier than I was and bent the trucks so that the deck was pinching against the wheel. My stomach squeezed tight.

He tried a kickflip. The board flipped upside down.

"See! That was pretty close!"

He fixed the board and bent down again. He was awkward on the board, with his butt sticking out and his arms waving in the air like he was surfing, though he was just standing still. His bare feet in his goofy sandals didn't look right on the grip tape of the skate-board, and they looked too big, too, half hanging off and twisting the trucks. He was off balance and had all his weight on one edge of the board for the kickflip, but he tried again. You could tell he had indeed once skateboarded because the board went in the air though he was nowhere close to landing it.

"Woah! Sick!" He said and righted the board to try again. There became less time between his attempts, and the attempts became frenzied. He alternated between optimistic encouragement—"Oh, that was close!"—to angry self-deprecation—"Dammit! Come on, Brad! Come on!" We stood in a semi-circle watching in silence. There was something pathetic about it. Each time he bent down and all his weight went on the heelside edge of the board and the trucks were stressed more than I would have ever stressed them the anxiety grew inside me, growing with each successive try, the knot in my stomach tightening as I stared at his bare toes straining in the colorful straps until—

"Hey, man, do you think I could have my board back?"

"Oh, yeah. Of course. Here you go, dude."

He picked the board up. Instead of returning it, he held my skateboard with both hands and considered it, as if struggling to part with it, perhaps like Boromir with the Ring in the Pass of Caradhras. Then, like Boromir, the transfixion passed, he looked up, smiled, and handed the skateboard back to me.

"Anyways, you kids have fun, alright?"

"Yep."

He walked back to his minivan and drove away.

We went back to skateboarding and didn't talk about the man in Teva sandals. But there was something about him that my mind kept returning to that night and during the nights that followed. It was the way the tone of his voice had changed when he kept trying the kickflip, it was the juxtaposition of his sandals and the skateboard; it was the distance in his gaze when he thought about his childhood at the loading dock, it was the lust in his eyes when he held my skateboard, refusing to give it back.

Berrysville, Arkansas

THE SKY OF NORTHERN ARKANSAS IS ALTERNATING PATCHES of navy then baby blues, a never-ending flotilla of cumulus clouds with colorful hulls, separated by strips of emptiness, stretching over the flat landscape in every direction. It's the end of a warm afternoon. The road is empty between fields dotted with cows and lonely trees. The towns have populations of two or three hundred and grow around pawn shops decorated with images of guns. I consider stopping at a 'hillbilly glassblowing studio' advertising a 'hillbilly at work!' but keep driving. I'm close to my next skatepark.

The skatepark in Berrysville, Arkansas is isolated in a large field of mown grass. When you park your car and descend the grassy hill, the skatepark far below and across the field is an island of pavement surrounded by green. Your skate shoes on the grass seem discordant or somehow indecent, for these are items that belong on pavement.

A boy and girl are sitting at a picnic table in the corner of the park when I finally reach the pavement's shore. The table surface is a slippery plastic scarred with gashes—it is in fact meant for skateboarding. The two high schoolers have nevertheless spread out textbooks and papers between them, though their attention is on each other and not schoolwork.

"I wont be distracting you guys from studying if I skate for a bit?" I ask.

"No, we stopped studying a long time ago," the girl says.

"That's good. You should never study too much!"

A memory explodes like a flare above a nighttime battlefield: every seventh period study hall of spring, a girl and I go to the lawn behind the tennis courts, open our books, and speak quietly looking into each other's eyes.

The ramps in the skatepark are made with metal sheets, so the silence is broken with loud bangs as I ollie on the transitions. The park consists of a narrow bank ramp leading to an island pyramid with a small euro gap and a kink rail, and another quarterpipe. There's a box with one edge curved in a gentle crescent, a double kink, the (occupied) picnic table, and, at the far end, a mini-ramp covered in stickers and worn-away paint.

I land an ollie-manual and a small boardslide. When I stop on the bank before dropping back in, the high school kids are just below me.

"Wow, you're so good!" the girl says.

"Haha. Thank you. But I'm not that good at all, actually, especially for how long I've been doing it!"

"How long have you been skating for?"

"Oh, I'm twenty-seven now, I started skating when I was in the third grade, that's what, nine? Ten? So about seventeen years."

"What, really? You've been skating longer than I've been alive!"

"So really I should be much better after doing it for so long!"

"I wish *I* could skateboard."

"You can! You just have to try it and then practice."

"Um, no way."

I roll over the crest of the ramp and fly through the afternoon on four wheels.

That skateboarding is an individual sport is a misnomer: skateboarding is best enjoyed with friends, or simply with other people around you. When you skate alone you become sluggish, uninspired, and apathetic. When you skate alone there is no one to build with, to collaborate with, to play with, to impress. You are a child by himself in a sandbox surrounded by lifeless toys. You can use any bucket or truck you want, but your fun depends on your imagination alone, and no one else will pick up the thread when your narrative of pirates in dojos and ninjas in pirate ships runs aground. If you are a child inclined to loneliness, who cries when your mother drops you off at daycare, having a friend to talk to is always preferable to sitting in the sand by yourself.

The boy and girl leave and I am alone in the park. I soul-skate, pushing around and popping and grinding and sliding, manualing and pumping for my exclusive benefit, to see what I can do and how well I can skate. I varial-flip the pyramid because it feels good, because it's difficult and I want to accomplish something difficult, landing it one time and then trying to land it twice in a row, taking the same line and flipping the same trick over and over and over so that I have it on lock and can stomp on command. A mature and respectable skater values consistency. This is the ideal I strive for when I skate by myself, and during these times I always think of the Soul Skater. To be honest, though, I have never been such a gentleman skateboarder. I'm more the tattooed redneck drunk on Twisted Tea huffing down a Marb Red on top of a seventy-foot cliff, yelling down to his buddy filming on a flip phone: "Ready, Buzz? I'm about to send it!" So it is with a tick of joy that I see two people walking down the grassy hill to the skatepark.

They are young men around my age. One is tall and wears swishy basketball shorts and Adidas sandals; the other is a skateboarder in dirty skate jeans and dirty Converse high-tops with the tops rolled down. He goes directly to the mini-ramp and starts pumping back and forth. Swishy Shorts detaches from his friend without a word and heads to his spot at the picnic table. They form an odd couple—Swishy Shorts is spotless and neat, composed, albeit in a casual way, while Converse exemplifies bohemian skater grunge, someone who wakes up hungover and finds the nearest T-shirt regardless of the mustard or pizza dust or blood staining the front, grabs his only pair of jeans from their spot on the floor where they have spent every night for innumerable weeks without visiting a washer machine. People in small towns like Berrysville do not have the luxury of picking and choosing their friends. In a small town, you become friends with whoever is next to you, and sometimes you become friends with someone when you are three or four or five years old and remain friends despite your growth into divergent personalities. So two small town contemporaries travel together to the skatepark where upon arrival one of them assumes his position on his phone at the picnic table, completely disinterested in the sport his friend practises with such devotion.

Swishy Shorts says hello as he walks below the bank ramp and I'm catching my breath. I drop in and try a kickflip over the euro gap. It's an easy trick, but I'm having a hard time executing and I feel silly now that people are there to watch me struggle. I right my board and push down the pyramid, rolling into the quarterpipe and cruising around the various features in the park, though every line brings me back to the top of the bank ramp because my focus is on the kickflip over the euro. When I lose my balance popping a frontside disaster on the quarter I have to jog after my board as it rolls away. "The metal's a bit slick, isn't it?" Converse says, chiming in from the deck of the mini. The comment acknowledges that I'm an outsider.

"Yeah, a bit."

"That's a sick trick, though."

"Yeah, man. I'm trying to get them back. It's been a few years!"

"Right?"

I push off towards the pyramid's hip. Converse eventually leaves the mini-ramp and skates around the park. I act like I don't care, but, like all skateboarders in a skatepark with another skater (especially one they don't know), I keep track of what tricks he tries, what he's landing, and how sketchy or clean his style is, always compiling and calculating to reach an answer to the inevitable, lamentable question: is he better than me?

"What are you trying over that thing, a kickflip?" Converse asks as he joins me on top of the bank ramp.

"Yeah, can't land it though."

"Those things are hard, dude." (Proper skate etiquette.)

"They should be easy. But I can't figure this transition out."

"Can I try?" (Again, proper skate etiquette.)

"Of course."

He drops in at the pyramid. He pops, his board does a half flip, and he lands on its painted underside.

"See! Fucking hard!"

"Haha."

A few tries later I land it, and Converse gives me tappies. As if he can finally stop messing around, Converse drops in and floats an exquisite kickflip over the euro gap, catching the board at the bolts and stomping back down on the metal deck of the pyramid.

Tappies.

Swishy Shorts yells from the picnic table. Converse tries a 5-0 on the quarterpipe but has too much speed and slides out.

"Yeeeewwww. Nice, man," I say.

"Yeah."

"Alright, how about this double kink?"

"What you wanna grind it?"

"No, boardslide it!"

"Alright, let's do it."

And so we go around the park, challenging each other to tricks, challenging our collective team to see if both or one of us can conquer the goals we set before us. He feebles down the double kink, while I go across and down in a boardslide; we varial-flip the pyramid-hip; we ollie nose manual the box; we noseslide the C-curve; we disaster the quarterpipe; we grind the pyramid's rail. When I land this last trick, after Converse had already stomped it before me, a newcomer sitting at the picnic table stands up and screams a long and held-out "Ohhhhhhh!!" like I had done something amazing.

"Yo, are you pro or somethin', man!?" he asks when I'm back near the picnic table.

"Haha. No way!"

"You gotta start your own YouTube channel, man."

"That's not a bad idea."

"Start your own YouTube channel, man, and show the world what you can do."

"Haha. I don't think the world would be that interested in what I can do. I just like skateboarding, that's it."

"Haha, you guys love that shit!"

"Haha. Yes we do!"

"No, start your own YouTube channel, man. Doesn't matter if other people think you're good or not. You gotta show the world what you're passionate about. And if doing it makes you happy, then keep doing it. Go deeper in and make yourself even happier. You've found a great source of happiness, man, and that's special."

"Yeah. How about I write a book about it?"

"About skateboarding?"

"Yeah, man. About me traveling around to different skateparks and talking to people."

"That would be *tight*, man."

We laugh.

"So where's your skateboard, then?" I say.

"Me? Oh hell no! I would stand on that thing for all of two seconds before I broke my ass! No joke! I would break... something, I don't know what!"

"Haha."

Sweat drips off the tip of my nose in steady drops, and the denim of my jeans is damp around the shins and thighs. There's a final trick I need to land.

"Alright, dude," I say to Converse. "How about 360 flips?"

"Tre bombs?"

"It's the proper way to end a skate."

"Alright."

We move to the flat and get to work.

No trick has caused more tears, elicited more screams, or appeared in so many nightmares. The marriage of a kickflip and a 360 shove-it (rotations on both axes), the 360 flip AKA the tre bomb, is greater than the sum of its composite parts. It is their product.

We stand in one corner of the pavement leaning on our skateboards like they're canes. Suddenly one of us springs forward, assumes a narrow stance with all of his front foot's heel hanging off the board and his back foot poised over the toe-side edge of his tail. He rolls at a cautious and measured speed (too slow and it's harder to flip, too fast and it's harder to control). A low crouch, total focus—you can do it, scoop and flick—a low crouch so that his butt is just above the calves, his eyes fixed and his toes fidgeting on the grip tape. Pop! He pops with his back foot, pushing the tail down and scooping it behind while *simultaneously* flicking the board with the toes of his front foot, both spinning and flipping the board while his eyes bulge and he's airborne above this madly gyrating skateboard, and he forgets everything so complete is his concentration. He watches the board hurl through space without him until he stops its revolutions with his feet and pushes it back to the pavement, gravity or momentum or God hopefully keeping it stuck in place.

Converse and I take turns dropping tre bombs. Neither of us can land one. Something is always off: the pop, the balance, the flick, the landing. Sometimes we're close—the board flips perfectly beneath the skater only for one foot to slip off the grip tape and grab the pavement. Then you skate to the other end of the park and wait through the other skater's turn. I try twenty times, then thirty, then I lose count of the number of attempts and could be on the first or thousandth for I have been dislocated from space and time.

My first tre bomb sessions took place at the skatepark. I began each session like Sisyphus running his calloused hands over the cracks and crevices of the rock he knew so well. And after caressing the boulder good morning I would push, and push, and push! And the attempts would start, and they would continue, and after forty or fifty I would say to myself, "OK, this time I'm *really* going to focus!" or "Enough playing around, this is it," or "Oh, Dear Jesus, please help me land this tre flip, I'm too weak to do it on my own!"—and I would push myself and crouch with great seriousness only to pop and flick and jump already knowing that I wasn't going to land anything. Hours would pass teamed up with Keith and Tommy and Mike and my brother, and we would battle the tre flip, waging war on our unholy master, desperate for the day the board would spin and flip and we would land back with two feet on the bolts, and we would be able to sleep in peace. Defeated, inevitably, we would collapse on the bench at the elementary school, the car-blocking boulders at the basketball court, in the grass at the skatepark, or onto the dirty, hot pavement, and we would pant like dogs and talk about *how close we had been.*

All these memories surface during the tre bomb session in Berrysville, Arkansas, or, more precisely, the memory of the sensation of being fourteen in a tre bomb session surfaces and overlaps with the sensation produced by reality so that the two filters produce a single image. My focus comes in waves: at times I pop and spin my board with purpose, as if I intend to land something, and at others I simply go through the motions. I drift further into the trance of the tre bomb, and the rest of the world drifts further away. The people I knew in Vermont, my existential anxieties about jobs, my ex-girlfriend in Burlington—all of it recedes like a planet from whence my ship departs, a marble disappearing into blackness as I speed towards some dimension belonging to dreams.

Once you hit a certain level of determination, or you have invested a certain amount of effort and sweat into landing a trick—*I will land this fucking tre flip*—success becomes an existential matter. You start imagining scenes from Tom Brady documentaries and the finale of *Rudy*; locker room clichés intrude uninvited into your head. This is a sort of revery or meditative high, for your mind becomes freed from the issues that have been hanging on its sensitive tissues. There is only the 360 flip. When you finish the session, and catch your breath, you might remember the thing that had been bothering you and it returns like a weight flung onto your spirit: "Oh, yes, Melissa…" But in the trenches, in the midst of a frenzied tre bomb session, you forget everything as you sink into your manic delirium.

"Three taps, brush the nose, spit, focus, visualize—board spins, bolts—scoop, remember to scoop, scooping is the most important, three taps, don't flick too much, toes not too low, but not too high, three taps, right in the sweet spot, where does it go, scoop and flick, three taps, medium speed, three taps, brush the nose, spit, focus, visualize…"

Converse gives up, pushes himself to the picnic table, and sits down across from his friend. I become the only movement and the only noise in the sunny afternoon stillness. I keep going. It's me versus the tre flip: I will land it, I am good, I will show them, I will show fucking all of them, and they will rue ever having doubted—

I pop, the board spins and rolls over itself a few inches off the ground, the four wheels hit the pavement, and I land back on top, the heel of my left foot scraping the ground before I roll away.

Count it?

Count it, fucker.

Converse and Swishy Shorts are hunched over their phones at the picnic table.

"Got it?" Converse says, quickly looking up and flashing a smile as I skate over.

"Nice man," Swishy says.

"Yew. Took me long enough."

I sit down with my gallon jug of water and take long gulps. There's the noise of cicadas, and a herd of overweight clouds migrates above us. The sun is warm on my arms and neck and face, and it coats the thick green grass on the hill above us. I take out my phone and open Google Maps. I punch in Tulsa and study the route I have to drive that night. Then I open the news and read the headlines Apple wants me to read. I open Instagram. I open Tinder, then Bumble. The three of us sit at the picnic table for ten or fifteen or twenty minutes without saying a word, each engrossed in the separate worlds contained in our smartphones. And it's a strange feeling, for I feel comfortable, as if I'd been with these people many times before.

I put my phone in my pocket and click the circular lid back onto the gallon jug. The sweat is crusting on my face and arms.

"Alright, guys, catch you later," I say.

"Ah, you out? Later, man."

"Later, dude. Take it easy."

I cross the lawn towards my car, and I identify the strange feeling of sitting at the picnic table. It had felt like friendship.

TOMMY ALWAYS BOUGHT more food than he could eat and there were always leftovers, and he always gave the leftovers to me. He always showed up to town with more money in his pocket than the rest of us, though his family was in no way wealthier. So if we went to the gas station and the rest of us just bought a fountain soda for fifty-nine cents, which we paid for in change, or perhaps broke the crullers inside a doughnut pack so we could buy them at a discount, Tommy would buy a cheeseburger and a bag of chips and a large bottle of Gatorade. I knew he wouldn't be able to finish his cheeseburger, but I didn't say anything. I waited patiently, like a well-trained dog, sitting with Tommy and whoever else on the high cement wall behind the gas station while our feet dangled and kicked and we spit and threw bits of food down to the pebbles twenty feet below. Tommy would set the half of cheeseburger aside, and I would have to wait an appropriate amount of time until we both knew he wasn't going to finish it, though we had both known as soon as he bought it that he wouldn't, and only then could I ask the question with an ironic or perhaps embarrassed grin. "You gonna finish that?"

And he would groan and act irritated, and reply, "Go ahead."

Whether at the gas station or at the pizza shop where all the skatepark kids hung out or at the Americana family restaurant, where the waitresses were friendly even though we wasted all their sugar packets and never tipped, we always played the same game—Tommy ordered more food than he could eat and then gave me the leftovers, and I never failed to finish everything.

Tommy never tried new tricks in the summer. Summer was for refining old tricks, he said. Only in autumn when it became cold enough to skate in a hoody would he allow himself to try new tricks, though he rarely did all the things he had said he was going to do "as soon as hoody season's here". As soon as there was an overcast day with even a hint of crisp air, Tommy would show up to the skatepark in a hoody and all day would sigh to himself and those around him, "Ahhh. Hoody skating."

Readers sometimes mistake the narrator as the main character in certain novels written in the first person, while it is in fact the narrator's friend who is the focus of the story. The friend is the main character, and the story of the book becomes the story of their friendship. *On the Road* is a book Jack Kerouac wrote about his friend. *On the Road* is not an adventure novel, it is not socio-cultural investigation, nor is it an introspective examination of the narrator/writer per Proust or Knausgaard. *On the Road* is about Dean Moriarty. Moriarty is the planet around which the narrator spins, forever pulled in by the weight and gravity of his friend. He is the force that pushes the narrative forward: the story starts when the narrator (Kerouac) meets Moriarty (Neal Cassady), and it ends when Moriarty abandons the sick narrator in Mexico, signifying the end of their time together. The book is simply a thorough description of a friend who has so dramatically marked the life of the writer, who the writer knew so intimately, in all his richness and complexity of character, his uniqueness, his charisma, but with all of his flaws, too, for all great stories are tragedies and tragic heroes always possess greatness but are destroyed by dangerous qualities related to this greatness.

If I were to write a novel about my time at the skatepark, it would be about Tommy. I would be the unobtrusive narrator, and Tommy would be the main character, for this is how I remember my childhood.

This is not a novel, however. I will leave Tommy alone in my memories, where he commands kingdoms more wonderful than anything I could create in these pages.

Tulsa, OK

THE AIRBNB IS CLUTTERED WITH ARTWORK AND PHOTO-graphs that, along with the bright couches, rugs, and pillows, suggest a heavy-handed yet distinct decorative touch. Throughout the clean and comfortable living room is a robust smell that greets me as soon as I open the heavy front door. I will later conclude that the scent is a mixture of plug-in air freshener and cat pee, for I recognize the latter from Mike's old house where we slept over when we skated late in the summer, and later when we went to parties. His parents were bohemians who kept weed in a drawer in the kitchen and didn't clean up after the three skinny cats who wandered around the house and hid under the bed in Mike's room.

"Hello, Clinton," my host says. She stands up from the couch and walks to the doorway.

"Hi, Kathy, is it? How are you?"

"I'm good, I'm good. So you made it. The driving wasn't too difficult?"

"No, it was fine. Your house is so nice!"

"Oh, thanks. Where are you coming from?"

"I'm coming from Arkansas. Well, I was out in Missouri last night, and I drove through Arkansas this afternoon, skateboarded a bit, then came into Oklahoma..."

"So what is it you're doing again? Driving around on your skateboard?"

"Yeah, basically. I'm visiting skateparks all over the US."

"State parks?"

"No, *skate*parks."

"Ah. Skateparks. So are you here to see the Gathering Place?"

"What is it?"

"The Gathering Place. Oh you have to check it out. It's this big

109

project they've been working on for two years, down in a park by the river. There's a skatepark, there's a bunch of other stuff, too."

"Oh. Cool."

"Yes, you definitely need to go see it."

"OK, yes."

"Yeah."

…

"Well, anyway, this is your room over here."

"Should I take my shoes off?"

"Yes, if you don't mind. I never used to, but most people just take their shoes off when they come here, so it's kind of become a thing, haha."

Kathy shows me my room, then the kitchen and the dining table where there's an array of breakfast items and snacks left in a large bowl. I'm not sure if "help myself" only applies to the morning, so I don't touch the bowl even though I'm hungry. Later, though, when the house is quiet and dark and it seems Kathy has gone to bed, I sneak out of my room and raid the snacks, foraging a couple peanut butter bars, a banana, and an orange. Back in my room, I eat my dinner watching old *Simpsons* episodes until I'm finally sleepy enough to know that I won't think much when I brush my teeth and turn off the lights.

The next day I skate around Tulsa—up to the university, over through the Blue Dome neighborhood with its breweries and ramen shops, into downtown—making my way with my skateboard sometimes under my arm and sometimes under my feet, clacking over the cracks between the squares of cement on the sidewalk. It is hot. The high, lonely sun accentuates the dry heat of the plains. The back of my cotton shirt fills with sweat against my backpack, and I am embarrassed when I stop for a coffee in an austere warehouse turned café (ubiquitous in Tulsa, all of them pumping out subdued House and avocado toast).

The Arkansas River is brown and shallow. I skate on a bike

path that follows the bends of its eroded bank and look out over the expanse at the factories and smoke stacks, the pumps and rusted machinery across the dirty flume. I pass a young woman walking slowly with her head fixed forwards. When I find a bench and stop to drink from the two-liter water bottle I bought at a gas station, and sit dazed in shaded daydream, completely oblivious to pressing matters or responsibilities, the girl passes me, walking as calmly as before, and though her passing jars me into feeling like it is time to go, I wait until she is far enough away so that when I skate past she doesn't think I stopped just to see her again, for she is in fact beautiful.

It's the opening weekend of the Gathering Place, and the park brims with a festive atmosphere. Families, couples, skaters, college kids, retirees, and others crowd the pathways by the music lawn, by the playgrounds and terraced coffee shops, by the obstacle course, the maze, and the skateparks. The people of Tulsa have waited years, watching as the spectacle was planned, discussed, and built: a city park turned amusement space of ambiguous character and purpose gifted by the benevolent Kaiser, one of the city's patriarchs. His family made its money in oil, as many in the city have over the past 100 years, my host's brother explained that morning as the two of us stood in the sun-filled lawn. He was round and wore his hair in a ponytail. After he caught me fetching a pair of socks from the trunk of the Saab, we chatted about Trump, Hunter Thompson, *Rolling Stone*, and the history of Tulsa as dogs and their owners and cars passed in relaxed third gear. He was a journalist and had once run a newspaper, which explained why he was so cynical.

"Kaiser's playing it off like he's so generous, and is some god to the city of Tulsa," he said. "But really, you know why he's doing it?"

"Why?"

"It's all a tax write-off. He's doing it so he can hold on to his millions—so he can keep his money safe from taxes."

"Huh. I wouldn't put it past him."

"No, sir."

"I'm sure it's some kind of ego trip, too. What could be more satisfying than building a huge park in your hometown, for all your ex-girlfriends and childhood enemies to walk through, and have everyone in the city talking about how great of a guy you are. It's better than a bronze statue!"

"Sure is."

Whatever Kaiser's motivations, he did a good job with the skatepark. It's concrete, modern, and stylish. Three lines branch from a starting point and re-converge at the skatepark's other end so that the skater flows through a line hitting gaps, ledges, and pyramids linked together instead of left in isolation. The proportions and angles of transition are immaculate, and even a mediocre skater like myself can, once he finds the balls to try, ollie up to a high ledge over a pyramid and lock into a backside 50-50.

I can back 50-50 a ledge?

The ledge is long, perhaps fifteen or twenty feet across and curved in the middle so that the goofy-footed grinder has to lean over his toes in order to stay balanced. The angle-iron is smooth and slick and designed for skateboarding unlike the rusty metal I'm used to. On my first try, the ramp pops me up, and I grind through the bend until I fall off the board. Like so many first tries, it feels much easier than I thought it would be.

You just have to give it a try, and you'll be amazed at the things you can accomplish.

Given the layout of the park, it doesn't make sense to dwell. Each time I fall off the curved ledge I right my board and finish the line, doing an ollie-manual over a box, trying a kickflip up a ramp, stalling on top of a quarterpipe to reverse directions. Another guy is trying the same backside 50-50. He seems about my age and ability. He has bright blue eyes and tattoos up and down his arms.

"Alright, first one to grind that ledge wins," I say to him.

112

"Ha. That thing's a bitch, man! I can't stay on through the curve!"

"Are you trying to pop off onto the transition or grind the whole thing and drop off to flat?"

"I wanna go to the end, but either way man. Landing tranny would be sick."

We both keep trying and both keep ejecting our boards shortly after the curve.

It is mid-afternoon. The sun is directly above the skatepark. Five drops of sweat break from my chin and nose each time I bend to pop, making dark spots on the fresh, clean cement. The park is filled with skateboarders and bikers and a couple of kids on scooters. Because the park is brand new, I feel like the local crowd is not yet established and that everyone is a newcomer. No one asks me where I'm from or what I'm doing there; they assume I'm just another Tulsa skater checking out the new spot. I like pretending that I'm a local, as I always do when I'm traveling, and I play along, making general comments to the different skaters as we catch our breath on top of the lines, sweat streaming down our faces.

"So, what do you think? Better than the other park, right?" I ask a chubby high school kid on a BMX. He looks fifteen or sixteen but has several inches and sixty pounds on me.

He grunts and doesn't say anything, and I receive the distinct impression he doesn't like me.

Another time, to the best skater in the park, a black man with dreadlocks hanging against his back: "About time we got a decent park, right?"

He's listening to ear buds and doesn't hear me at first. He turns and takes one out. "What?"

"What do you think of the new park?"

"Oh. It's fantastic, man. Love it."

"Best in the city?"

"Absolutely." He returns the ear bud and jumps on his board, pops some technical flip trick and lands first try.

The chubby BMX teenager suddenly gets a nosebleed. Blood streams around his mouth and coats his chin, decorating the white-gray cement with vivid red dots. He holds his hand to his nose and glossy trails streak from his knuckles down his arm.

"You been doing too much blow, dude!" the blue-eyed blond guy says, laughing. I figure he's making the joke for someone else's benefit, so I don't react. Then he nudges me on the shoulder: "You see that, man? That boy's been doing too much blow!"

And me, just to say something: "Why'd you give it to him? He's too young for that shit!"

"No he's not! I was smoking ice at twelve, bro'! No joke!" And he starts laughing, revealing brown, yellow teeth.

The ice-smoking blondie is also a father, it turns out—his wife and young daughter are there with skateboards. He occasionally visits them and helps his young girl push herself around and down various inclines in the park. Dad soon lands the 50-50 on the ledge and comes back to the top of the drop-in with a large smile on his face. He offers me a pound and we tap knuckles.

"Sick, dude."

"Now you gotta land it!"

"I can't stay on!"

"You gotta lean back a bit. Don't lean into the bend. Stay upright on your heels. Try sticking your butt out behind you."

"Alright."

I pump down the double transition of the drop-in. I ollie, lock on, start grinding, swing through the bend, and feel physics once again pulling me off to the left. I resist, arch my back and lean on my heels, then over-correct again, pushing my torso forward and straightening my legs to stick out my butt. I find the goldilocks spot and grind the rest of the ledge in easy control to drop off the end without even ollieing.

A board taps behind me, but I act cool, pushing myself into a big backside heelflip up a tiny euro gap which I don't come close to landing.

When skating with friends, execution is contagious.

I become lackadaisical, purposeless, and sunburned after landing the trick I've been working on all day. But I'm having too much fun to stop, and I skate for another hour. I skate the pool and work on frontside 5-0 grinds in the snaking mini-ramp. I try board slides down a small rail above a baby stair set. I can't leave the park. No one else can leave, either: my 50-50 buddy, the pudgy high-schooler, and everyone else I've been skating with all afternoon stay as long as I do. Nobody complains about the heat or their bruises (mine, a big bump on the outside of my knee). Everyone just keeps trying new tricks and landing new tricks, flying around and slapping the tails of their boards when someone stomps.

It's after five when I finally leave the park. I'm dazed and unsteady as I shuffle my feet on the sidewalk crowded with families. But I'm high. I'm clear-headed, as if racing thoughts have been pounded into submission—a Zen-like rapture of post-workout oblivion—and I smile, stoned on endorphins, grinning in the sunshine with my board in my arm, playing back that backside 50-50 over and over in my mind. There are dark moments in life—times when anxiety wraps its heavy fabric around you and squeezes, and you lose sight of hope, times when you are lonely, and wretched because of it—but just as inexplicably you sometimes find yourself buffeted above torment with appreciation for breath and pumping blood and each passing moment they bestow; briefly charmed by caprice, you realize that life is simple, beautiful, and precious.

Life is simple: skateboarding makes you happy.

I open Google Maps and plug in my Airbnb address.

Shit.

It's an hour and twenty minutes on foot. And my phone's on one per cent battery. *And*—more significantly—I've arranged a Tinder date with a pale-skinned chemist.

I quickly study the route. I have to go north to 21st Street then follow that east to Florence Park. Easy enough. When I zoom in on my location, the phone suddenly dies.

I start east on 31st Street. The crowds thin, and I skateboard. When an inviting road presents itself, I turn left and push down the side street, roaring over the pavement, ollieing over manholes and drainage grates. The houses become nicer—old, brick or plaster walls crisscrossed with wooden beams and A-frame gables, colorful shutters beside each window. The lawns are lush and trim with sprinklers stuttering water over the grass and the sidewalk. If a homeowner is in their driveway or yard they look up and glare, silently interrogating: "Whatchya doing in this neighborhood?" and I remember that *The Outsiders* is set in Tulsa.

This is a city of old oil money piled up for more than a century. Those that have the money—"the Soc's", as they're called in Hinton's book and Coppola's film—live in communities isolated from but tangential to those that do not—the Greasers. The Tulsan lives touched and untouched by money become different, as the reader sees when Sherri Valance (Soc) and Ponyboy (Greaser) spend time together and try to connect. The Soc's wear letterman jackets and drive around in shiny blue Mustangs. They're rich and judgemental, privileged and suspicious of those who are not. The Greasers, meanwhile, get together to spit in dirt and comb their hair and smoke cigarettes. Their adolescence is marked by fraternal community and a glaring lack of supervision. They identify in the way they talk and they way they dress relative to the rest of society and the boys with nicer clothes. The twenty-first century equivalent, of course, is the skateboarder: that cool, slightly dangerous rebel who mothers in big houses try to keep blonde daughters from dating. Like the Greaser, the skateboarder scoffs at the popular and relishes the alternative, resenting the football player in khakis and rocking instead dirty ripped jeans, dirty ripped shoes, dirty shirts, and hats with holes in them. Like the Greasers, few of the skaters I had hung out with that afternoon come from the blue-blood Tulsa I'm navigating on my skateboarded.

However, it could hardly be said that skateboarding is still fringe or dangerous. The anti-establishment identity that skateboarding assumed in the eighties and nineties softened as skateboarding became more mainstream. The very thing that made skateboarding edgy and exciting attracted so many people that skateboarding eventually lost its outsider status. Now ripped jeans are typical of Abercrombie and Fitch, Vans are ubiquitous among civilians, the X Games are on ESPN, Justin Bieber skates, parents send their children to skateboard camps, and in 2021 skateboarding will be an Olympic sport. People my age started skateboarding because it signaled dissidence, but the corporations cashed in on its popularity so that the dissidence became a farce. The sport was further commercialized and commodified, so skateparks became clean and the scooters came in, so dawn goes down to day, nothing gold can stay. Nevertheless, still, deep within the primitive DNA of every skateboarder remain strands of the rule-breaker, of the fringe-dweller, of the Greaser. Or so we like to think.

I half-skate, half-walk through Tulsa imagining myself Ponyboy. The sun falls down the horizon, shadows lengthen, the sides of homes and the hundreds of leaves on each tree catch the orange and pink light, and glow. When I enter the cool, dark house that smells like cats, I go to my bathroom, take off the sopping clothes, step into the shower and drink long gulps from the 1950s faucet.

THE GIRL FROM Tinder sends a message:

"Soooo, my friends Im hanging out with rn are hungry too, so would it be cool if they came too??"

To which I respond:

"Of course!! Absolutely fine w me—would be happy to meet them! Looking forward 😁"

But I think: Hmm.

As I walk through dark hazy twilight, I feel the distinct happiness of having said "Yes" to something that my initial impulse may have been to avoid. The feeling is a revelation, because I've wallowed for so long in an opposing state of consciousness, waking to drag myself through unremarkable days in which I ran at the prospect of any discomfort. When traveling we know that we are only somewhere temporarily and therefore must reap experiences as urgently as possible. So the traveler learns to make "Yes" instinctive and forgets the hushed "No", though the latter is habitual when we are at home drifting imperceptibly but constantly towards routine and comfort. While Vermont means stasis in the familiar, and a suffocating grayness, the road signifies movement through the unknown and colors that have never been so bright.

I walk onto a restaurant's patio in the trendy Cherry Hill neighborhood looking for a group of girls, one of whom has curly black hair.

Nope.

Nope.

Not there.

Oh—

I make eye contact with a young blonde woman at a table of three. She kind of waves at me. I kind of wave back. Her black-haired friend turns and waves, too, and I smile and wave back. I go over to their table.

"Hello!"

"Hi."

"Hey."

"I'm Mary, nice to meet you."

"Hi, I'm Clint."

"I'm Jen."

"Nice to meet you."

"Nice to meet you, too."

"And you must be Sophie."

"Yeah! Nice to meet you."

I sit down. The blonde girl who had waved, Mary, does most of the talking, though she isn't my date. She's attractive, and half-way through dinner I become wary of giving her too much attention and suggesting to Sophie that I'm falling for her assertive blonde friend, which, of course, I am. I detect that this is entirely Mary's intention even though she's not single. Girls that are as good-looking and focused as her rarely are, and briefly so if they find themselves out of a relationship. I suspect that she has a long-term boyfriend and may even spend Thanksgiving or Christmas at his family's house. She likes this arrangement, but when her friend said she was going on a Tinder date with a traveler visiting from out of town, a pang of jealousy struck, or perhaps one of simple curiosity. She wanted to prove to herself and her friends that this could not be as good as what she had, that she was as good if not better than them, that she could have this too, if she wanted.

Secretly, though, I like the quiet friend the best. Jen is slim and pretty with straight black hair and dark features. I can't focus my attentions on her, either, so when the food arrives (taproom burgers for everyone) and Mary's dominance over the table is temporarily interrupted, I turn to my left and address Sophie. We speak in a slightly softer tone that separates our conversation from that of the table.

We're the same age. She's a chemist with a job at the university. She's direct in a down-to-earth way I associate with people in the scientific and mathematical fields, people who are smart and confident in a practical way and don't care about affectation or appearing fashionable. She goes hiking in New Mexico and Colorado and tells me about the time she was lost in a lightning storm in a desert famous for its sand dunes. She camps by herself in the middle of the prairie and scales vertical cliffs using her hands and feet. Thus, in addition to our contrasting complexions—mine

Nordic, hers Mediterranean—our personalities also diverge, for I relish daydreaming and poetry, books and beer and inactivity. In short, I enjoy all that is impractical and useless, unproductive, and meaningless. I am unemployed and homeless. I live in a tent and go skateboarding every day. She is a scientist who works at a globally-ranked university and is responsible for the success or failure of million-dollar research projects. Yet we make eye contact very comfortably, and as we do the world beyond our stare fades as the world within sharpens. The details within her eyes sharpen and expand and relax. Pretense and the polite veneer of strangers evaporates; we become two naked humans blinking equal parts vulnerability and curiosity.

The table orders more beers, and the specter of awkwardness that had haunted our group when I sat down—I was on a Tinder date with a stranger and her two friends, in Oklahoma—disappears. We talk about *The Outsiders.* Jen (of course!) is the only one who has read it. They tell me about social stratification in Tulsa and about the neighborhoods being gentrified. The evening air is balmy and clean, the lights of the patio are bright, glass pints and silverware sparkle. I start to buzz on IPA, on a Tinder date with a beautiful stranger and her two beautiful friends—in Oklahoma!

The plates have long been cleared by the time we put our four cards into the skinny leather book and think about leaving. Jen and Mary say they'll carpool home.

"Feel like having another drink?" Sophie asks.

"More beer? Of course."

We hop into her Jeep and she backs out into the wide, stretched-out street. The seats are high off the ground, and the car drives smoothly on its large tires. The floor is messy with papers and crushed Dunkin' Donuts coffee cups. The square berth within the center console contains a sticky blend of pennies, nickels, dimes, gum wrappers, and receipts. I buckle the seatbelt and experience the excitement of being in a strange place in a stranger's car.

The bar's a dive that shows Premier League matches on the weekend. A board covered in neon marker advertises a Tecate-tequila special, so we order a beer and a shot each and clink glasses before we lick the salt off our hands, swallow a mouthful of sour liquor, and suck the juice out of fresh wedges of limes. We take our beer cans to the patio and sit in plastic chairs around a circular table. The sun that towered above the prairie only hours before, making the people of Tulsa sweat and groan and cover their eyes, is gone. It's cold, colder than I thought it would be, and I shiver in my long-sleeved shirt.

We talk through one beer and then another, and then a third and a fourth. The two of us become drunk as we look at each other and explain more about our lives, our relationships with our families, our goals and disillusionments and hopes. We talked about the difference between East and West, and conclude that 'East-coast types' are, among other things, more open about sex.

"You really think that girls on the East Coast don't have a problem with sleeping around?"

I was thoughtful for a moment.

"No. No problem at all!"

"Huh. And what about guys?"

"What about them?"

"Do they judge the girls?"

"I don't think so. I know a lot of girls that go out trying to get laid but aren't necessarily looking for a relationship. I don't think any less of them for it. They want to have sex—who doesn't! It's good for you."

"So if you knew some girl slept around a bunch, would you want to date her any less?"

I was thoughtful again.

Mmmmmmm.

"It depends on how attractive she was, and how much she loved me."

We laugh, then stare at each other, visualizing the maneuvers of the pawns, bishops, and rooks yet to pass.

We kiss when the other table on the patio empties, first holding hands and playing with fingers, then kissing. The door to the patio opens, and we break apart like teenagers caught doing something forbidden.

"Well, shall I close out my tab?" I say.

"Yeah, I think so."

"Should we go back to your place?"

"Haha, well, I would but … like I said, I live with my parents."

"Oh, right. We can't sneak in the back door?"

"Well we could, but you'd have to say hello to my dad in the morning."

"Hmmmm."

"I was thinking we would go back to your place."

"I'm staying with the crazy cat lady!"

"Haha. So it would be impossible for me to come over, then?"

"What about my flawless Airbnb rating!"

"I can picture her review already: 'Clinton was mostly a well-mannered and polite guest. However, he brought some girl back in the middle of the night and had sex in my guest bed!'"

"Haha!"

What do I care what Kathy thinks. She's a nice lady, sure, but I'll never see her again. She can judge me all she wants, she means nothing to me.

Maybe she'll even be OK with it? Sophie and I can have breakfast with her in the morning and talk about the weather?

Maybe the eccentric brother will stop by.

"Who's this, Clint? Sampling the local wildlife?"

"Please, sir, this is Sophie. She's my friend."

"Back in my day we would say 'girlfriend'. Then again, we had more morals than you libertines these days."

No, it wouldn't work.

But I can also just enjoy the night and face the consequences tomorrow, whatever they might be. Tomorrow is always a life-time away.

"OK, let's go then."

I finish my Tecate, and we leave. I give Sophie directions as we drive east, retracing the route I had taken walking to dinner. Though we listened to the radio going to the bar, now she hits the CD button and we listen to British rock from the eighties.

The street is deserted when we pull up at my Airbnb, and the house is dark. It's two AM. Sophie turns off the ignition. The car is silent.

"So, do you want to come in?" I ask.

"Now that I'm here, it doesn't feel right."

"That's fine. Happy to preserve my five stars."

She laughs.

"OK, then," I say, "Well, it was nice hanging out tonight."

"Yeah, I had fun, too. If you're free tomorrow, I might go to that soccer game."

"I would love to go."

"OK."

"Well, goodnight."

"Goodnight."

And we kiss again, kissing in the dark in her car until we are suddenly kissing too much, perhaps, and she pulls away, and I'm left leaning over the center console with my eyes closed. When I open them, there are just the whites of her eyes in the shadow of the cab. I step out of her car, and we separate without ever having done that which we both wanted to do.

I wake up with a hangover. The headache is ripe, and I haven't slept enough. I roll over and grab my phone.

8:30.

No messages.

Ohhh.

Shit.

Did I really drink that much?

It must have been a combination of the drinking and the dehydration from skateboarding all day.

And I had tried bringing Sophie into Kathy's house!

Christ.

What had I been thinking?

What am I doing with my life?

What will I do when money runs out?

Should I get a job?

Christ, kids five years younger than me already have careers.

Does my ex-girlfriend hate me?

What is she doing now? Does she miss me? Does she have a new boyfriend?

Christ.

I stay in bed all morning, getting up only to have a cup of orange juice and a bowl of granola in the kitchen. I chat with Kathy about her cats and about the weather. Then it's back to the Eorlingas and my Tempur-Pedic mattress on which I alternate between napping and reading. In the afternoon, still hungover, I shower and drive to a coffee shop downtown, sit at a table with two people doing a job interview. I try writing about going to the skatepark in Arkansas, but I can't focus or find the energy to think of something to say. I can't create; I can only consume. So I take out Tolkien and pick up where I left off, reading despite the questions and answers of the two young men in ties and the dull throb of the lo-fi electronica.

I text with Sophie. She's hungover at work, and tired. Each time I see her name on the screen warmth pings in my chest. I tell her I want to see the Gilcrease Museum. She says she'll meet me there when she gets out of work. So when I finish my coffee and get to the part with the wild men of the Druadan Forest and Dernhelm, who is really Eowyn filled with a horrible unrequited love for Aragorn, I pack up and drive to the outskirts of the city, where the Gilcrease is perched on a hill crowned with gardens.

The Gilcrease is dedicated to telling the story (or myth) of the Wild West. I pass through a hall dedicated to Native American history: colorful headdresses, moccasins, beads woven into bright geometric patterns on papooses and bridal gowns. I walk down another lined with Mayan masks, then one filled with totem poles, another populated by the life-like busts of former presidents and heroes—Lincoln, Lafayette, Washington. I pass into the next room and am paralyzed, abruptly, by a large rectangular canvas.

A dim green hue fills the painting, as if depicting an underwater scene. The strange color alone lends the piece a sense of eeriness and impending drama. Despite its aquamarine tint, the scene is not of the ocean: on a desert plain, in the middle of torrential rain, a galloping horse carries a lone rider. In the background, a single lightning bolt streaks from the sky, and a herd of cattle jostle in a stampede, mad with fear.

Oh.

The slanting rain, the vivid lightning bolt, the airborne horse and its cowboy upright in the stirrups, both hands on the reigns, his head bent low, the shadows of a thousand charging cattle, all of it a visualization of urgency, of man's lonely fight against indifferent nature, in a completely lonely place. The image is powerful because of what it depicts and how it's executed, but the experience of stumbling on Frederic Remington's 'Stampede' is more disturbing due to its associations in my memory.

I remember dust sparkling in the sunlight of a clear winter morning. Less the memory of a distinct scene than the memory of what consciousness had felt like at a certain age, the careful, timid way I had thought and experienced fascination at seeing pictures of faraway places. The light was warm on my face and hands, and the living room smelled of must. I was sitting on the cat hair-covered couch with a large book opened across my lap, staring at the image of a cattle drive caught in a lightning storm. A fire crackled in the kitchen's wood stove. And as I stand riveted in front of the canvas in the Gilcrease Museum, my eyes as wide as they had been at five, I suddenly feel the security of home, the warm oblivion of childhood, the tenderness of a mother who loved me unconditionally.

"Clint?"

I look up.

Sophie is in the opposite corner of the empty, silent room. We look at each other for a moment. I kind of wave, and she kind of waves back.

"Hey," I say. My voice echoes in the cavernous space.

"Hey." Her hard-soled footsteps fill the room as she walks towards me. "Do you like this painting?"

"Yeah, I do. I remember it from when I was a kid."

"It's interesting. What a strange color."

"Yes."

...

"How are you though? How was work?"

"Ha, it was a little tough! For some reason I was tired and hungover today."

"How strange. You must have been up late drinking with someone."

"Yes, must have, some sort of out-of-towner."

"How irresponsible of you."

"How was writing?"

"I went to a coffee shop, but I was completely useless. I was thinking about Hemingway, who used to be famous for partying all night and waking up at the crack of dawn to start writing, no matter what."

"Maybe if you drink as much as Hemingway you'll get used to writing hungover?"

"Worth a try."

We continue through the exhibit, pausing to chat in front of Remington's paintings and statues about things unrelated to Remington's paintings and statues. We leave the museum as it's closing and find a wooden bench in the dappled shade of a tree. Two parents are posing for photos with their newborn baby between colorful bushes of flowers and a stone fountain. The baby flails its arms and legs, and the photographer tries in vain to capture its wandering attention. Sophie and I talk quietly on the bench, while, concurrent with our conversation, another runs in my head: What would happen if we dated? Would we fall in love? How long would it take for me, or for her, to grow tired of the other? How long before one of us felt stifled and trapped? In five years, could we go out to dinner and still have anything to talk about? What would be left when the excitement waned? What would we find on the riverbed when the waters ran low?

Now, though, her eyes hold me and make me happy to be within them instead of anywhere else, which is perhaps how she feels, sitting with me on the bench on the sunny, quiet hilltop. And that might be as good a definition of love as any: when two people can be alone together, separated from all else in the world, and desire nothing more; when two people can drift away and create their own private realm for themselves and no other, and a secluded bench on a remote hilltop can become the center of the universe far from New York or Paris and the parties of the world.

Sophie says it would be better for me not to go to the soccer game because she's going with old friends she hasn't seen in a while. But she still has two hours before the game, so we could go eat something? She suggests a deli chain, and we go to our cars and drive back into Tulsa, me following her black Jeep in my rusty Saab over interstates and interchanges, switching lanes and passing cars, braking down exit ramps and accelerating through yellow lights.

The restaurant is in the same neighborhood we had been in the night before. The place is known for its salad bar. It has tubs of bright greens and reds, purple onions and black olives and dressings in translucent shades of brown, white, and yellow. "I always come here with my dad," Sophie whispers to me as we get in line to order at a cash register. "Nothing fancy, but I like it."

"Looks good. What should I get?"

"Get a half a sandwich, and the salad bar!"

So I order half a Reuben and load a plate of greens with as many toppings as might outweigh any health benefit the spinach provides. Sophie leads me to a booth with tall maroon seats, but after we've finished our food and are licking soft-serve from sugar cones she says she's cold and we move to a circular table caught directly in a square blast of orange sunlight. The table is in the middle of the floor, but because of the sun's low position over the distant plain the stained light pours into the second-story room at a low trajectory and smothers our table, our chairs and faces, our hair and ice cream cones in the orange-gold of an Oklahoman sunset. I feel completely at ease. And even more than the calm, I feel present: totally invested in the time and space enveloping me, aware of the streaks on the windows, of the silhouettes of buildings across the street, of my feelings, of the depth and designs in Sophie's eyes as light enters them, shrinking the pupils and transforming the black to brown. And with the sense of presence in the chilled, grimy diner comes the affirmation that, for me, this is the greatest joy in traveling: to leave one's life behind and pretend, for a brief yet true moment, that we live somewhere else, in a different place, surrounded by different faces and a different climate than those we have always known. In the alternate universe in which Tulsa is home, this diner is a familiar facet of my life, as it is for Sophie and her father in this universe. It is specifically the mundanity of the diner that allows me to imagine an everyday existence in this city, in the sunlight of the plains, under never-moving clouds, with this woman sitting across from me. But even as the screw tightens on the experience, so the sun sinks below the office building across from us, and our square island of sunshine goes dark, and cold, and I think again of Ponyboy:

Nature's first green is gold, Her hardest hue to hold...

And after I drive back to Kathy's house, and Sophie texts me that she's too tired after the game, and I wake the next morning and bring all my things to my car and leave, I'm driving west towards Oklahoma City across empty plains when the feeling of home that had so hastily been constructed falls apart, collapsing in a cloud of dust. I am again filled with the sweet melancholy of the road, and I think over and over: nothing gold can stay, nothing gold can stay.

A SPRING DAY in seventh grade—seventh period, the second to last before we could leave. People were finding their seats before science class began. I was tired. Jon and I were talking when our conversation was interrupted. Nikki had stopped and was standing next to us, so that she was looking down at me.

"Hey, Clint," she said.

"Hey."

"I think you're hot."

"Wh—what?"

"I said, I think you're hot."

"Oh."

She looked and waited to see what I would say. She had been new that fall, and I had barely talked to her before. She was beautiful and different from the other girls in our grade. Most notably, she was fully developed whereas few of our other classmates had begun to pass through puberty. In other words, Nikki had breasts.

There were other factors that set her apart and made her as alluring as she was intimidating so that no boy dared talk to her. She was an Italian girl from Philadelphia suddenly in a small town in Vermont. She was bold and direct; she talked back to the teachers and didn't try to be nice to the girls she didn't like, who were the popular girls. She wore lip gloss and hoop earrings, low-cut shirts, and foreign jeans. All of the white Vermont boys feared her and lusted after her, and some were in love with her. And now she was confronting me.

"Oh... Oh," I said.

She continued to look at me, waiting. She had large brown eyes. When she realized I wasn't going to say anything, she laughed and walked away.

I lost a lot of sleep thinking about Nikki. Keeping me awake was desire, of course, and love, but also shame and regret and self-loathing. I grew to hate myself for not being able to confront her as she had me and tell her that I thought *she* was hot, and that I liked her. Every night I would decide that tomorrow would be the day, but the morning would come, the periods would pass one after the next, and after not talking to her at recess I would think about when I would see her again, and when that moment came, later in the afternoon, when she was at her locker by herself and I was walking by with my friends, I would again say nothing. The rest of the school year went like that, and so did the summer.

By fall, the misery had not dissipated but had congealed into something hard I lived with. Perhaps its edges finally became too sharp, or I finally passed a certain threshold of maturity, but one night I told myself that I was going to make a move and it felt different. It was simple—Nikki had already said she thought I was hot, so there was nothing in doubt. I might as well just ask her if she wanted to make out with me.

The next day was a sunny Indian summer Saturday. I took extra care washing in the shower because I knew Nikki and Ashley were coming to the skatepark. As I was drying off I was overcome with happiness and started to laugh because I already knew what the day had in store.

Tommy and Mike were at the skatepark when I biked up at noon. We started skating. Soon after, Nikki and Ashley arrived. Nikki was wearing a tie-dye tanktop that showed off the top of her breasts. The two girls sat on the bank ramp and chatted as we skateboarded. At some point Ashley came down to use Tommy's skateboard, leaving Nikki by herself. I skated up the ramp and sat next to her.

It was just the two of us sitting on top of the bank ramp.

It was midday, sunshine coated the skatepark and the cicadas were still whining in lazy voices as if it were summer.

I racked my brain for something clever to say. But awkward seconds were passing between us, so I turned to Nikki and blurted out the first thing that came to mind.

"Wanna go in the woods?"

She looked at me.

"Sure," she said.

We ran down the bank ramp and walked across the skatepark to the edge of the forest. We were both silent as we walked uphill. The steep slope was covered in orange pine needles and tree roots. We used tree trunks to pull and push ourselves further and further up. Near the top, not far from the cliff with the two couches where people smoked weed, we reached a spot where the pitch flattened in a large tree well.

"How's this?" she asked.

"This is fine."

We turned and stood looking at each other for a moment before—and it was the most bizarre, delightful sensation—plung-

131

ing our tongues into each other's mouths.

I thought to myself, oh, so this is why people kiss one another. It was the first time I had ever experienced it.

Years later I was piss drunk in a college bar, a dark, crowded bar where you stepped on broken glass and there was always the smell of stale spilled beer, and I saw Nikki. She was in town visiting friends. We talked and looked at each other again, and again we started making out. Her tongue was the same shape and had the same strength and made the same motions as before, it felt the same in my mouth, and tasted the same, too, and all the sweetness and intensity I had experienced on the hill above the skatepark exploded inside me, and to the same degree, a degree which I had not experienced since that day in September in the eighth grade. With the emotions and intensity came the memory of what it had felt like to be at the skatepark. Suddenly, I remembered the high sun above you when you were lying on plywood, the odor of the plywood close against your cheek, your bunched up boxer shorts in a hot pair of jeans, the perspiring wax of a Maplefield's soda cup. Suddenly I experienced being thirteen at the skatepark as a twenty-two-year-old. I was somewhere between memory and reality, and exploding through all of it was the smell of strawberry shampoo and the softness of the lips which had taught me to kiss—Proust's *madeleine* in the form of a woman's tongue.

Amarillo, TX & Lubbock, TX

THE NAME HOLDS PRESENCE ON THE MAP, A LONELY DOT THAT signifies 'Panhandle' and a million things I don't know, and a million things I imagine: wind and tumbleweed, houses with desert for front yards, rusty trucks and cowboys at the gas pump. When I arrive in Amarillo, I'm surprised and pleased to find these things are real. I stop at a convenience store on the corner of Route 66 then drive through neighborhoods of small houses separated by dusty fences, toys and tires and ripped lawn chairs. The houses are spread out, the roads wide, the people walking on streets without sidewalks stone-faced and cold, like cowboys in a film even when they're wearing long jean shorts and dew-rags beneath flat-brim hats.

On Google Maps, the skatepark seems the centerpiece of a busy neighborhood, but when I pull into an empty parking lot that stretches for a quarter of a mile and see the circular cement park surrounded by rocks and dirt, I realize my map had been zoomed out. The wind is loud outside my car. It's four in the afternoon, the sun is harsh and stark and the air is hot, so dry I check to see if my lips are already chapped as I walk across the desolate expanse to the skatepark. Two families are having barbecues beneath separate awnings: one is Spanish-speaking, the other is white with a chubby young boy wearing football pads. Though both groups appear to be making a lot of noise, they are barely audible through the steady, insistent wind.

There are five people in the park: two teenagers, a boy and a girl, the boy in tight flannel pants, the girl in a baggy camo jacket and khaki Dickies; two boys on scooters (a bored father sits on a nearby bench); and a guy about my age, wearing a T-shirt and purple nurse's scrubs. I drop my gallon of water in the shade and start skating.

The park is an undulating cement strip bent into a circle so that the perfect skater—Nyjah Huston, perhaps—could skate around forever without stopping. Dropping in from a small quarterpipe, moving counterclockwise, the line goes: four-stair/DIY concrete step-down, steep pyramid, vert wall-ride, single kink and fun box, small and steep quarterpipe, down-ledge/kicker, box, death gap, and finally a three-foot drop before you're back at the quarterpipe where you started. The transitions of the ramps and quarterpipes are quick and the boxes are clunky with fat coping that sticks out over the edges. Pebbles and dust fill the creases and cracks and low points, such as where people skate in and out of the dirt area within the circle, a little patch of desert containing a boulder and a gnarled tree stripped of leaves.

I warm up with ollies and kickflips. When I land an ollie-manual on the box, it means I'm ready to skate. I ollie off the drop, then back-one it; back-one up the DIY euro into a fakie tail stall on the quarter and a kickflip attempt over the pyramid's hip, which isn't close.

That would've been sick, I think. And I've found my first puzzle to solve.

I keep trying the line. The teens are mostly sitting and chatting on the boulder in the middle, the hangout spot. At one point I say "Nice one!" when one of the scooter kids does a little air in front of me, and, like a hungry dog receiving a bit of bacon, from that point on he sees me as a viable source of attention, for which he is desperate. He follows me around and talks to me.

"Did you see that one?" he asks.

"Watch this!"

"Can you grind?"

"Hey!"

"Hey! Heyyyy!"

"Hey, dude! Hey! Are you watching?"

All while his overweight father or the father of his friend dozes on his bench. I'm angry for a moment, then realize: if I had a kid, I would most likely be too hungover, too, to feign concern about what my boy could do on his scooter. I might be able to muster just enough energy to make it to the skatepark where I would quickly fall asleep.

I approach the pyramid at a crawling pace, barely ollie and catch my back wheels on the edge of transition. I lurch forward onto the dirt and sprawl in a dust cloud. The scooter kid confronts me.

"Hey, hey dude."

"What?"

"You know something?"

"What?"

"You're actually pretty bad."

"Oh, thanks."

"I just thought I would let you know."

And I had thought I was Nyjah Huston.

Scrubs is skating hard, linking creative lines and topping out on the wall-ride each time he passes. He tries popping off the up-ramp to 50-50 the flat of the kink rail. It's a skinny barrel rail, and the grind impresses me when he finally lands it.

"How do you grind that thing?" I say to him on top of the pyramid's flat deck, now our drop-in.

"Ha. I've busted my ass on that thing so many times, man."

"It's a dangerous height."

"Yeah, you can definitely nut yourself on it."

"It's not hard to grind on? It looks skinny."

"It's not too bad once you get on there."

Then, as if to prove his point, he drops in and approaches the rail with speed. He pops high into a delicate backside feeble grind with his front wheels poked to the side. I pick up my board and slap the wooden tail against cement.

I take the same line but try a heelflip off the up-ramp. The board rotates beneath my feet but drifts too far away from me.

Still, Scrubs gives a little *woop* to reciprocate. I spin my board around and go back to the pyramid.

I keep trying the heelflip with little success. As I do, the park gains skaters. They are friends of the teenage boy and girl: high school kids with elaborate cut-outs on their grip tape, skater chic beanies and Janoski shoes. They toss their boards into the dirt upon arriving and take their spots on the boulder, doing the slap-pound hello to each friend, some of them lighting up cigarettes. When I pause to listen, I hear them speaking both Spanish and English. Besides the high school crowd, another guy around my age shows up, as does a younger kid that's probably nine or ten. He has gel in his hair and wears pre-ripped jeans.

Now that there's a crowd sitting around the boulder, I feel self-conscious doing my heelflip. Pre-Ripped pushes himself around and rides down transitions with his hands in the air like a surfer on a wave. The new guy my age skates with a driving pace that separates him from the high school kids, who are there mostly to hang out, though he's friendly with them. Scrubs, meanwhile, has taken a seat on the boulder and is drinking a tall Tecate. When I finally land the heelflip there are a few *woop-woop*s from the boulder and a "Hell yeah!", that I think comes from him. He isn't cheering because the heelflip was impressive, only because he had seen me trying for so long.

Soon after I notice Pre-Ripped fidgeting on top of the short quarterpipe, toeing the coping and staring down at the transition with pursed lips and frightened eyes. Every skateboarder knows those eyes and what's behind that face drained of blood. I remember the feeling, remember how your stomach rises into your throat and you feel like you're going to throw up; your pulse pounds in the veins in your neck and your hands tremble when you hold them out in front of you. He puts the tail of his board on the coping, puts one foot on the tail, stares dumbly at the board and the ramp for a half a minute, then lifts the board and begins pacing again. When he puts the tail back on the coping, the boulder starts shouting encouragement.

"You got it, little man!"

"You just gotta go for it, dude!"

"It's super easy, you'll see!"

"You can do it!"

"Go for it!"

"You got it!"

I skate over to him.

"Just put all your weight on your front foot. Just slam down on your front foot and lean forward, and you'll land it, easy. If you're unsure of yourself, and you lean back, the board's gonna kick out and you're gonna eat it."

"I don't know if I can do it."

"You definitely can do it! It's just a matter of whether you'll do it or not."

He looks at me, trying to process the words.

He places his front foot on the board.

He stares down the small quarterpipe.

Breathing…

Then he picks his board up and yells in frustration.

"It might be easier if you tried dropping in on that ramp," I said. "It's bigger, but the transition is super mellow. This transition is super quick."

"That ramp over there?"

"Yeah."

"He told me to try this one." He nods towards the boulder.

"You think this one would be easier?" I say.

"Yeah, I mean, that's the one I learned how to drop in on," Plaid Pants says. "It's less scary than the other one."

"Yeah, probably. Either way, dude, you can do it. All you have to do is keep your weight on your front foot."

The boy puts his board back on the coping.

"Just have to keep your weight forward. Don't lean back!"

He stands on the skateboard's tail. The nose sticks out into the air over the quarterpipe. The boy moves his front foot onto the front of his skateboard. The wind is strong, dust rises and swirls in brown clouds over the parched earth.

The board tips forward, the front wheels descend. The boy rides to the bottom and jumps off his board without skating away. All the skaters who had stopped to watch cheer. The boy's face explodes in excitement.

"Wow!"

"See, man? It's easy!" I say. "You didn't commit all the way, though. This time, just commit. Think, 'I'm gonna stay on my board and ride away'."

"OK."

He climbs back up to the deck. When he's on top of the transition, we hear a voice calling from the parking lot.

"Jeremy! Jeremy! Jeremy, get over here! Let's go!"

The boy turns.

"Crap," he says. "It's my grandma. I gotta go."

"Give it one more try," Scrubs says. "You gotta land it."

"Jeremy! Goddammit Jeremy, let's go!"

The boy looks over his shoulder. Grandma is walking over the dry, dusty dirt.

"Jeremy!?" she asks, the name an accusation. Jeremy puts his board back on the coping. He takes quick, sharp breaths. Without waiting to think about what he's doing, he transitions his weight from his back foot to his front, and he drops in. He rides away from the quarterpipe with his hands in the air. People clap and slap their boards on cement and metal. Jeremy jumps off his board and hugs it to his chest, smiling the pure and total smile that only an elated child can create. Some of the high school kids get up to give him a high five.

"Jeremy!" Grandma yells.

"I'm comin', grandma," he says. "But watch this."

And Jeremy runs back up the quarterpipe and drops in again. Grandma makes no reaction.

"Did you see that!?" he asks.

"Yeah. Now let's go!"

"OK."

And they walk off together across the dirt to the parking lot.

I go back to fooling around on the pyramid and the box on the upper plateau. I land a nollie backside 270 on the pyramid after too many tries. I hide my excitement when I land it, but really I want to smile like Jeremy had smiled. And that's the joy of skateboarding, I think: the joy of landing tricks we thought we would never be able to do, of independently creating confidence and a feeling of self-worth. Skateboarders become addicted to progression and the high writ on Jeremy's face when he dropped in on the quarterpipe. Progression thus becomes a habit. While the child that doesn't skateboard might think "I can't do that—that's impossible", the child that does skateboard will think "I haven't learned to do that yet, but I will", and will relish the dripping blood and bruises and time required to make this true.

When I leave, I go to pick up my water jug by the tree in the middle of the park. Scrubs is still sitting there, smoking a cig and drinking a fresh Tecate.

"You leavin', man?" he asks.

"Yep."

"Have a good one, dude, see you around then."

"You too, man. Take it easy."

And I skate away to my car. Scrubs had seemed cold at first, but the truth is he's just shy.

I drive through Amarillo on my way out of town. Every street displays poverty, from abandoned or empty buildings to a city block lined with homeless people. Exploded bugs and the dust on my windshield catch the desert afternoon's late light, an effect that depresses me in a poignant sort of way, and the depression only settles as I bounce over a bridge and am back on the highway. The speed limit on I-27 South is seventy-five, but the Saab shakes if I drive over seventy so I set cruise control at sixty-nine and slouch low in the driver's seat. The occasional pickup passes, the farmer inside looking with curiosity at this rusty Saab with green plates from ... Vermont! ... driving so slowly on his highway. The road is mostly empty, though, a straight line through featureless flat prairie and faraway farms. The sun is low just above the western horizon. I pack Grizzly Wintergreen and play a Bill Evans album. I've never listened to Bill Evans while driving, but when I'm scrolling through iTunes and see the wistful bare branches and the sparse font of the album art—*You Must Believe in Spring*—my thumb taps instinctively. The first gloomy notes of For Elaine fill the car. I spit brown tobacco juice through the small hole of an empty coffee cup's plastic lid and drive defenseless to the feelings, inciting the feelings, simmering with feelings as I sail through time and space, south through the Texas Panhandle and forward through the fading autumn evening.

I ENTER THE city limits of Lubbock during the last moments of dusk, when the highway finally breaks from its infinitely straight trajectory to bend around the town's refineries and factories and industrial skeletal structures, the pipes and sand piles and oozing smoke stacks. All of the shapes are silhouettes against an orange strip of sunset above the flat horizon.

The skatepark is a community of fenced-in ramps covered in graffiti and the bright illumination of floodlights. There are no buildings nearby, only darkness. This is a neighborhood of factories and fast food stores and parking lots, and nobody lives here. There is the noise of cars and trucks on the busy three-lane highway at the top of the long side street I had driven in on. In the other direction, the tops of radio towers or power lines flash red dots across an expanse of swamp, and, further on, beyond the nothingness, orange streetlamps forty feet in the air shine down on another teeming boulevard, a highway between asteroids in space. This is not a place meant for human beings. This is a network of runways at an airport—painted roads and blinking lamps intended for titanic metal crafts, not flatulent bipeds made of flesh and pumping blood. The long stretches of emptiness amplify one's sense of isolation, of being an organic form lost within non-organic structures, of being the pedestrian walking down the shoulder or meridian of a highway to buy cigarettes at an all-night 7/11, at the far end of a vacuous parking lot...

Or, at least this was what *Paris, Texas* had been about, and I had been applying my memories of the film to everything I saw as I drove from Amarillo to Lubbock. When I grab my skateboard from the passenger seat and push myself down the cement path to the chainlink gate, I remember the sunken eyes of Harry Dean Stanton, confused at the wilderness of western Texas, frightened, impassive, mute...

It had required a German filmmaker to make the most American movie of all time, though this should perhaps be expected: outsiders often have a more unbiased vision, while insiders cannot separate previous experience from present perception.

The surrounding environment is sparse and inhuman, but it's inexplicably beautiful, too. The isolation of the skatepark amid so much emptiness, the hundreds of faraway lights, the faraway sigh of heavy traffic, the distant headlights and taillights and towering streetlamps, the balmy breeze (tropical compared to the air of Amarillo). The moon in the middle of the huge sky and the first of the emerging stars, no cloud or hill in sight—all of it was beautiful and peaceful in a unique way that stirs poignancy. An excitement bubbles, as it did when Florida-air evenings arrived in Vermont for one week each summer. I roll onto the smooth cement and dive into the light of the skatepark.

The tall floodlights are only on one side of the park so that ramps and rails cast shadows on the spray-painted murals of the cement, and your board is sometimes hard to catch if it's flipping in darkness. On the opposite side from the lights, in the blurry umbrage beyond their range, a row of benches hosts the peanut gallery: a mother, looking bored, and a father with his girlfriend. Bouncing around the park like screensaver graphics are two children on scooters plus a stoic college student in a T-shirt and beanie. He's been trying a small boardslide but stops when I start skating around him.

The skatepark in Lubbock, Texas offers plenty of space to kick and push between features. Flanking one end are two quarterpipes, one bigger that's scary and exciting, one smaller that's perfect for trying new tricks (I relearn frontside disasters and front slash 5-0s). After riding away from the quarterpipes, you encounter a pyramid that's so big you can't get enough speed to hit it properly, or a small section of rails and boxes that lead into a mellow bank ramp with a ledge on top. A long, low-incline bank ramp (with a deck instead of a ledge) serve as the turn-around, mirroring the quarterpipes at the other end of the park. All the metal ramps are covered in innumerable layers of graffiti so that their surfaces are slippery and the clang of your wheels is muted like a stroke on a drum covered in rubber.

I find the graffiti intriguing from an anthropological perspective. Could deciphering these bright letters and shapes yield insight into the minds of the skaters of Lubbock? Is there anything unique in the design and style that separates this spray-painting from all the rest in the world? I read sharpie messages etched onto the ramps: 'Human Centipede Booty Party 2017', 'Allison is a LOSER' (suggesting Allison is cool and hot, while the author is the loser), 'Your comfort zone will KILL YOU'.

My eyes return to this last note whenever I stop on top of the bank ramp. It's dumb, but I like it. This is the sentiment that made me leave Vermont, where I felt myself sinking, like an elephant into a tar pit, into my comfort zone. And the more I sank into this passive spectatorship, the more my translucent frame faded to nothingness. To exist I needed to participate. And to participate I needed to move. "To be or not to be" was, for me, "To go or not to go", or perhaps even "To skate, or not to skate", for only by skating could I take arms against a sea of troubles, and by opposing end them.

I begin amusing myself on the bank ramps—rolling up and popping kickflips, heelflips, shove-its, backside and frontside flips and big-flips, switch frontside 360s. I session the rails and boxes in front of the peanut gallery, which embarrasses me. A young couple shows up with one skateboard to share between them. The mother on the bench, meanwhile, is becoming impatient.

"Ryder! Let's go!"

"No!"

And his assertive response makes her go back to her phone, silent, and Ryder goes back to pushing around his scooter with a soft smile on his face, a song he heard on TV running through his head.

The couple is college-aged. He's tall and lanky, bearded and skinny, and she's blonde and athletic, wearing skate shoes and jeans and a T-shirt. When I kick up my board on the flat of the bank ramp, he's giving a tutorial on how to ride its transition.

"It's a lot faster than that one, though," he says. "Like, a hell of a lot faster!" To demonstrate, he carefully stands on the board and—arms out wide—rolls over the brink and down to the cement. The girl and I watch him glide away. There is the warm breeze and the whisper of ambiguous traffic, the lights in the distance, and very much a peaceful sense of being surrounded by open space. The guy turns around on the pyramid and comes pushing back up the bank ramp.

"See? Think you got it?"

"Sure," she says, and takes the board. She steps on and pushes herself forward with much less fuss than Jeremy had earlier in the day. She drifts down the ramp with her torso bent at the waist, her legs straight, and her arms outstretched like a person walking on a tight rope. The guy claps and cheers. She's beaming when she walks back up to us. He offers a high five, and so do I.

"Nice!" I say.

"Haha, thanks, but it's not that good! You're so good!"

I indulge my ego for a moment: yes, I am so good. I'm better than Nyjah Huston. She must have seen that backside 5-0 on the mini-box!

"I'm not good!" I say. "I used to skate a lot, but I've just started again."

"Where are you from?" the guy asks. And I launch into it: skateboard safari to see small skateparks across the US, etc. Right on cue, he laughs and asks, "But why would you come to Lubbock!?"

I learn their names, then forget them immediately. I ask about the change in climate from Amarillo.

"Oh, yeah, man, it's because of the jet stream, or something like that."

"So the air here comes up from the Gulf? Or does it come from the Pacific?"

"I don't know, dude."

"The air is just so different down here than it was up in Amarillo."

"Yeah, maybe. Don't make it up that way too much. We kind of just stay put in Lubbock."

"Ryder!" the mother screams, breaking the skatepark's twilight spell.

"Alright!"

I hear her berating him as they walk through the chainlink gate. Soon after, the tires of a pickup truck screech on the road, pebbles ping undercarriage pipes, and the truck's engine roars towards the highway.

The skinny boyfriend tells me he spray-painted all the graffiti in the park. Kids had kept drawing dicks and swear words on the ramps, so the town had commissioned him and a friend to paint over everything. He had used puffy, squished-together letters to write the word BEANS on the bank ramps, pyramid, and cement. The other recurring tag is FWD or 'fiends with dreams', the name of his crew.

"We realized, like, we were crack heads for making art. And our dream was to keep tagging, and to make it big, ya know? So we were fiends with dreams, man."

"You gotta have dreams."

"You gotta have dreams, man. If you don't have dreams, your life is... Your life is what? Meaningless, right?" And he looks at me with eyes that say he had once known what that felt like.

The girlfriend skates over. Everyone else has left. The three of us talk in quiet voices that seem appropriate for western Texas. The sentences taper off and we listen to the sounds of the wind and the traffic with our eyes raised to the sky, as if we've simultaneously forgotten the thread of our conversation. They tell me about the DIY skatepark someone built in an abandoned factory. It had been overrun by drug addicts, and there had been piles of used needles at the bottom of ramps. The town chained up the doors, but there was still a second-story window you could climb through to go and skate. Boyfriend and his friend sneak in to tag the walls, more to practice than to show off. I say I wish I could see it: a skate cathedral glowing with colors from floor to vault; poetry and paintings overlapping in neon pinks and greens from the rime-covered beams fifty feet down to the floor, and continuing there over the ramps and cement factory floor like moss spreading from the bark of trees to the rocks beneath roots. Lubbock's not great, he says, but there's skateboarding, at least.

And your girlfriend, I want to add. She even likes skateboarding.

Before they leave, I ask to take a picture. They run up the short quarterpipe. The guy stretches his arms over the railing behind him, and she stands close. At their feet is the skateboard. Half of each face is in shadow, while the other halves are incandescent. Her protruding bangs hide her eyes. His smile is bashful. Later, when I look at the photo, the figures are blurry, and I cannot help but ask: Who are these people? In what lifetime did I meet them?

I keep skating when they leave. I'm tired and keep thinking 'one more trick', but the warm air is too good. After a 360 flip, I think, and push lightly on the flats between the ramps trying them again and again. Another lone skater arrives. We don't acknowledge each other but pass in opposite directions, each focused on our individual tricks. I land the 360 flip. The air is warm and the breeze is soft, there are a million stars above the skatepark and we're surrounded by highways, and faraway streetlamps sparkle like the flashing pinpricks above them. I am skateboarding on an infinite plain, alone and happy, because it's beautiful—the street-lamps bring tears to my eyes when I stop to stare through the chainlink squares. I'm glad to be alive. I think, well, after a half-cab flip, then, and I push fakie back and forth across the flats, and when I land the half-cab flip, I start work on a fakie big flip, popping and flicking beside the man trying boardslides in a similarly thoughtless way. The two of us skate back and forth in complete concentration, or oblivion, consumed by the game we're playing like toddlers lost in the construction of a sandcastle as the tide climbs further and further up the beach.

THE ICE RINK opened in November. Overnight our oasis on the hill was invaded by cars, parents and kids with bulky bags and taped hockey sticks. The town plowed the pyramid and the boxes and rails off to the sides and then forgot about them for the winter, which of course ruined them. But the quarterpipes and the bank ramp remained where they always were, so if we wanted we could still skate beyond and between all the cars on the patch of smoother asphalt we knew as our skatepark.

This was stick season in Vermont: dreary tones of gray and brown, mud hard like cement, the wind making naked trees dance and clap their skeletal branches. The sky was dark; the dim air was intermittently filled with the faintest flakes of snow. Tommy, my brother, and I had come down to skate, though I was still in that embryonic form where I rode my brother's hand-me-down board but didn't see myself as a skateboarder. I didn't buy the clothes so wore a fuzzy black fleece, the kind Vermont children used to wear that financiers would later appropriate, and my snow sneakers, the ones with gnarled tread and no laces.

I had been thinking about it all summer, but I hadn't been talking about it. So neither my brother nor Tommy believed me when I said I was going to drop in. I knew this would be the year's last day of skateboarding, something that seemed dramatic and deserved dramatic action.

I walked up the bank ramp to the deck of the quarterpipe. My hands trembled and my saliva was thick. Tommy and my brother stood below me. The ramp was much steeper and taller than it had looked from the bottom, as it always did. I had come up here many times before but had never put my skateboard to the coping.

This time felt the same, but I knew that this time would be different.

I secured the tail of my skateboard against the coping on top of the transition. I stood there for a long time with my back foot on the tail of my skateboard and my front foot planted on the deck of the ramp.

"You got this Clint!"

"You got it! Just all the weight on your front foot! Don't even think about it!"

I moved my front foot from the ramp to the front bolts of my skateboard. The front wheels stuck out into the open air, like I was on a diving board at the rim of a canyon. The board wobbled with my fear. I imagined leaning forward and dropping down into the ramp. I tried doing it, but it was impossible, my body would not respond to the commands coming from my brain.

I took my front foot off the board.

"Ah! Come on!"

"Don't think about it! Just go for it!"

"Ahh!"

"You got it!"

"It's scary!"

"You're thinking too much! Don't hesitate, just put your foot on and go! Don't give yourself time to think about it!"

I picked up my skateboard and held it in my hands as I paced in circles on top of the quarterpipe.

Visualizing.

All my weight on the front foot.

I secured the tail back on the coping, placed my front foot above the front bolts, and pushed down, transferring my weight from my back foot to my front foot, though without conviction and without believing that I would ride away, and I didn't. My balance was too far back, the board shot forward at the bottom of the transition, I flew up in the air, my legs stretched out above my head, and gravity pulled me down on the rusty strip of sheet metal connecting the rotten plywood and the pavement.

Owf.

I tried to breathe, but couldn't.

Ohhh.

Tommy and my brother were bent over laughing.

"You had it!"

"You didn't lean forward enough! You gotta commit the

whole way!"

I lay there for a long time looking up into the murky currents and the white soot floating down from the sky. This was the worst that could happen, and this wasn't so bad. And now I knew what I had to do differently: I just had to keep my weight forward.

I retrieved my board from the bamboo bushes and skipped back to the top of the quarterpipe. I felt like Tony Hawk, who my brother and I had stayed up to watch at the X Games when he kept trying the 900 and the other skaters stopped dropping to give him more tries.

I put the skateboard's tail on the coping and fell forward with all my weight on my front foot, and even before I was at the bottom of the ramp I thought to myself, Ah! It's that easy! And I rode away fast over the pavement, the wind and snowflakes in my face, smiling as I stood rolling and Tommy and my brother chased after me.

Roswell, New Mexico

IF YOU HEAD WEST FROM THE TEXAS PANHANDLE, THE DESERT turns into mountains, suddenly, so that when you're driving in the morning from Lubbock the mountains are silhouetted black against the morning sun, and it somehow feels dramatic because you are driving straight towards them, and all around the sage brush is silver as far as you can see, and you are alone on the single lane highway. You weave through the mountains, and then you come down again, and again you are in the desert though this time something is different. The desert is empty for a long time. Eventually you see a bent green sign. The green and the white of its letters are faded by decades of wind and sand:

ROSWELL 96 MILES

And you instantly think of green creatures you have seen on TV and in movies, you hear whirring noises, and your perception of the desert around you suddenly changes, and you are ashamed because you know how silly it is to let one's imagination cloud one's understanding of reality.

The first thing I do in Roswell, of course, is visit the UFO museum. I spend two hours with 1940s laminated newspaper clippings more disturbing than any website or Joe Rogan episode. The voices come from before the term UFO was part of the national lexicon, before the History Channel filled its slots with *Ancient Aliens* or *The Simpsons* spoofed *The X-Files*. In other words, these local and national journalists were writing when 'Roswell' simply meant a small town no one knew about.

I leave the museum with questions swirling for Mr Rogan (why did the government send in troops after the rancher met with the sheriff? And why did the rancher and the sheriff never speak about it again?) but remember I'm there to skateboard. I leave for the skatepark but am delayed again when I realize the Patriots are playing. I pull over into the crowded parking lot of a sports bar.

It's already the second quarter.

Fuck!

We're losing to the Titans.

As I walk towards a table by the TV with the Pats playing, I see a Tom Brady jersey.

"Go Pats!" I say.

"Let's go!" he says, and gives me a pound. "You a Pats fan?"

"Yeah, man. I'm from New England."

"Really? You're here to watch the game? Man, pull up a seat."

I do, and though I told myself I'd only have one beer and watch one quarter before I went back to the skatepark, I have several and watch the entire game, all the while talking to my new friend, the most die-hard Patriots fan in all of Roswell, New Mexico.

He says his cousins live on Cape Cod and once sent him a Brady jersey, so he's always been a fan. Is Cape Cod close to Vermont? Kind of. Then we talk shop: Oh, that Eagles game... Can Brady win another? But he has no receivers... He doesn't need one, etc., etc.

At the end of the game, my friend gives me his email and tells me to let him know if I was ever watching another Patriots game in Roswell.

We lose to the Titans, and I'm upset because of it. I'm also buzzed, the sunlight is harsh coming through the Saab's dusty glass, and I don't feel like skateboarding. I drive to the park, take my skateboard from its seat next to me, and roll out onto the baby blue swimming pool cement.

The skatepark in Roswell, New Mexico is surrounded by desert. Sand accumulates in the basin of its bowls and at the bottom of its quarterpipes. Wind scours its surface, and when you catch your breath in between lines, you squint out across the open desert and see plumes of sand swirling above faraway sage brush. You squint the entire time you skate at the skatepark in Roswell, New Mexico, and you always gaze out into the distance, squinting, and you never laugh or talk quickly or excitedly, so you begin to feel like a Clint Eastwood character the more you skate there.

The skatepark is divided into two sections, each large and interesting enough to be a stand-alone skatepark in its own right, and each with its own distinct characteristics, which gives the impression the sections were built separately and in different time periods.

The newer feeling section, which is on the left when you skate in, has a typical surface of black asphalt. The asphalt is smooth and of good quality. This section feels more like an East Coast skatepark, with nailed-together steel ramps laid out in an arrangement someone thought would be pleasing for the skater. There is a larger-sized mini-ramp with slippery steel walls and perfect transitions, a steep, short pyramid, a death gap, a box, a series of quarterpipes lined up together, one of which is high and vertical at its top. This vert quarterpipe is aligned with a five-stair descending from the deck of the pyramid and then a roller drop-in going down from the deck of the mini-ramp. There is a low C-rail at the edge of the park.

The second, older section of the skatepark is made of the soft cement they used to use in swimming pools. The cement is baby blue and makes a dull noise when you ollie on it. This section of the park is taken up almost entirely by a pool/bowl. The bowl has bizarre walls which makes you feel like someone who didn't know anything about skateboarding built them. The sides are bank ramps of mellow pitch, interrupted by stair-sets and handrails no one ever hits; the deep end comprises two C-quarterpipes that might be fun to skate if there weren't sandy storm drains at the bottom of their transitions. In the shallow end, there is a circular stair set and a gradual downward pitch. Beside the pool, this section of the park has a box and an exceptionally long, low, slippery flat rail.

The two separate sections of park meet in strips on either side of a square of dirt which sits between the two skateparks like a plaza between two buildings. The dirt patch is covered by a canvas awning filled with tears and gaping holes; the loose flaps slap and wriggle in the never-ending wind, and patches of bright sunlight dot the square of dirt in abstract puzzle-piece shapes. The Swiss cheese canvas of the awning, the wind and sand, the distant sand plumes and squinted eyes remind one of a set from *Mad Max*, especially if one is drunk and very much from out of town.

There are scooter kids in the bowl so I skate the newer park and its mini-ramp. I land a kickflip-to-fakie on the steep pyramid, a nose stall-to-180 revert on the top of the box, and I ollie the five-stair after dropping in the steep vert quarterpipe. It is hot, dry, and I have to squint to see anything. A headache creeps from skating in the sun after drinking a football game's worth of beers. Another skater shows up as I'm skating the mini. We take turns dropping in and going up and down the walls; his runs last longer than mine and contain more complex and original tricks.

When I roll to the older park the scooter kids are still mindlessly bouncing between the walls. I make a few lines but grow disinterested. Instead I gravitate towards the long flat rail.

The long, low, slippery tube is in the very corner of the park, on the deck of the pool, so if you're a goofy you have to stand with your heels hanging off the cement then sprint forward and jump on your board just before you pop and lock into a boardslide, which you pray takes you all the way to the rail's end some thirty or fifty or 500 feet away. My first attempts at sliding the whole thing go surprisingly well so I start a session. Unfortunately the moms of the scooter kids are sitting at a picnic table directly behind me, and I feel uncomfortable right in front of them, as if I'm trying to impress them or something, perhaps in order to sleep with them or charm them. A few tries later, I slide across the entire rail in a perfect boardslide, drop off the end, pivot on my back wheel and ride away with speed.

My head hurts and I'm feeling dizzy. Heat stroke comes fast skateboarding in the desert. The sun is crashing down towards jagged mountains and I still have two hours to drive to the state forest where I'm hoping to find a spot to pitch my tent. I leave the skatepark and head south and then west through parched lands of sagebrush and barbed wire.

Later that night, the dark, silent revery between the fire, Tolkien, and me is suddenly and violently interrupted when a pickup truck speeds into a neighboring campsite. A raised mound is between me and the truck, but its headlights, taillights, and the lights on top of its cab are bright, illuminating the air and the underside of the canopy above me. The truck stays idling. I grow nervous.

A woman screams.

A loud, horrible scream.

She is screaming at the top of her lungs.

Jesus.

Jesus fucking Christ.

Is she getting murdered?

Should I save her?

Should I hide in the hillside?

Does he have a gun?

Then, something else becomes discernible in the screams:

"Ye-ye-yes! Yes! Yes!"

Oh.

They're having sex.

Soon—surprisingly soon—the screaming stops, car doors slam, tires spray gravel and screech on pavement, and the truck is gone.

Even later that night, when I'm drowsily reading *Return of the King* by the campfire, my drowsiness is again suddenly and violently shattered by a startling noise.

Oohhhhaahhhhhhhhewwwwww!!!

It's sounds like a demon crawling from the earth, just on the hillside behind me.

Ewwwwwahhhhhhhoohhhh!!!

What the fuck.

Fuck New Mexico.

Fuck this place.

Ewwwwwwewwwwwohhh!!!

Then, like Gollum scrounging in the depths of a cave, I pluck a nugget of pub quiz trivia from the back of my mind: elks bugle. I've never heard what an elk bugle sounds like before, but now it makes sense.

I sit still for several minutes. Twice more the elks bugle; twice more my blood freezes in its veins. And then the screams stop. I remain still. My headlamp illuminates my breath in the cold air and the smoke rising above the fire. It's cold, cold with a chill that makes me remember what winter feels like. I sit still for a very long time in the silence left by the elks, and I'm gradually overcome with the sensation that no one I've ever loved or cared about knows where I am or what I'm doing at that moment. And with that sensation comes a great wave of sadness.

I start crying.

The tears come out fast and are hot on my cheeks.

Then, just as fast as the desperation and the panic surfaced, they disappear, and I realize:

I'm by a campfire in the woods of New Mexico, with Tolkien, and no one knows where I am.

I take a gulp of Tecate.

What could be better than this?

That night I dream of my best friend's father milking a cow. He's in the shed where they used to keep their goats, where Hansen and I would crawl through the hay and droppings to pretend we had a fort. Each time Hansen's dad pulls on the cow's udder, it bugles like an elk.

WE WERE IN the town over, maybe in the back of a school bus on the way to a soccer game, when Tommy pointed out the drop.

"Clint," he said, "do you see that drop?"

"Where?"

"There. From the upper parking lot down to the lower." He pointed across the road. The upper parking lot ended in a cement wall the height of a car's hood. Beyond the short barrier was open air—a fifteen foot drop and a ten foot stretch of lawn to the parking lot of a gas station.

"Holy shit."

"Soy Sauce tried that."

"No way. Did he land it?"

"No. Broke his ankle on it."

So we received the news with some disbelief when, the following summer, we heard that Sawyer had landed the Morrisville Drop. Since Tommy was the only one Sawyer knew by name, he was the one who asked about it the next day. "Oh, you heard about that?" Sawyer said. "Yeah, I did. Finally—took long enough!" And as if he was embarrassed, like he felt more comfortable skateboarding than talking, he jumped on his board and pushed at the ramps.

I knew Sawyer at different stages in my life, and in each stage he seemed a different person. He was changing, but my perception and understanding of the universe was also evolving as I grew so that everything I saw was constantly being cast in different lights, or in different shades and luminosities of the same light so that I saw either more or less of them. Generally as I approached adulthood I saw things more objectively, and things within my gaze were less colored by subjective feelings than they are when you are a child.

I first remember Sawyer as a rocker. He was one of the central figures of the Older Crew. I was a little kid nervously tick-tacking in a corner of the skatepark with my friends. He wore black shirts and his jeans were ripped at the knees and butt so you could see his boxers. The tongues of his dark skate shoes puffed out like exploded airbags, which was the style back then. Everyone in the Older Crowd seemed scary to me, but Sawyer was friends with Tommy and was never mean to us, so he was less intimidating than the others. His style was aggressive in a frantic way, not smooth and easy like the Soul Skater, but more its opposite—choppy, angry, determined—like a carpenter trying to manipulate a stubborn piece of wood.

Next, I remember Sawyer as I did when I was in high school and had become part of the Older Crowd myself, though I didn't think of it that way. The real Older Crowd—that which had been the Older Crowd when I was a kid—had mostly dissolved, though some of its members still came around to skate, usually by themselves. One of these was Sawyer, who we still called Soy Sauce. He had gone from rocker to hippy. Gone were the dark shirts and jeans; now he wore cargo shorts and colorful shirts, drug rug sweaters, ankle bracelets made of hemp and sea shells. He skated barefoot and didn't even use a real skateboard—he skated on one of the old school set-ups with a pointed nose and wide trucks, big wheels and plastic boardslide bars underneath. He no longer ollied or kickflipped or grinded like he used to; now he just came to push around in his bare feet, going up and down the ramps and carving on the pavement. He would park his Jeep close and blast jam band music. Sometimes he would walk up the hill behind the skatepark, and we could smell the weed floating down through the trees in invisible clouds. Once or twice he ripped a bowl in front of us, discreetly when we weren't close, but I still saw and was shocked to see what smoking weed really looked like.

The Sawyer of this period was less intimidating because I felt more comfortable at the skatepark. It didn't feel inappropriate for me to talk to Sawyer when we were skating together, though he still probably referred to me in his own head as 'that curly-haired friend of Tommy's'. Now his aura of intimidation was replaced with one of mystery. What kind of life was this guy living? What kind of stuff did he do when he wasn't at the skatepark, where he seemed to come less and less? What had made him change so much?

The final stage in my understanding of Sawyer was the most objective, when I had become an adult and saw myself on equal footing. This is maybe like in Christianity when you finally make it to heaven and can meet everyone who has lived and died before you and can ask grandma something that you had always wondered or even Abraham Lincoln what he was thinking during the Civil War. So it is in small towns when children finally turn twenty-one and start hanging out in the bars with everyone who has turned twenty-one before them.

I was back in town painting houses for the summer, and my boss, after some barroom negotiations, subbed me out to Sawyer for two weeks to help on a project. "Hey, I remember you!" Sawyer said when I showed up at the job site one rainy morning. For two weeks we stripped the paint off a single wall of a large home. It rained most days, so Sawyer nailed a tarp to the roof and made a shelter we could work under. The plastic tarp trapped the fumes released by the heat gun and cast the wall, the ladders, and Sawyer in a dim blue glow.

Sawyer was chatty and friendly, and I realized he always had been, just that my own personality had prevented me from recognizing it. We passed the heat gun back and forth between our ladders and talked about "the days of the skatepark" or "the old skatepark days". Our conversations were a revelation, for I was able to see the skatepark as he had, and to align his memories with my own in some kind of triangulation, in so doing creating a more complete picture of what had happened on that hill above the basketball court.

"That skatepark's the one good thing this town's ever done," he kept saying. "Too bad they fucked it up!"

"You know what I remember most about you from the skatepark days," I said to him one day. "It's when you broke your ankle on that drop in Morrisville, then went back and stomped it the next summer."

"Ha! That's right!"

And Sawyer told me the story.

His skating idol had always been Jamie Thomas, who he thought was the most badass, fearless skater in the world. Sawyer used to watch *Misled Youth* on repeat, especially when he was upset. Jamie Thomas's song was Baba O'Riley. He watched the tape and the anger and aggression of the skateboarding and the music, everything about it—the editing, the crashes, the blood—resonated with the anger and aggression Sawyer felt, and he turned more towards it, more towards his idol and the feelings he got from the video he watched multiple times a day. "Back then skateboard decks were something you identified with," Sawyer said. "I skated Zero because I wanted to be like Jamie Thomas. Skating anything else wouldn't have felt right."

But he couldn't just skate on the same decks as Jamie Thomas; he had to skate *like* Jamie Thomas, too. That meant hitting the drops other people were too afraid to hit. That meant eating shit, hard, and trying again.

"I tried that drop dozens of times," Sawyer said. "Dozens and dozens of times over three years. It kind of became an obsession. All winter I would watch Jamie Thomas Zero videos and think about that drop in Morrisville, and spring would come and I would start trying again. I would stay up late thinking about it. That drop terrified me, but I felt like I had to hit it. I had no choice. I had to land it, to prove it to myself, ya know?"

"Kind of like, that you were actually Jamie Thomas. You didn't just listen to the same music or whatever, you skated like him, too, which is the most important."

"Yeah. Yeah, maybe. One time I tried it and landed kind of funny, and there was a snap. Right away I knew I had fucked my ankle. I drove myself to the hospital with my left foot. Sure enough—it was broken."

"Why would you go back and try again?"

"I had to! The whole time I had my foot in a cast I knew I would have to go back and land that drop."

"Fuck."

"It took a year. But I went back and landed it. Hands down the sickest thing I've ever done on a skateboard."

"What did it feel like when you landed it?"

"Oh, man. It felt so good. It felt so, so good."

We became quiet as we kept working, scouring the clapboards to strip the paint from the wood.

"Did you get it on camera?"

"No, man. It was just me and Critter. Critter was the only one who saw it."

Sawyer also told me the origin story of the skatepark. He did a lot of the initial fundraising and helped build the ramps even though he was only in high school. All the money came from private sources, and all the work was done by townspeople like Sawyer and my father. The town merely laid the square of fresh pavement, which the fundraising paid for. And now Sawyer wanted to get the skatepark rebuilt, it was almost all he could talk about as we worked together.

"Yeah, I've raised about four grand," he said. "It's got to be a proper park this time around, though. None of this ice rink bullshit where they snowplow the ramps to the side each winter. It's gonna be a cement park, fenced off in its own spot. We're gonna get some legit skatepark designers to come in, there's gonna be a snake run, a bowl…" And he would elaborate, once again, on the skatepark flourishing in his mind.

He told me how he went to every town hall meeting and every select board meeting and brought up the skatepark and made the same arguments every time, so that the town officials knew what he was going to say as soon as they saw him walk into the room.

"We're not gonna make that mistake again," some wrinkly select board member had said. "That skatepark was nothing but a dangerous pile of splinters and rusty nails where kids went to do drugs. A *skatepark* is *not* something we want in *this* community!"

During those two weeks I worked with Sawyer, he flushed out another legend I had long since forgotten about.

"Remember when I smashed the windshield of Frank Bouchon's truck?" Sawyer asked.

"When was that?"

"Remember when he ran over the pyramid and broke it?"

I thought for a moment. And though I didn't remember a truck driving over a ramp, I did remember showing up to the skatepark one day and seeing the pyramid disfigured. Its flat top had been bent inwards, there were gaps at the joints so you couldn't skate over the pieces of plywood, and the board of the vertical ledge had fallen off, so now you could crawl into the pyramid like it was a cave.

Sawyer explained that Frank Bouchon had gotten a new Ford F-150 from his grandma for his sixteenth birthday. The first thing he did with his new truck was to drive it to the skatepark and ride over the pyramid like he was in a monster truck. The pyramid compressed under the weight, boards broke, beams snapped, joints came apart. Frank then drove down to the courts. He parked his new truck alongside the boulders and laughed when he told people the story of what he had done. Sawyer went up to the park, saw the pyramid, and skated back down to the courts. He jumped on the hood of Frank's truck and used his skateboard as a sledge-hammer against the clean, new windshield, smashing the board into the glass, again and again, making one crack, then another, until finally, with one hard swing, he punched his skateboard through the windshield of Frank Bouchon's new F-150, scattering shards of glass throughout the fragrant leather interior.

El Paso, Texas

IT'S DARK WHEN WE ARRIVE AT THE LARGE SKATEPARK OUT-side El Paso. Floodlights illuminate the tall cement quarterpipes and bowls and all the sloping transitions. We park the Yukon and each crack a Modelo. The car engine's off but we keep the windows down, and a strong wind washes through our cab with a freshness so foreign to warmth I've known.

There are four of us in the Yukon. Arturo, which no one calls him, sits in the driver's seat. He's the owner of the downtown skate shop I walked into that afternoon. He's slightly older and shorter than the rest of us and runs on a restless and perhaps eccentric energy. Conversations with Arturo change directions dramatically and often. If he senses the hint of a pause or an over-ripening of a certain thread, he pivots and we'll be talking about something else, his "So, anyways" said in a single breath before a new digression begins. We talk for all of five minutes about my project and five minutes reviewing the questions I'd been formulating since a friend gave me Arturo's name and number back in Vermont. The structured formality between us in which I'm a writer and he the subject of interest lasts ten minutes and then I'm just another guy hanging out in a skate shop flipping through indie skate mags, watching skate videos on an iPhone next to three other people, listening to how much more Arturo needs before he can order a shipment of a dozen decks.

Jorge and Ivan insisted I take the front and now sit in the dark backseat, speaking Spanish with each other while Arturo and I carry on in English. Jorge has bushy black hair and a bushy black beard. He's more reserved, or just prefers not saying much in English. Jorge greeted me when I first entered the cave-like dimness of the skate shop, and the whole time I explained myself he focused

163

on his computer screen, not because he was rude but because he reflected my anxiety. Ivan is chattier. He's cleanshaven and heavy, with wavy black hair he wears pulled to one side. When, later, he shows me a picture from high school, I realize his hair is the one remnant of the emo punk look he rocked as a teenager. Both Jorge and Ivan are Mexican and speak English as a second language, though Ivan is more fluent.

Our first stop after leaving the skate shop was the Van Buren drainage ditch, a giant cement amphitheater set into a steep mountainside. At the foot of the stadium's waist-high steps was a pool with walls sculpted into quarterpipes, in the middle of which stood two vertical hips. Ivan told me the city built the ditches after a huge storm in 2006 to prevent wash-outs. With just a little extra cement and labor, they turned the ditches into skate attractions.

Ivan said he once saw a pro skater from Oregon launch up and over one of the hips with a 360, turning it into a spine.

The last storm had yet to drain from the pool's floor, and the bottom was coated with a thick layer of mud and trash. So instead of skating Ivan and I clambered up the cement ledges to the top of the amphitheater. We reached the summit out of breath and turned around to look out over the steps, the mountains, the streets, streetlights, homes and buildings descending to the heart of El Paso, to Juarez, to the river that separated the US from Mexico. This singular urban entity comprising two tangential cities and nations glowed with tens of thousands of lights sparkling at dusk. From here, it was impossible to distinguish the two cities from one another. Above me the sky deepened into unusual colors, and the clouds were beginning to brighten, too. There was a breeze on our perch, and it was quiet; the sound of traffic was a whisper less audible than the wind. It was beautiful, and for a moment poignancy swelled, smacked, and crackled. I tasted that rare treat one is sometimes privileged to experience, a certain joy of traveling: an acute awareness of beauty and its brevity.

Twilight hangs over the desert, then becomes night; a fat cherry blossom sags upon a branch, then falls. As a traveler your defining act is movement—nothing you see will remain in sight for long, only in your memory and in your notebook may the faces and landscapes linger, though soon they too shall pass.

We drove from the ditch as night fell and now we're parked in front of a large cement skatepark drinking beers in the temperate breeze passing through the car's open windows, a balmy, Florida breeze that reminds me of skating the courts on certain summer nights.

Arturo tells me about how much grittier it had been skating in El Paso before there were skateparks. It was a scene, he explains—if you skated you were a skateboarder and nothing else. Now people have jobs and skateboard on the weekends and all different types of people skateboard, not just the hardcore types. He explains how El Paso became a skate hub and he thought it would be smart to open a skate shop, but he learned it wasn't a good business to be in—skateboarders aren't the type of customer you want to target. Nor are your friends. Wealthy people, who splashed out on luxuries, those were the types you want as customers. Arturo wants to move to Colorado and start a ride service company, shepherding rich people from the airport to Vail in his SUV.

"When I move to Colorado..." he says over and over, his refrain of dreams.

"Kids are always trying to come give me their videos," he says. "Like, 'Oh, sponsor me, give me this, give me that.' It doesn't work that way, man." He takes a swig of beer. "I do hook up the homies. You gotta. And it's always more important to support the MVP than the top dog. You know what I mean?"

Aren't the Most Valuable Player and the top dog the same?

"Yeah, man, I feel that."

"Support the kid who's coming next, you know?"

"For sure."

After one beer we crack another, and when that one's finished we skate into the park. The undulating cement expanse is filled with skaters: they fly up and over ramps and pass one another at high speeds, they congregate on ledges and corners like flotsam swirling in the eddies of a river. The park is a snaking flow section wrapping around a plaza interior. Tall quarterpipes and bank ramps lead from the outside to the inside, as do, in several parts, down rails and stairs, a euro gap, ledges and drops. There's a large bowl with a deep end and a shallow end.

It's the proper sort of West coast cement skatepark that suits proper skateboarders. Which is to say, it suits people that didn't grow up skating in splinter-and-nails, cracked pavement, anthill sand New England hangouts. I can putz around with little flatground flip tricks, but I can't grind across high ledges, I can't link cement transitions with big mute grabs or lofty kickflips I catch with my feet. I can't actually skateboard. I'm a New England small town skatepark skateboarder skating in a big cement skatepark in El Paso, Texas, a fact that becomes obvious to me and everyone else as soon as I drop in.

I'm tentative. Skaters jostle at drop-in spots like rodents on top of a cliff. Every few seconds a skater springs forth, jumps on his board and charges at the double ledge rising above a pyramid. As soon as he's out of the way, you seize your chance—anyone else going? No? Then GO!—jump on your own board and try to forget about all the people watching you. I work on an ollie-manual over the ledge (of course) while Ivan tries a noseslide on the top of the kink ledge after the pyramid. It's a big park, though, and I feel obliged to at least try linking lines in different sections, treating the skatepark like a snowboarder treats a mountain. I stick to the outside line with its mini-quarterpipes and ramps, returning to a small gap over a cement parking blocker that makes for nice backside 180s. I always stop in the small waiting space by the pool where Ivan's usually tinkering with kickflips and nollies.

"How you like that new board, man?" He asks.

"It's sick!"

"Yeah, you like it?"

"It's for sure wider than I'm used to. But it's crazy how much easier it is to pop!"

"Yeah now you can actually ollie, bro!"

"For sure! What are you working on?"

"Ah, I'm just trying to get this noseslide bro. I landed this shit last week! But I'm too fat and old, I can't skate!"

"Haha. You're getting close!"

"Not really, man. But the important thing is to keep trying."

"Yeah."

Throughout the park, the noise of wind and of dozens of skateboards pounding down, wood and wheels against cement and steel.

"How about a back 50-50 across this ledge?" I ask.

"The high one?"

"Or the low one."

"Yeah, that would be sick. Can you do it?"

"Maybe. I've been working on 'em. Think you can?"

"No way man!"

"Let's see."

I drop in, turn on the far bank ramp, and crouch low as I approach the ramp into the ledge. It's a similar setup to the grind I landed in Tulsa, so I commit fully to grinding across the metal corner of the box. Only my front foot lands on the board, though, while my back foot plants on the cement. My legs split apart as the board shoots forward, I totter backwards and crash on my butt.

I look over at Ivan. He's clapping and laughing.

Most of the other skaters are much better than Ivan and I. Two skaters in particular impress. One's younger, perhaps still in high school. He rocks a trendy hip-hop style—baggy Dickies, baggy shirt, beanie, smart Janoski skate shoes—and skates with a matching trendiness. He skates each section in a unique way just for the sake of being different. He lands varial heelflips and nollie backside flips, fakie double kickflip and big spins over gaps I can't imagine hitting. The other skater is older, maybe in his mid-thirties, and skates with a nineties vibe that emphasizes speed and amplitude over creative originality. He launches grabs from quarterpipes, turns pyramids into hips when he clears over the landing and stomps on a distant transition the park's designers hadn't created for that purpose.

There are perhaps sixty or seventy skaters in the park, all different ages, some of them girls, some covered in tattoos, some with collared shirts and haircuts you might wear for a job interview. All besides myself are Latino, though. This is something I notice fairly soon after beginning to skate. Being a minority, it turns out, is a fairly palpable sensation, especially when the majority of people around you are speaking a language you don't understand.

The nineties charger-skater is inspiring me, and I find myself pushing hard through the middle lines of the park, ollieing over pyramid table-tops and grinding though the curves of high quarterpipes. I start sending the large euro gap step-up. It feels good popping off transition on my new board—the board is wide, the tail pristine, the pop fresh—and I'm filled with delusions of cement skatepark grandeur. A couple of kickflip tries are perfectly flipped beneath me, but I wimp out and kick the board away before I land. Finally, after psyching myself up, I pop off the euro and *catch the board with my feet*, go to land and—my back wheels clip the ledge, I'm flung forward and slam hard on my elbow and my sides. There's an audible groan around me.

"You alright, dude?" someone says.

Me, still on the cement: "Yeah!"

I stand up. The skin on my right elbow is ripped open. A guy is offering me my skateboard.

"Almost had it, dude."

"Yeah. Thanks."

I had felt like a real skateboarder, for a moment…

I go back to line up for the euro gap again, charge forward across the flats, pop, catch, and, again—*oof!* My back wheels hang up, I'm tossed hard onto the ground right elbow first.

Bone on cement, blood on cement.

Fuck!

Ow.

Owwwwwwww.

Ow ow ow ow.

Owwwwwwww.

This time I'm much slower to my feet. I don't want to show how hurt I am, so I jump back on my board and skate off. But when I'm in a corner I cradle my elbow and grimace.

"You about ready to go, man?" Ivan says to me. "Those guys just went to the car."

"Alright. Can I try one more time? I'm so close to this kickflip up the euro."

"I think they're waiting for us, bro."

"One more try."

"Alright."

Deep breaths on the quarterpipe opposite the euro gap, my elbow throbbing.

Focus.

When the coast is clear, I drop. Push hard through the park. Again, I commit, and this time…

The exact same thing happens.

Back truck hangs up on the ledge, I fly headfirst through the air, my weight comes down on the tip of my elbow.

This time I don't pretend anything—I scowl and swear and skate out the front gate, where Ivan is waiting for me, smiling and applauding.

"Haha, oh man!"

169

Jorge is in the front next to Arturo. I get in the back with Ivan, and we drive into El Paso. Arturo parks at the skate shop. The streets are empty, the storefronts shuttered. Soon the four of us are sitting behind cold cans of PBR at an otherwise empty sports bar, recapping the session and sharing videos of skaters on Instagram. My elbow has turned purple and oozes blood so that I have to be careful not to place it on the wooden bar.

"You should be happy about that, man," Ivan says. "You should be happy. Do you know why? Cause when you skate and come back with some shit like that, you know you were trying hard enough. You tried hard today, man. Good for you! You come back at the end of the day and nothing's fucked up, then you weren't pushing yourself! You weren't trying anything new!"

"Cheers to that."

The beers feel fine, as do the simple pleasure of company. After one Pabst Arturo says he has to get home. Jorge is done, too, but Ivan wants to keep drinking. The two of us say goodbye to the others and skate through the empty, silent city to a bar near my hostel.

There are two other men at the bar. One is old and fat, with a mustache and aviator-style prescription glasses. The other man is young and apparently homeless, drunk, high, unstable, or all of the above.

We order half-liter bottles of Heineken. The older gentleman is in the mood to chat. He's friendly but heavily intoxicated so that he slurs his words and is difficult to understand. Underlying our conversation about politics and Trump is a persistent uneasiness stemming from the sense that this is a lonely old man desperate for someone to talk to.

The young homeless man spills a pocketful of coins onto the bar top. He can't count the coins, so the bartender comes over and begins pulling nickels, dimes, and quarters from one pile into another. Sorry, he says, there isn't enough. The young man swears and mumbles something about discrimination, then leaves. I notice he left his half-full pack of cigarettes on the bar. I run after him.

"Hey, you forgot your smokes," I say on the corner of the sidewalk.

He turns around and looks at me. Behind his glasses, he squints as if struggling to see who's talking to him.

"Give me my cigarettes!" he yells.

"Here." I make a frisbee toss with the packet, but he makes no effort to catch. The cigarettes bounce off his chest and fall to the sidewalk. He looks down for a moment, then begins shouting.

"I just want people to treat me with respect..."

I go back to the bar.

"You know, you seem like a nice guy," Mustache says. "Nice guys don't last long in the desert."

Ivan and I finish our beers and leave.

"Sorry, those guys were kind of crazy. I go there all the time with this girl I know. She loves that place!"

"No, no, it's fine."

We continue skating down the road to a corner lined with two bars. The first is filled with people dressed nicely: through the window I see them lining up at the bar, screaming, laughing, dancing with each other. Men's hair glistens with product, a techno remix of a familiar pop song pumps out onto the street. In front of the next bar is a crowd of people smoking in a little patio. We pass through the gate. Ivan stops to say hello to several people, alternating between English and Spanish with each of them. People are standing around in clip-in bike shoes, flannels and jean shorts or jeans. The commotion in both of the bars contrasts with the sleepy inactivity we had passed on our skate through the city.

It's karaoke night inside fixed gear-hipster bar. Ivan orders the beers and we move to the back patio. Here, too, the seats are filled—people lean back in their chairs and talk across circular tables decorated with cigarette packs stacked beneath lighters and pints of hazy IPA. We find a counter attached to the wall and stand next to each other.

"Cheers!"

"Cheers!"

"Yeahhhhh!"

"Ehhhhh!"

The beer is a lager, though unfamiliar and slightly more substantive than a PBR or Labatt, with its own unique pattern classifying it as something local I've never tasted before, a flavor I know I'd never be able to describe or articulate but would, if encountered again, recognize like a little melody heard many summers before.

Ivan takes out his phone and shows me pictures of his daughter. She's standing on a skateboard and smiling, a young girl wearing knee pads and a helmet too big for her head, excited to be out having a day with her dad. I tentatively prod with questions. Ivan, drunk, I suspect, has no reservations about fleshing out details.

The daughter lives with her mom. The mom is Ivan's ex who he dated for many years; she dumped Ivan not so many months ago. The baby momma, it seems, was convinced by her own mom to find someone whose job didn't involve making T-shirts at a skate shop. They had been together since they were young, and it seems the loss still stings Ivan.

"But that's sweet that you get to bring your daughter skateboarding!" I say.

"Yeah, man, she loves it. She really loves it. I bought her a board and everything, even a helmet and pads. It's something I can share with her."

"She's lucky to have a cool dad who likes skateboarding with her."

"Thanks, man."

I buy the next round, plunging into the karaoke zone to acquire two pints of pale ale. I want to dig about our president, searching for my Mexican friend to confirm my pre-existing notions of what

Mexican people think. But Ivan is measured—it's clear he's left-of-center, but there's no vitriol. It seems he wants to avoid politics and the Trump question, which is fine with me—we're having such a nice conversation anyway. Instead he tells me about how he was born in a faraway Mexican territory I don't know about and moved to Juarez then Colorado when he was in elementary school. When he arrived in the US he didn't speak English, and he had a hard time making friends.

"Then one day, man," Ivan continues, "I saw these kids playing outside this house we were living in. I was like, 'Hey mom, what are they doing?' She said, 'Don't go play with them Ivan!' But one day I stopped and said hi to them anyway. They were skateboarding. These kids were Latino, too, so they spoke Spanish. When I came home, my mom could tell how happy I was, and she asked, 'What happened, Ivan? Why are you so happy?' I told her, 'Mom, I tried the skateboarding! I love it!' She grounded me for two weeks. The funny thing is the whole time I was grounded, I was thinking about skateboarding. I forget exactly what happened, but finally my mom realized how much I really loved it, and one day she bought me a skateboard. I went out to those kids and started to skate with them."

"And did they become your friends?"

"They became the best friends of my life, man. And then when I moved from Colorado to El Paso, it was back to the beginning, I didn't know anybody. But I had my skateboard. Guess what? I had my skateboard. Pretty soon I had new best friends."

"Wow."

Ivan holds up his board in front of him.

"You know what, man? This piece of wood, right here—this stupid fucking piece of wood—every single friend I've had in my life, every single fucking friend, I have had because of this piece of wood. This piece of wood has given me everything! It has made me who I am."

"I know what you mean, man. I feel the same way."

"You do?"

"Yes. I mean, it's funny—I'm a white guy from Vermont. I never had to move to a new country when I was a kid. I grew up in a small town in a nice house with two parents. But the best friends of my life were the ones I met through skateboarding. And when I was a kid, skateboarding was all I could think about. And me and my friends had a little skate crew—we all wore the same shoes and the same jeans, we bought skate hoodies and skated around town thinking we were like the pros we watched in the movies."

"Yeah, man."

"So me and you are different, but I feel like, in some ways, we're kind of the same." I have a gulp of ale. The booze is setting in. "We share something from our past that is important to both of us. It's kind of like we're both *built on the same thing,* ya know? And that makes us similar, and I feel like I know you very well, even though I just met you … today, I guess."

"Uh-huh."

"Would I feel like that if it weren't for skateboarding? A white guy from Vermont who feels like he shares something deep with a Mexican guy he's never met before, who lives in Texas?"

"No, man. That's crazy. But I get you!"

"And I feel like so many people our age experience the same thing. Skateboarding is so important to so many people, even if they don't skate anymore. Skateparks are important to people, even if they don't go there anymore."

"Yes."

"That's why I feel like I have to write this book."

"Yes, man. You have to write it. Write that fucking book. For anyone that grew up with skateboarding."

I'm standing with one foot crossed over the other, and as I go to guzzle the last of my beer I lose my balance and tip sideways. I catch the counter, my cheeks still puffed with beer.

"Haha, are you drunk, bro?"

"No, no, I'm sober."

"You're a lightweight? Damn, I wouldn't have expected it."

"I'm no lightweight! Here, I'll buy the next round."

"You got the last one, this one's on me. Come on."

We pick up our backpacks and skateboards and go into the bar. After the tattooed pin-up bartender gives us two cans of beer, she sets down two shot glasses and fills them with tequila.

"You like tequila?" Ivan asks.

"Of course!"

"*Salud!*"

We find seats at a round table in the back patio, sit down, and dump our boards and backpacks between our feet. The guy sitting in the chair next to me leans over. "You guys were skating today?" he asks. He's wearing a tanktop, and his chest and arms are coated in colorful tattoos. His teeth slant diagonally away from his upper gums, and I have to tell myself not to stare at them.

"Yeah, man."

"Where at?"

"Carolina," Ivan says.

"Fuck, man. I love Carolina."

"Yeah, it's sick. It was my first time there today."

"I used to skate Carolina *every day*, dude."

"You ever kickflip up the euro?"

"For sure."

"I couldn't stomp it today. This is what happened when I tried." I show him my elbow.

"Fuck, dude!"

"So do you still skate?"

"No…" He looks down at his can of PBR, hunches his shoulders forward and takes a sip. His hands clutch underneath his knees.

"How come?"

"I don't really know, man. Just kinda stopped. I used to skate all the time. I even got really fuckin' good a few years ago… Then, I don't know…I hurt my ankle a couple times, and I had my baby… I miss it though."

"Yeah, dude. You should start skating again."

He looks up into my eyes, as if I had said something he never thought of before.

"I should, shouldn't I?"

"Yeah, man," and I think of when I had the same revelation. It was in Montreal earlier that summer. It was after two AM, I was double-vision drunk in a dive off Saint Laurent. The bar had a mini-bowl surrounded by chicken wire fence. I borrowed someone's deck and skated the ramp. I did an axle stall, a rock-to-fakie, and when I thought I was still going down I started going up and shoulder-slammed into the ramp's transition. I handed the guy back his skateboard.

"Sorry, dude. I'm so drunk! And I've stopped skateboarding."

He was a tall black man who spoke English with a French accent. He took his skateboard back and spoke very seriously.

"*You must not stop skateboarding.*"

I looked at him. He looked at me.

"No, I shouldn't, should I?"

"You *must not* stop skateboarding. You *cannot!* You can't stop skating!"

And it seemed like he was talking to me after having learned the same lesson himself.

So I say to this man covered in tattoos in El Paso:

"*You must not stop skateboarding.*"

He's my age, which makes me sympathize with him more, as it always does, like we're teammates, and I imagine that my life could have been very similar to his had I been born as he had. But I hadn't—I had been born in Vermont, he had been born in Texas, or Mexico, and now here we were.

"You're right, man. I should get back to skating."

"You can't stop skating!" I plead, drunk.

"I won't!"

Ivan introduces me to some friends. I bum cigarettes and drink more beer. Soon we leave because Ivan wants to show me the bar next door. Most of the people have filtered out, and Bingo is happening. The numbers are shouted over the pop music by a man with a microphone.

"This is a *caguama*!" Ivan says to me through the noise.

"What!?"

"This is *caguama*—big ass beer from Mexico!"

Big ass beer indeed—a cold 40 oz. bottle of Corona.

"*Salud!*"

"*Salud!*" We drink. Ivan yells at me, "So you're really gonna leave tomorrow!?"

"Yeah! It sucks! I wanna stay, man! I love El Paso!"

"Man, you gotta come to Mexico with me. You would love it!"

"Dude!"

"Stay an extra day, man. Tomorrow night we're going to *Mexico!* Let's go drinking in *Juarez!*"

"What's it like?"

"Man. Just picture a street full of bars. *Soooo* many bars. And at every bar, people come around and sell you *tacos*. You have a quarter? Buy a taco. How about a little *burrito*? Cheese and beans, fifty cents. Another *caguama*? One fucking dollar! And every bar is full of hot Mexican girls, man."

"What are Mexican girls like?"

"Bro! They're so much cooler than American girls!"

"Really?"

"Mexican girls are so chill, man! Plus, they love *gringos!* A white boy like you walks into the bar, the girls will be all over you!"

"Alright, I'm staying. *¡Vamos a Mexico!*"

"*¡Vamos a Mexico!*"

We smash our bottles together and drink.

"Is Juarez dangerous, though?"

"Don't listen to that shit, man! It's not dangerous at all. People like to say shit about Juarez, but they've never even been. It's a normal fucking city, man. We'll go and get some tacos, drink some *caguama*. Then we'll come back. A few beers, a few tacos, a little bar hopping, then we'll walk right back into the USA. Nothing to worry about!"

"OK! Let's do it!"

When we finish our *caguama* and more shots of tequila and lose at Bingo, we skate through the still empty and sleeping city back to my hostel, ollieing over sewer drains and manholes, manualing under red lights from one crosswalk to another, popping on and off sidewalks, yelling at each other as we carve back and forth down an invisible slalom course in the deserted street. When I arrive at my hostel, I tell the young woman at the front desk that I love El Paso and will be staying at least an extra night. She has to lead me to the staircase up to the second floor. I find my room, take my shoes off, and collapse on the thin mattress in my smelly skate socks, dusty T-shirt, and blood-stained jeans. Soon, very soon, I am asleep.

I wake up, and the room is unbearably hot. I wake suddenly and gasp like someone bursting through the surface of the ocean. Orange morning light filters through cheap blinds and illuminates bars of floating dust. A sixty-something Asian man is standing across the room in a T-shirt and whitey-tighties. There is no air conditioning; my face is covered in resting beads of sweat, and my green T-shirt is dark with perspiration.

"Good morning!" the man yells. He has a thick Chinese accent.

"Good morning," I say. I'm in my jeans on top of the blankets.

"What's your name?" he asks.

Fuck.

So hungover.

"Clinton."

"What!?"

Too hungover for this shit.

"Clinton."

"Clinton? Like the President?"

"Yep."

"Oh my God!"

"What's your name?"

"Cory."

"Huh?"

"Cory."

"Cory?"

"Yes."

"Nice to meet you, Cory."

"Nice to meet you Clinton!"

Cory comes over and sits at the foot of my bed. My head is filled with sap, and my tongue and gums are coated in a thick paste that tastes like tequila.

"Where are you from?" he asks.

"I'm from Vermont."

"Eh?"

"Ver-mont-uh."

"Ah! Vermont! Yes! I just went to Vermont!"

"Really?"

"Yes! I am traveling by Amtrak! One month free pass! I traveled to Montpelier!"

"Montpelier! Ha!"

We talk about Vermont, where we're both traveling from. I ask Cory where he's from.

"Santa Barbara."

"Huh?"

"Santa Barbara."

"Where?" I've never heard of that city in China.

"Santa Barbara."

"Santa Barbara?"

"Yes! Santa Barbara!"

"Ah! Are you from there originally?"

"No, I am from China. But I have lived in Santa Barbara for twenty-eight years!"

"Oh."

Cory has lived in California for twenty-eight years but never acted on an impulse to travel around America by rail. Now in his sixties he finally took off, on his own, on the trip of his dreams. In this sense we're experiencing the same thing: a solo trip across America, giddy with the names of the unfamiliar states, living moments that would become memories for none but ourselves. The difference, of course, is that I'm a white person from a middle class family, and he's a Chinese immigrant; I'm twenty-seven, and he's in his sixties. I'm a careless Vermonter who has little money saved and few concerns, while he's a no-nonsense adult dedicated to the American Dream, who left behind unknown circumstances in China to strive in a foreign country with resolve and purpose. So we come from very different contexts but are now in the same moment experiencing a similar sentiment: traveling, freedom, the excitement brought about by the open road and adventures from one side of America to the other. We have each found ourselves in an old hotel in El Paso, in a stifling room filled with dust, and perhaps for that reason we talk for an hour, listing the places we've visited on our trip, what we've done, what we've seen, and where we're planning on going next.

Eventually, Cory puts on his pants. His bags are otherwise packed. There's a train to Yuma he has to catch.

"Goodbye, Clinton!"

"Goodbye Cory!"

"I hope you enjoy your trip."

"You too. I hope it's the trip of a lifetime."

"It is already."

"Safe travels."

"Goodbye."

With that, he waves and rolls his bag out the door, and I am left alone with my hangover and its strange thoughts.

Hungover in downtown El Paso.

Stark shadows and buildings bathed in sunlight, wide streets and quiet sidewalks. Art deco facades and granite government buildings.

I have a cold shower and put on my least smelly underwear and socks, my stained jeans and a wrinkly, smelly T-shirt. I go to a coffee shop and fill several pages with notes from the previous day. I intend to start writing but open *Return of the King* instead and settle in with Tolkien's prose, indulging in passive receptivity.

Jorge and Ivan are working at the skate shop when I arrive in the early afternoon.

"How are you feeling, man?" Jorge asks, a smile on his face. "Heard you guys had a big night."

"Yeah. Fuck."

"Haha."

"What up, man?" Ivan says.

"Hey, dude."

"How are you feeling?"

"Rough."

"Me too!"

The shop is silent save for the dull hum of an industrial fan set on the floor. The door is open, and occasionally a car rolls by in the sunlight.

"When do you wanna go skate?" I ask.

"Soon, man, soon," Ivan says. "I just need to do a few things."

I sit down on the leather couch and start reading a skate magazine. It's from the UK, and I read several interviews with skaters living in London before my eyes become heavy, I lean back and fall asleep.

181

I doze, dreaming of the voices of teenagers with their mothers and of young men speaking Spanish. I dream that I call Karl Ove Knausgård. When Karl Ove picks up he says, "*Allo*", but when I ask him a question he tells me in Norwegian that he doesn't understand English. My question is urgent, I need the answer, I begin shouting at him, but Karl Ove only replies in Norwegian: "Sorry, I don't understand… Sorry, I don't understand."

My dream dissolves and I am again in the quiet, dark, cavernous skate shop. The store is empty, but I hear faint music in the back. I walk slowly to the door behind the glass counter.

Ivan is working the screen-printing press. There are bright halogen work lights shining on the machine, and a bluetooth speaker plays music. This part of the old building is unfinished and filled with debris.

"'Sup man," I say.

"Hey."

"What are you doing?"

"Making you a shirt, man!"

"Sweet!"

I hoist myself onto a table covered in blank T-shirts and sweaters and watch him work. First, Ivan arranges a shirt on an arm of the press. Once he has made a dozen small adjustments so the shirt is perfectly flat and there are no wrinkles, Ivan places the wooden-framed screen on top. When the screen is clamped into place, he uses a putty knife to remove a healthy glob of colorful goo from a jar. He globs the goo onto the screen and uses a wooden scraper to slowly and smoothly level it out, applying consistent pressure so as to make a consistent coat over the cut-out skate shop name and logo. He removes the screen, rotates the arm so that the shirt with the wet goo moves underneath a heater a quarter-hour around the circle.

A few minutes later he spins the platform back, peels the shirt from its position and holds it up for me to appreciate.

"Check it out!"

The white T-shirt has the skate shop's name printed on the left breast above the graphic of a fluttering hummingbird.

"Sick!"

"Now we just need to do the back."

He repositions the shirt with its front facing down and repeats the process, this time using a different screen. When he lifts the shirt off the press, the back features a large graphic of a maze and the skate shop's name in a heavy metal font.

"Here you go."

"This is for me?"

"Yeah, dude."

"Thank you."

"No problem, man. Glad you like it."

Ivan begins working on hoodies, one of which he makes for me. I become impatient and doze amid the blank T-shirts crisp from the factory in China. Their smell makes me think of Walmart and back-to-school shopping with my mother at the end of August.

"Hey man, you ready?"

The heating unit and the lights are off, a pile of neatly folded sweaters sits on a table.

"Yeah. Let's do it."

We skate on the sidewalk in the direction of the border. The sun is bright and I'm still half asleep, still dreaming while skating down the sidewalk in El Paso. We stop in a small restaurant for fish tacos and micheladas. The server is Ivan's friend, a beautiful young woman with purple glitter on her cheeks. Her voice becomes more high pitched when she switches from Spanish to English to shake my hand and say hello, switching from familiar and affable to polite, distant, and self-conscious, and I want to tell her to talk to me the way she talks to Ivan.

We have the tacos and the micheladas and discuss going to Mexico. The girl laughs and looks more at Ivan as she speaks to us. We order another *cauguama*, this time without the michelada mix. It's nice drinking the cold beer listening to the Mexican ballads sung by the man from Juarez. At my request, Ivan translates the ballads into English: words of not being able to continue, of memories too potent to disappear.

When we leave we skate through the city parallel to the border that's only two blocks away. The city changes as we push along: gradually the crowds of the busy commercial streets dissipate, as does the traffic on the roads. Businesses and shops give way to houses and short apartment buildings, the smartly dressed office workers turn to old women carrying groceries in the baskets of their four-legged walkers. This is El Segundo Barrio, Ivan tells me, or Second Ward: El Paso's historically Hispanic neighborhood.

Segundo Barrio is also known as 'the other Ellis Island' due to its role as a point of entry for Mexicans coming into America. Since the 1800s, Mexican immigrants, many of them *campesinos* or farm workers, landed in Segundo Barrio to begin their lives in the United States. Immigration continued, and in the 1930s and forties the barrio became overcrowded. Families lived in tenements, and living conditions generally lagged far behind the level experienced throughout the rest of the United States—it wasn't until the 1960s that streets were paved and illuminated. Today, the neighborhood retains its distinct Mexican or Mexican-American character. El Paso is an American city marked by its Mexican heritage, and Segundo Barrio is the heart of that heritage.

The skatepark in Segundo Barrio is modest. It comprises a series of ramps and rails placed on a former basketball court. The surface of the court is soft, so that the sound of your ollie's pop is different than it would be on cement. Cracks crisscross the court in straight lines filled with sprouting grass. There is a box, a double kink, a short straight rail, a tall pyramid, a short pyramid, and two series of opposing quarterpipes. The features are all crammed together on the single basketball court so that there is little time to push between them. Next to the park is a playground filled with the laughter of children, like trees with the songs of birds. A sidewalk wraps around the other two edges of the park so that you can skate from the street directly into a quarterpipe and people walk through the skatepark as a shortcut.

Ivan and I begin skating. I flow around, grinding across the coping of the shorter quarterpipes, dinking boardslides on the ends of rails, ollieing on and off the boxes and popping weeny airs over the transitions of the pyramid. It's hot, and I start sweating immediately. The park is empty besides Ivan and I. Pedestrians—many of them old people or kids returning from school—stare with bored curiosity as they pass. The beer buzz is good and it's fine being outside under the sun and blue sky, and we're both happy in a relaxed sort of way, like when you relish standing in the rustling shade of a tree, closing your eyes to better feel the soft breeze on your skin, raising your gaze to watch an unflinching bird traverse the sky.

Skateboarding requires a certain kinetic enthusiasm we lack this afternoon. Still, we try to push the issue.

"Want me to film you, man?" Ivan asks.

"Sure."

"What do you wanna do?"

"Think I could boardslide that double kink?"

"Go for it."

The run-in is short, so I leave my board on the basketball court cement of the skatepark, run across the sidewalk and jump on, crouch and pop onto the top flat of the double kink. I make it to the second kink and stick. In the ensuing tries, I alternately slip out or stick, fly forward or backward but fail to stay balanced throughout the rail. As I get closer and closer, I become excited and take shorter breaks between attempts.

Try.

Grab my board.

Back to the starting spot.

Try again.

Ivan films on his phone.

"Almost, man. You got it!"

"Alright, this time for sure!"

Or I say:

"This is definitely it!"

"This time for real!"

"This time I'm actually going to focus."

I try again and again, I swear I'm close when, suddenly, the skatepark begins dissolving in flashing blotches of black.

"What's up, man?"

"Shit…"

"You alright bro?"

"I'm dizzy…"

I lie down on the soft cement under the leaves and the pale blue everywhere above them.

When I've recovered, we skate past the playground and down the street. Colorful murals coat the tall sides of brick buildings. We skate to a general store advertising tacos and burritos and empanadas. The clerk speaks Spanish with Ivan, and I prepare my best "*Pardon, señor*" for when I place my two bottles on the counter.

"$2.40," he says.

"OK."

There's a bench in the sun outside. I keep sweating and drink a liter of water, then open the other. A man pulls up in a small pickup truck. He's slim and wears his T-shirt tucked into his jeans. As he walks into the store, he gives a surprised shout.

They're speaking Spanish. Based on their tones, it seems the chat goes something like:

"Ivan! No shit! Long time since you've shown yourself around here, you punk."

"Hey, Ricky."

"What's new with you?"

"Oh, you know, still working at the skate shop."

"Still over there with Arturo, eh? Alright."

"How's your family?"

"Everyone is good, thanks for asking. Jane just went back to school, so that's exciting."

Ivan must have said something about me, for the blue-collar dude looks at me, nods disinterestedly, and the conversation continues, to my delight, and I am left alone in dehydrated delirium.

Blue-collar dude goes inside the store. Just as I am about to ask Ivan about the conversation, two other guys show up. They're like Ivan in terms of age and hair, though they both have more videogame nerd style (basketball shorts and sandals) than skater style (jeans and skate shoes). One of the guys has his entire face covered in a tattoo emulating the villain's mask from *Saw*. The three of them begin talking. Pickup Truck comes outside with a six-pack of beer. He wants to say something else to Ivan, but when he sees the guy with a *Saw* tattoo on his face, he does a little wave and changes trajectory straight to his truck.

Saw and his friend go into the store. They come out a moment later with Styrofoam containers and plastic forks.

"Alright, Ivan, take it easy dude, and see you around," maybe they say, and walk off.

"I went to school with that guy," Ivan whispers. "He was the smartest guy in our class. Everyone knew he was going to go to college and get a nice job. He went to college, graduated, which is something, man, then a few weeks before he started doing job interviews, he got the *Saw* tattoo on his face. All these companies had wanted him, but then no one would hire him."

"So what does he do now?"

"I don't know. I don't think he has a job."

We're quiet. An old car drives by on the dusty road.

"Why did he get a tattoo of the guy's face from *Saw*?"

"I don't know. I guess he just really liked *Saw*."

We laugh.

When we skate back to the park, I notice a large mural I hadn't seen before. It shows an old man in a cowboy hat playing guitar and another on the accordion. Beside and below them is the image of a grandmother washing a baby in a metal tub in what looks to be a colonial city in Mexico. In the other corner are three men walking down a set of train tracks towards the sunset, their backpacks overflowing with clothing and water bottles.

"You coming, man?" Ivan asks.

"Hold on."

"Cool mural, right?"

"Yeah. It's amazing."

I take a picture on my phone.

"Alright, dude," I say to Ivan, "Go get in the photo!"

"Me? Why would I be in the photo? Give me your phone and you go pose, man."

He's probably self-conscious about playing the Mexican posing with the Mexican-pride mural. I feel guilty when I realize I'd embarrassed him, so I give him my phone and stand with my back against the wall.

I like the photo, but it lacks the potency of the one I selfishly requested of Ivan, of the young Mexican man and his skateboard posing beside the old musicians and the Mexican baby and her grandmother and the migrants crossing the border. Ivan, too, is what it means to be Mexican-American: he too is part of that experience. Hanging out at the skatepark, making friends who skateboard, Ivan in his torn black jeans and black T-shirt and ripped red skate shoes standing beside the Mexican grandma, the mustachioed men with their bolo ties and their instruments: different iterations of the Mexican in America from different generations, wholly unique individuals with different values and goals who nevertheless share a common background and form an integral part of the United States. And just as Ivan before the mural seems somehow meaningful, I think, so the skatepark within this neighborhood seems significant in relation to my project.

Objectively, Carolina was one of the best skateparks I had been to in my life. I prefer, however, this small skatepark on an old basketball court in El Segundo Barrio. This skatepark is in the heart of El Paso, but it epitomizes the space and institution I've been chasing: the small town skatepark. The Segundo Barrio skatepark has the feeling of the rainy skatepark I visited in Spencer, West Virginia, and the one where I grew up in Vermont. The ramps and rails are small, the surface is bumpy and cracked, the features are cramped and poorly organized. But the Segundo skatepark is more than enough. It's a place for young people to escape their families and be together on their own, yelling when they keep trying the same trick over and over without landing it, sitting on the ramps watching someone skating in the sun, gossiping, debating, laughing. It's a space where you see the same faces day after day, where it's hard to skate without talking to the others skating around you. For them, it's a space for growing up.

Should it have surprised me when Ivan said this was his favorite place in the world to skate?

What is charming about this small skatepark? Do all small town skateparks have a charm caused by empty, sleepy roads and somnambulant spectators? Is it just that they make me remember my childhood, and so are charming only to me?

Ivan tries but cannot tell me why he prefers skating the Segundo Barrio skatepark, just as I, after thousands and thousands of words, cannot explain why I am drawn to the skateparks found in American small towns.

I simply am.

The double kink is now submerged in the outstretched shadow of the sidewalk's tree. I lock into a boardslide on the top flat, lean forward over the down, survive the second kink by flailing my arms in circles with my back arched and belly forward, then drop off the end, managing to turn my board 90 and land switch. Ivan keeps filming. In the video I see myself pivot back to goofy, push once, gently, into the next flat rail. I'm wearing the white Barrio shirt Ivan made for me. I ollie and muscle my back trucks over the rail, smack a lipslide down and land regular. With what little speed I have left, I pop a little kickflip. The board barely leaves the ground, but I land perfectly on the trucks. Ivan skates toward me. I raise my hands and look at the camera, grinning in a way that's surprising, for I don't associate myself with such happiness.

We stop by another bar on our way back to the skate shop. The interior is a scene by David Lynch—red leather lit by neon blue, neon red, shadows and shadowy faces and the glowing pink square of a jukebox, the crimson rectangles of pool tables. A long bar with stools that spin, the damp smell of spilled beer and decades of cigarette smoke.

We take two stools and put our skateboards and backpacks between our feet, upright against the bar. One of the two bartenders comes over. She knows Ivan, and they speak Spanish together. She has shiny fingernails and the frazzled hair and face of a heavy smoker. We order Tecate. She cracks the cans and puts them on the bar with a slice of lime on top. I squeeze the lime so the little pods pop and break loose and drip into the beer.

We drink the beers, then order more.

A man approaches us. He's slightly older than middle-aged, wearing a wife-beater tanktop that shows off his huge arms. Ivan and him begin talking, and it seems they, too, know each other. After they've been talking a while the man looks at me and switches to English.

"You boys are crossing the border today?"

"Yes, sir."

"You shouldn't do that. It's no good down there. Especially for guys like you."

"I'm sure we'll be fine."

"You'll be dead, is what you'll be!"

"Come on," Ivan says. "When was the last time you crossed the border?"

"Ten years ago. And I don't plan on doing it again in my life, if I can help it."

"Then you wouldn't know."

"Maybe, maybe not." He tips his Budweiser bottle upside down and takes a large gulp. "Well, boys, enjoy then. And be careful. Watch yourselves."

"Yikes."

"Don't listen to that guy, man," Ivan says. "He's just trying to scare you. I go to Juarez all the time. It's a normal place. You're going to be fine. Then you're going to be amazed at all these people saying crazy things when they don't even know the situation."

The sun is low now, and the light and fresh air startle me when we step outside the bar: life had continued without us. We skate back to the shop. Jorge is pissed we took so long, but Ivan and I are drunk and laugh at him.

We have to wait for the shop to close before we can go to Mexico. Jorge leaves to buy dinner, and I go back to my UK skate mags. Customers come and go as the light entering the front window dissipates, and then it's night. The shop is dim like a jazz lounge, empty, and silent. Far away, across the room, Ivan stands in Jorge's position behind the laptop. His blank face and unblinking eyes are illuminated in the blue-white glow of the computer's screen.

When Jorge comes back they start counting the money in the register while I slouch on the couch with my chin on my chest and my belly sticking out. I dig my passport out and leave my bag and skateboard behind the counter, and then it's time to go. We lock the doors and walk south through El Paso towards Mexico.

The city's sidewalks and roads are devoid of people and quiet enough that we can talk in whispers. Then, the darkness and the tranquility recede in the hum of floodlights. Brighter than anything else in the city, the border appears. The sidewalk turns into a footpath over the bridge. Chainlink fence arches above us as we begin to climb. To our left is four lanes of stopped traffic, to the right the river, really more of an industrial void filled with the debris of a fault line between estranged states—cement, metal, and mud.

"Where's customs?" I ask.

Ivan laughs. "There's no customs going this way, man. You got a quarter?"

"Yeah."

"That's all you need to get through."

We continue over the bridge until we're high above the Rio Grande and the bridge's slope plateaus. There's a plaque fastened to the fence. The sign is divided vertically—on the right, the words are in English, "PASO DEL NORTE BRIDGE," and on the left, Spanish, "PUENTE PASO DEL NORTE." Ahead, the material and construction of the fence and sidewalk change.

"One more step and you're in Mexico, man," Ivan says.

"One more step, and it's the furthest from the Shire I've ever been."

"What?"

"Nothing."

"Haha. Alright, after you!"

And with that, I cross the Rio Grande and step into Mexico.

Everything feels different immediately—the streets are lit differently, there's a different smell, there are cars we don't have in the United States that make different noises, the sidewalks are different with yellow tactile pads for blind people, there are food carts and convenience stores with names I don't recognize. Yet, for all the differences I notice as Ivan and Jorge lead me to their favorite bar, they are nevertheless small differences. The dramatic transformation of surroundings is less objective than subjective and related to the fact that with one step I have become a foreigner. Now I am at fault for not being able to speak the lingua franca; now I feel out of place, confused, and wary of my surroundings. Mixed in with this excitement of being abroad is the excitement associated with the place name Ciudad Juarez, which I have heard is a city more violent than Damascus. However, just as Proust had been disappointed when he finally reached the tranquil shores of Balbec, so I am somewhat disappointed when our group peaceably strolls down Main Street in Ciudad Juarez and stop for a bean and cheese burrito and a pack of cigarettes from a friendly old man at his food cart.

Well, not disappointed. More accurately, I am thrilled. I'm in Mexico! And with the delight is a sense of embarrassment and shame that I had been so ignorant, that I had let Fox News shape my opinion of a place I knew nothing about.

We light up and walk down the wide avenue. The sidewalk is mostly empty, but now and then we pass someone—someone heading home from work, someone heading to a bar to meet a friend, someone heading to a lover's apartment. As we walk further into the city, the jarring sense that I am somewhere completely different than El Paso changes, replaced by the epiphany I always experience when traveling.

This place isn't so different after all.

People are the same wherever you go.

We turn into an unmarked door through which we have to crouch to avoid bumping our heads. Inside is a long narrow room with a bar and its fifteen stools and two tables in the back next to a jukebox. When you sit at the bar your back is nearly against the wall so people have to squeeze by if they're walking past. All along the back wall and on the sloped ceiling is a collage of old *Playboy* centerfolds, a mosaic of 1970s boobs that steals your gaze if your eyes wander from those of the person you're talking to.

There are two groups of two in the bar: a pair of young professional buddies, each in a crisp plaid button-down, and two older men who hunch on their stools and speak in softer tones. Our group of three fills the stools between them. Ivan orders three *cuagama* and the bartender places the large bottles of Indio on the counter along with three mugs filled with ice. We pour the beer from the bottles into the mugs then hold them up.

"Hey, *salut!*"

"Salut!"

"Salut!"

Jorge orders a plate of beef jerky. The bartender empties a packet of dried meat onto a deep-rimmed plate and proceeds to douse the pile in Worcestershire sauce, hot sauce, and several other types of sauces. When she sets the plate down before Jorge, the chunks of jerky are swimming in a pool of brown salt. He nibbles at the plate for a while, then, to my shock, tips the plate above his mug and dumps the meat and the sauce into the beer. The beer turns dark and the chunks of beef mix in with the ice cubes.

"Wait, what—?"

"What?"

"Did you just add the jerky to your beer?"

"Yeah, you've never seen that before?"

When Ivan orders something, the bartender opens a bag of tortilla chips—they're in a plastic bag stapled together, as if produced locally—and proceeds to fill the bag with a similar assortment of sauces, though this time emphasizing the red sauces instead of the brown. She folds the top to seal the bag and shakes the chips like a cocktail shaker, saturating each and every crispy shard of *tortilla* with the viscous sauce combination. When the plate arrives on the bar, she squeezes the empty bag like a tube of toothpaste to drizzle the last of the sauce over the soggy mound of chips.

We drink the beer on ice and beef jerky and talk about skateboarding. By the time I order a second *cuagama* in nervous Spanish Ivan and Jorge are already on their third. Ivan goes to the jukebox. He stands for a while in the glow of its display while I try to spark conversation with Jorge. Ivan enters his pesos and makes a selection. The quiet Spanish murmuring in the bar is suddenly and immediately replaced by the full sound of music. I forget about the bar and am transfixed, pinned to the same voice that moved me in Tulsa.

There is a light and it never goes out.

I had heard the same song with Sophie in Oklahoma. Where and when, and what we had been talking about I can't remember, but I had been buzzed and ecstatic, possessed by an inexplicable human happiness. The song had come on and reacted to my mood or fused with my mood or combusted due to my mood, and I melted, my heart ballooned with the poignancy of ephemeral experience, the supreme joy of ephemeral existence, so now it doesn't surprise me that the song speaks of death.

I have the distinct sensation the universe is speaking to me. Sophie, Ivan, the man in purple scrubs, the man trying 360 flips in Fayetteville, the toothless man in Charlestown, the boy with the Spider-Man bike in Keene. Somehow they are related, somehow they are pieces in a puzzle I am intent on solving. The story isn't about skateboarding. No, it's about life, about living, about the earth spinning and the smile of a child, the sunshine of summer afternoon in Vermont...

SMALL TOWN SKATEPARKS

SMALL TOWNS ARE like islands, each unique with their own flora and fauna, topography and coastline, but in other ways each island is the same, too. The gaze of islanders out to sea is filled with the same emotions no matter where they are: curiosity, fear, yearning. The sea represents the unknown, a tremendous force in opposition to everything around them on the island, the intimately known and familiar. The unknown is appealing for the same reasons as a mystery box lottery prize—what's inside could be bad, but it could be good, it could be very good. Either way, many islanders think (though few act upon these thoughts) that whatever's out there has to be better than what's here. And they leave, and when they come back, they will try hard to look and act differently, though this is just affectation, for they really have not changed very much at all.

The islanders who leave, as well as some of those who stay, will hold deep within their identity this conflict between the outside world and the island. It is an existential crisis that lingers well past adolescence: Are they an islander, or are they someone of the outside world? Can they live somewhere with no connections to the people and families they grew up knowing? And if they are not a lifetime islander, then what are they? Who are they? What is their identity?

For the young person from the small town, the 'outside world', that empty blue horizon filled with mystery and potential, is represented by 'the big city'. Few young people in a small town dream of staying in the same small town their entire lives, though many of them will do just that. No, they think of their futures and envision themselves in Manhattan, in a sky rise with big windows, hosting a cocktail party attended by beautiful and interesting people. That this vision of what they want their life to be is so ill-defined is perhaps why it so rarely comes to fruition, and why they experience so much existential turmoil as they become adults.

Perhaps these young islanders with delusions of far-off landscapes will eventually join the older islanders strewn on the beach with bottles of rum and a pile of limes within easy reach. These older, fatter individuals meet in the same place every day, they are content, and there is no inner conflict. They are very sure about who they are and where their place is on earth. It is here, on this beach, with these people they know well, with whom they share healthy portions of rum and vast quantities of familiar food. They are at peace and they are happy. These islanders gaze out to sea and view the empty horizon in opposition to what they experience on the island. Since they nestle themselves increasingly into the comfort and safety of the familiar, the outside world comes to represent discomfort, danger, and suffering. And when a boat arrives and delivers people from the outside world—foreigners— these older people look at them with suspicion and malice.

Our hidden corner of the island was the skatepark, and from that private beach we looked out over waves and clouds and discussed the universe. We had little perspective from this vantage point, so it was more our imaginations than our eyes that revealed to us what lay beyond the horizon. And when one's imagination assumes primacy over the senses, the unknown becomes unbearably enticing. We would have long conversations about the places we wanted to go and the things we wanted to do. These conversations only became more heartfelt the older we got, because, for most of our earlier time at the skatepark, we were consumed in the happenings of the island, especially at the beach reserved for the people we thought were the coolest.

Still, we were in awe of the outside world. So when a shipwrecked sailor or pirate washed up on our shores, we were fascinated by this sudden injection of the foreign.

The first outsider I remember hanging with us at the skatepark was Pablo. He was from Chile and worked at the ski resort on a student exchange visa. He was nineteen or twenty, and we were thirteen or fourteen, but he was looking for people to skateboard with and so became our friend. In the winter he drove us to the indoor skatepark in Essex in his old van filled with all his things. This never felt quite right, because I felt that the skateboard was meant to be put away in November and not taken out until spring. Pablo was happy and friendly and told us things about Chile like, "We've got some sick mountains, man," and "Yeah, it snows a ton, and that's when it's summer for you guys—June and July!" and we talked about how we were going to get to Chile.

Then there was the kid from New Zealand. He just showed up one day, hung out with us for a few weeks, then left. He was just like us, completely unremarkable except that he was from New Zealand. He became the celebrity of the skatepark, and we invited him to join us wherever we went.

Dee arrived the spring of my senior year, in his oversized maroon SUV that oozed bass you felt in your limbs. He was a white guy with tattoos and dreadlocks, and he always skated with his shirt off to show the jagged scars across his gut and back.

Dee was from Baltimore. He had gotten into some trouble and had been sent to live with his grandparents in Vermont. Said trouble, I found out when I asked about the scars, involved a crack deal gone wrong and multiple stab wounds. "It was over five bucks, dude," he said to me. "Swear to God, five bucks, this crackhead stabbed me outside a J.C. Penney. I walked into the store bleeding everywhere, went up to someone and was like, 'You gotta help me', and he was like, 'Sorry I don't work here.'"

"Haha."

"And then I passed out. When I woke up I was in the ambulance. There was blood everywhere, and there was this doctor working on me. I remember just asking him 'Am I gonna die?' and him looking at me and saying, 'Doesn't look good, kid.'"

"Damn."

"And then I was in the hospital for a few months, and then I came up here. Aha! Funny shit, right!?"

I had experienced a falling out with many of my friends and was already orienting myself towards the foreign, so we became friends. During the summer before I first left town, I hung out with Dee more than I did with people I had known since childhood. We skated together in the afternoons and evenings and then would drive around smoking joints in his SUV. He was looking for a friend in a foreign place, and I was looking for a foreign friend in a familiar place, because I had, in my mind, embarrassed myself in front of everyone I knew. Plus, the foreign seemed good—to move to the foreign was to move in the right direction. The foreign was interesting and exciting, the foreign signified experience over innocence. Most importantly, though, this foreigner was a friend who could listen to all the things I wanted to say. And sometimes someone we don't know is the only person who can do that.

I left town at the end of the summer, and my friend from Baltimore stayed. He was there for a few years. I saw him when I was back in town, but then one time I came back and asked about him, my friend told me, "Oh, you didn't hear? He moved back to Baltimore."

"Oh," I said. And that was the last I ever heard of him.

Phoenix, AZ

A SANDSTORM HITS ON THE HIGHWAY PAST LAS CRUCES. THE southern sky is dark with navy tones, ominous and dramatic, there's light traffic on the highway, and then beneath the darkness to my left I see huge pillars of dust and sand crawling over the surface of the desert. Some are like tornadoes while others are indistinct, opaque masses. The light brown of the swirling sand contrasts with the dark blue of the sky, and it's beautiful—shades and shapes I have never seen before, in such empty space. The forms shift and morph, slowly, gracefully. Their leisurely pace across the surface of the desert reminds me of the somnambulant migration of a pod of whales.

Except, the sand clouds aren't moving slowly.

They are moving quite fast, in fact.

And coming right towards me.

Shit.

They're coming right for us!

The eastbound highway disappears. A second later, my car is consumed in the storm. The road vanishes. All I can see is a dense fog of sideways-flying sand. My instinct is to hit the brakes, but I remember those billboards I keep seeing and keep driving straight, praying the road won't bend.

Seconds later, the desert, the highway, the indigo clouds, and the mountains reappear. When I glance into my rearview, all I see is a wall of dust. I bring the Saab to ninety and leave it there.

Later, after I've turned off the interstate in Lordsburg and driven into Arizona on one of those empty single lane desert highways that East Coast people dream of, the sky finally does what it's been promising. The rain falls so thick I have to drive slow with the wipers on at max. The rain falls until I'm a half hour outside Phoenix and start descending from the highlands. Ahead, the orange and violet of an Arizona sunset emerges from the clouds.

From the east, Phoenix begins suddenly. You're in the desert, and then you're in the sprawl, one never-ending city which is in fact many cities that have grown together so that you can no longer tell them apart. The highways are thick with cars and no one walks. I go to the skatepark in the first of these cities. The storm has passed through—there are puddles all across the large cement skatepark. There's a padlock around the gate and a sign that says the park is closed during rainstorms.

Shit.

I stand in the wet grass looking into the park through the tall iron fence.

"It's locked?" someone asks.

I turn. There's a skinny guy in his early twenties or late teens with a skateboard under his arm.

"Yeah, unfortunately."

"Looks dry enough to me."

"Yeah."

Without saying anything, the guy begins walking the perimeter of the fence. When he reaches a section where it curves to make an acute angle around a tree, he tosses his board over and uses the wedge in the fence to hoist himself up and over the top. He navigates the spiked tips of the iron bars and drops the seven or eight feet down to the skatepark's cement like he's done it before, flips his board over and drops in.

I go around and trespass using the same technique.

It's just the two of us skating in the humongous park. There's the excitement of having so much space to ourselves, which we take advantage of by pushing fast and going up tall ramps for no other reason than to come back down. Added to this excitement is the thrill of breaking the rules, of ducking a rope and skiing a trail filled with untouched powder.

I gravitate towards the street section. I find two hits in a line that suit me perfectly. One's a mellow bank ramp you can connect with a long, low tube rail (the upper flat of a long kink rail). I get a boardslide, a kickflip and a varial flip and a backside heelflip off the bank ramp, then, to cap off my night, a frontside boardslide to switch, which even gets tappies from my friend. Going back the other way is a steeper bank ramp crowned with a ledge like the setup I grew up on. I can always skate above my level on a bank ramp-to-ledge, like a song an otherwise unmusical person learned as a child and can impress people by singing, and my friend might be surprised when he sees me land a nose stall-to-180, a nose stall-to-switch, axle and feeble stalls and an axle stall that moved just enough to be considered a 50-50 grind.

Then again, perhaps he doesn't even notice.

I'm skating well and having fun. Twilight is falling, the tricks are becoming more difficult in the hazy half-light of the gray evening sky, but both of us seem content to keep going until it is too dark to skate. Then, a police cruiser pulls up. The officer steps out, slams his door, and walks towards us.

He has a crewcut and a belly and thumbs tucked into his belt.

My friend and I are in the middle of the park.

"Hey!" the cop yells. "Hey, come over here!"

"Well, we're fucked," I say.

"Yep."

We skate over. The cop's hands are wrapped around the bars of the fence.

"You guys seen two little kids on scooters around here?" he asks.

"No, I haven't seen them."

"No, sir," Skate Guy replies.

"Two little boys, maybe in middle school? Both of 'em on scooters."

"No, I haven't. I've haven't been here long, though."

"Nope, me neither. Haven't seen 'em."

"OK, OK…" The cop nods and looks off in both directions, scanning the area for the sinister scooter kids and strategizing his next move. "Alright, well thanks, you two, have a good night."

"No problem."

"Thank you, officer."

The officer goes back to his car and speeds out of the parking lot.

"You think he realized we hopped the fence to get in here?" I ask.

"Not sure. But I don't feel like sticking around to see if he comes back."

"Me neither."

We skate around the fence looking for a spot to climb out. Skate Guy's cool impassivity has been replaced with nervous chatter and a higher tone of voice.

I keep skating along the fence without noticing that he stopped, threw his board over, and is attempting to climb the fence. He's struggling frantically—the flat soles of his skate shoes keep slipping on the smooth black metal bars of the high fence.

"Shit, shit! I can't get over!"

"It's alright, man."

"I can't get hold, man!"

"It's alright!"

"We're not gonna get out!"

"Here, come down for a minute."

He lets go and drops down.

Were those tears welling in his eyes?

I squat with my back against the fence and hold out my interlocked hands as a step.

"Here. Step on and I'll hoist you up."

"How are you gonna get over?"

"Don't worry about it."

Skate Guy puts his foot in my hands and takes hold of the fence. I hoist him up by his foot. He puts his other foot on the top beam of the fence and pops himself over, landing with a crash on the strip of little stones on the other side.

I toss my skateboard across then pull and kick myself over the fence and land in the stones next to him. He hands me my skateboard.

"Thanks, man," he says.

"No worries."

And he instantly reverts back to cool impassivity as if nothing had happened, for he's embarrassed that he had panicked and had needed my help, and perhaps more so that we had been forced to get so close. When we walk around the fence to the parking lot he pushes off without saying goodbye. I toss my board into its spot on the passenger seat and sit watching the faint shapes of the skatepark's ramps disappear. When they're all gone, I plug in my friend's address and start the car.

Something makes a very strange noise.

A friend once asked, "Do you have faith?"

"As in, Jesus?"

"No. In general. Like, are you the type of person that has faith that everything will turn out OK? Even if all signs point to 'no'?"

"Oh." I thought for a while. I thought about Tom Brady driving down the field in the fourth quarter, down by a score. "I would say I have faith."

He looked me in the eyes. "You have to have faith, man. You have to."

I think about this conversation a lot when I'm driving the old Saab across the country. I bought the car on Craigslist for $900. It has holes rusted into the undercarriage, the frame shakes violently when I go too fast, things sometimes fall out from its belly when I hit a bump. Still, I believe in my car. It's done me well for so long, and whenever I hear a new screeching or rattling, I stay calm, because I know my little Saab is not about to fail me, not after all we've been through together.

204

Driving a used car is a practice in having faith. One must trust a less-than-trustworthy character. We put the day-to-day functioning of our lives—our ability to bring our kids to school, to get to work, to drive to the restaurant where we have a date—in the hands of a klutz who might drop everything. We perhaps even ignore things that are likely to happen, covering our eyes with our fingers and saying, like Han Solo to worrywart C-3PO: "Never tell me the odds!" So drivers of decrepit hunks of junk picture themselves as Harrison Ford flashing a lop-sided grin as he hops from the wreckage of a bright monoplane on a California golf course.

Having faith is different than being faithful, though 'full of faith' makes one think of unquestioning loyalty and confidence. The faithful spouse is one who believes their husband or wife will never wrong them. When the person we love is 'unfaithful', we are crushed that our trust was betrayed, that our lover lost their belief that we were good enough for them. Similarly, when Lionel Messi misses a penalty, or Tom Brady is sacked at the end of a Super Bowl, they are being unfaithful, for they have acted in a way contrary to the faith we entrusted in them.

And the feeling that filled me when Chris Long finally reached our quarterback and the ball went spinning from his arm is similar to the feeling when, accelerating on the five-lane highway in Phoenix, there's a loud bang and the steering wheel suddenly refuses to turn so that I have to hit the emergency lights and drift to the shoulder as eighteen-wheelers roar past, pulling on their airhorns: the pain of hope being ripped apart, of faith being proven hollow. It is the despair produced when subjectivity comes into contact with objectivity and there is a discrepancy; when we realize that our wishes, no matter the fervor with which we whispered them, have had no bearing on reality, that all our incantations of "Oh, Ave Maria..." were, in the end, meaningless.

I get my car towed and go drinking with my friend and her boyfriend. The boyfriend teaches at Arizona State and lives in Tempe. His kids are away with their mom so I sleep in his little daughter's bed; there are dolls scattered on the floor and pink things hanging on the walls. I feel slightly uncomfortable, but when I finally lie down on the narrow mattress after the three of us drank tequila next to the pool as the stars disappeared, drinking and talking until the sky was blue and bright and we went swimming again, I fall asleep instantly.

When I wake up, I sell my car to a man for $100. His girlfriend sits smoking in the passenger seat of the tow truck as he and I talk. We had agreed to $200 over the phone.

"Where's bill of sale?"

"This is it."

"Not the bill of sale, man, that's registration."

"Oh."

"No bill of sale, I can only do $100."

"Whatever."

He gives me a hundred bucks and takes my Saab away.

I don't go skateboarding again until two days later. My friend has work, so in the afternoon I go to the western part of Phoenix, a different city, to another skatepark someone had told me about. I'm driving the white Kia I've rented to take me to California. The car is much cleaner and quieter than the Saab, with better air conditioning and an excellent sound system, but I wish I had my old car back.

The skatepark is as large and impressive as the last one. The general layout revolves around a central island made of stair-sets, euro gaps, kickers, down rails, boxes, and wedges. All around the perimeter are different little things that make me excited, each a highlight in a small town skatepark. The centerpiece of this perimeter of little cement features is a huge half-sphere, a giant cantaloupe sliced in two and stuck at the top of the skatepark, daring you to ride the upper portion of its inner face.

Of course, there's a vert pool, too.

There are maybe ten people scattered around the park. Most are by themselves, and no one is skateboarding—everyone is hunkered down in patches of shadow, waiting as if the all-clear signal has yet to be sounded following an air raid. One teenage guy sits within a triangle of shadow just large enough to contain him as long as he sucks his thighs to his chest and rests his cheek against a knee.

I start skating around, and everyone looks from their spots of refuge to stare as if I have broken a taboo or am just a crazy man asking for trouble.

Skateboarders in the Valley of the Sun are like vampires—they only come out at night, and if they find themselves at the skatepark before dusk, they hide in the dark until it's safe to emerge.

But maybe the vampires are the smart ones. I push around and jump and grind and my insides are squeezed of their moisture like an orange in a juicer. When I go for my gallon jug in the bushes, I drink so greedily the water splashes onto my face and down my front. It hardly does anything, though, for five minutes later my shirt's dry and I'm thirsty again. I don't have any water left.

It's an uninspired session. I try to ollie two inches to land on the downward transition of a pyramid. My back wheels catch and I'm flung, unprepared like an old lady tripping on a step, slamming onto my hip and shoulder on the pavement with a hollow thud that echoes in the quiet park. Snickers bounce across the cement from the shadows.

I land a backside heelflip up the euro gap, as well as a backside 180 off a fairly high ledge, but otherwise I am aimless and lackadaisical. After an hour and half of zombie skateboarding in the desert skatepark, while the sun goes from tenor to baritone as it approaches the horizon, turning increasingly orange, and more skateboarders show up and the shadows became longer and the sky goes from blue to navy to purple, I drive back downtown and go to my friend's restaurant. I sit at the bar and drink beer as she comes and goes with orders. When she gets off, we go drinking again, first to a roller disco and then to a series of dives with her friends. When the sun rises we are again drinking tequila on the rocks next to the still swimming pool.

I make it to the skatepark in Flagstaff just before five that afternoon. I'm still too hungover to take in anything. I'm empty—I notice nothing about the park or the town save that the air smells of pine and that it is cooler than it had been in the Valley of the Sun.

A SUNDAY IN spring, my senior year of high school.

Keith and I decided to go skate. The day had an unusual poignancy. High school was about to end, we were soon to leave town, and our days of skateboarding together were numbered, though we had once felt they would continue forever. We had already half-turned our backs to the town that once constituted our entire universe.

We skated the courts and then the curbs at the elementary school. Everything was quiet—there were few cars on the roads and in the parking lots. The dirt from a winter's worth of sanding lined the streets in strips where the snowbanks used to be. Our friends were away at tennis or baseball games, and the rest of the town, too, seemed to have things to do on that first day gripped by the lapping drowsiness of summer.

We continued our street expedition away from the skatepark and the courts. We skated behind the library, the gap by the coffee shop, the rock-ride boulder on the pathway above the hotel. As we skated by the bank, Keith popped into an ollie-manual on a wide section of sidewalk connecting the parking lot and the street. He landed it first try, then I skated back and tried it, almost got it, so tried again, and Keith came back around, and then we were sessioning this little manual-pad of a sidewalk. We were shocked we had never noticed it before.

I landed the manual, then we each got nose manual, which took longer, not least because we were sticklers about nollieing off the end and not having our back wheels tap. There was little traffic in the street but each time we headed into the manual pad we still checked to see if any cars were coming before we popped a trick. This was difficult because the bank blocked your view for most of the run-in and looking up right before you ollied threw off your rhythm.

After nose manual, we started fooling around with tricks on and off the curb. We did kickflips on and kickflips off, 180s to fakie tricks off, half-cabs on to backside-ones off. We each got a 360-flip off, stomping somewhat haphazardly in the pile of sand in the road. The taps of the other skater's deck echoed against the surrounding buildings.

I had never been able to do tricks in or out of manuals, but on a whim I tried kickflip-manual. I popped, flicked, caught the board, and landed on the sidewalk on my back two wheels. I was so surprised I put the front two down.

"Dude, did you see that?"

"You had it!"

I kept trying. Manualing was harder when you hadn't set your feet perfectly—sometimes you landed the kickflip with a toe or heel hanging off, and you had to fight to stay balanced. Keith started trying it with me, and then there was the excitement of two skaters of the same level working on a trick neither had landed before. We rushed back to the parking lot, pushed off, did a quick glance for cars, tried and failed, grabbed our board from the road, and rushed back again, both of us following the other so we made a continuous circuit.

One of us landed it first, and the other was not far behind. What about kickflip-out, we asked? So for the hell of it we tried, and we were again surprised by how close we came. We were both dripping sweat so that the faux-brick rectangles of the sidewalk were dotted with drops. We were in the flow zone, and it wasn't long before we landed another trick we had never done before, and the other was calling out and slapping the tail of his skateboard against the pavement.

"Ohhhhh!!"

Now, we asked... Surely not... But what if...?

Kickflip-on, kickflip-off?

We started trying. The session assumed an epic atmosphere, like we were Tony Hawk and Bucky Lasek duking it out in best trick at the X Games. We might actually be able to do it, we thought. We were locking in after the kickflip and sometimes popping something off the end, though it was hard popping a kickflip when you were off balance and your feet weren't set the way they had to be. There was the feeling that one of us might stick it and enter the next tier of skateboarding.

I watched Keith land on his upside-down board, pick it up, and then I dropped in.

Pushed at the sidewalk.

Focusing hard.

All my concentration on this one trick.

Kickflip on.

Land manual.

Manualed across the sidewalk, the grooves ticking beneath me.

Shuffled my front foot to the right side of the board.

Got ready to kickflip off.

Then, a large shape in the road.

Car coming at me.

I jumped off the board and landed in the street. A car screeched to a halt. Even before the car stopped I recognized the driver and knew how angry she was.

It was my old bus driver.

I used to ride the bus to and from school every day. The bus driver lived just up the road, so my brother and I were always the first to get on when she started her route in the morning and the last ones to get off her empty yellow school bus at the end of the day. She was an old-timey Vermont lady from an old-timey Vermont family. She had a real Vermont accent and barked at kids when they were making too much noise on her bus. Sometimes she even pulled the bus over, stood up in the aisle, and screamed as loud as she could for everyone to shut up, which everyone did instantly. You could hear a pencil drop; everyone squeezed their legs together and clenched their stomachs in terror, holding their breath, and only then would she begin her tirade, screaming at us in her gruffest, angriest, most accented voice.

Now she was staring at me through her windshield, only feet away, and, though I had forgotten, I suddenly remembered how she used to look when she stood up in the bus and screamed, and how scared I used to be. Her wide, livid eyes now looked the same.

She put her car in park. I picked up my skateboard and jumped back onto the sidewalk. She got out into the street, and yelled across the hood of her car.

"You guys are still up to this shit!? I figured you two would have grown out of this shit by now! Guess not! Grow the fuck up, you two! Grow up and cut this shit out!"

Then she got back into her car and slammed down the pedal so she peeled out and pebbles pinged off the metal of the undercarriage.

I was filled with shame and embarrassment.

I looked at Keith. He looked like the kids around me used to look when the bus driver yelled at us: gaunt, silent, ashamed, like puppies that had just been kicked.

Were we too old to skateboard?

Was skateboarding something just for kids?

It was a thought I had never considered before. But once it entered my head—shoved in there by a monster from my childhood nightmares—it resonated, either connecting with things that had already been forming, or entering with enough weight of its own to make an impression.

"What a fucking bitch," Keith said.

"She hasn't changed at all."

"Fuck you, lady."

"She's the worst."

We went back to the kickflip-on, kickflip-off, but something had changed, and neither of us could get any closer to landing it.

Las Vegas, Nevada

LAS VEGAS APPEARS SUDDENLY. THE MULTIPLE LANES OF THE downward sloping highway curve around a mountain's hip, and there it is: the tall hotels I recognize from films, roads lined with palm trees, a circular urban sprawl not as daunting as I expected. In fact, seen from the high bend of my highway, the city at dawn underwhelms, as if all the images of its buildings and fountains had been made so as to conceal a reality and promote a myth.

Few cities are so associated with myth as Las Vegas. The mystique tied to that name is recognized and appreciated by all Americans—even children know that Las Vegas means flashing lights, promiscuity, and excitement. Beyond the United States, too, the name holds potency. In America, Las Vegas means the antithesis of boring small town America, the real America for those from these sorts of places—apple pie and splintery ragtag skateparks. For people from Japan, or Norway or France or Nigeria, though, Las Vegas *is* America. Las Vegas is the distillation of America, the place where anything is possible, where sheep-shearing can be traded for roulette and the fortune of a lifetime can be won in minutes. For the Finnish fisherman whose brother left for New Jersey decades ago, a week in Las Vegas represents a week to discover what he's been missing, a week to suck on the tit of the American Dream and swap Old World village gossip for wild freedom and easy money, glamorous women with expensive haircuts and mini-skirts. When I was in Japan I was surprised time and time again when, after being asked where they went in America, or where they wanted to go, a smiling Japanese person was quiet then said quickly and in one breath, with a sparkle in their eye: "Las Vegas."

For Americans, that puritanical bunch, Las Vegas has less positive connotations, for it is a city of sin. This is a city of prostitutes, of hotel rooms decorated with crumpled lingerie, cocaine residue, empty liquor bottles. Anonymous hotel rooms filled with anonymous nude bodies, soft light on anonymous tan curtains, and, out the window, a million colorful lights. Sex, drugs, and rock 'n' roll. A place to cut loose from the umbilical cord of morality that tethers one to the space station—home, the small town—so that one spins wildly in the emptiness, out of control, terrified, sad, ecstatic, knee-deep in filthy experience, high on drugs and not yet nervous about what you've done.

This myth and all the other characteristics attached to Las Vegas derive, in part, from films. Even if you have never been there, you know what the city looks like, for images of its sunny boulevards and casino hotels are ubiquitous. "And then they go to Las Vegas!" we can almost hear the scriptwriters saying. *The Hangover, Leaving Las Vegas, Viva Las Vegas, Vegas Vacation, What Happens in Vegas, The Godfather, Diamonds Are Forever, Rat Race, Con Air, Ocean's Eleven, Rain Man.* All exploit the myth of Vegas to make their stories more interesting while simultaneously adding to and then retransmitting the myth to a global audience.

Unlike those Japanese daydreaming in smoky bars, I've always known enough about Las Vegas to not want to come here. The sex and drugs sound fun, yes, but not the anonymous motel rooms or the kitsch and glamor, or the pissing away of one's money. What has ultimately brought me to Vegas this bright, cool morning in September is not gambling but literary tourism. For of all the stories that contribute to the myth of Las Vegas, my favorite is the darkest, the most disturbing and drug-addled, the most deranged but also the most thoughtful.

Fear and Loathing in Las Vegas is ostensibly about a dune buggy race in the desert, but, of course, it has nothing to do with that. Rather, this is the story of a man's attempt to live without appeasing the societal forces swirling around him. What is the meaning of life? To work? To love? To bear children and protect them? And if not those things, then what? To answer the question, perhaps we consume a trunkful of drugs and plunge through the black hole of the American Dream and write about what we see in our hallucinations? It's less a book of journalism than a book of philosophy. What happens to a man with manic tendencies, seventy-five pellets of mescaline, five sheets of acid, a salt shaker of cocaine, two quarts of rum, and a pint of raw ether, who is intent on getting to the bottom of things? And when he gets there, what does he uncover?

It wasn't until I read William McKeen's biography, *Outlaw Journalist*, that I began to appreciate Hunter S. Thompson. I realized he did what every writer wants to do, but cannot: he took the editor's assignment, pissed all over it, and wrote *what he wanted* instead. So an article about dune buggies suddenly became a poetic meditation on American culture and the absurdity of the postmodern experience, if not the experience of existence itself. Or just the story of a wild weekend in Vegas.

McKeen says that Thompson told not the story but the story of getting the story. He flipped the convention of downplaying the writer in journalism, emphasizing the centrality of his own subjectivity and encouraging his own mad, incredulous voice to become more estranged, more strange, more carried away and convinced of the reality of his dreams. And when he was most carried away, he and his readers discovered something: it was fantastic.

The ideal act of writing is to express oneself without fear or pressure to conform. And though most writers appreciate this ideal, few respect it. Thompson was one who stayed true to this ideal, and for this reason is he a writer's writer. I thought of him when I set off on my own adventure in reportage and took *Fear and Loathing* with me, reading it by lamplight and jotting down notes in its endpapers in the silence of my cold tent, breaths of steam dissipating between his words and mine.

And now it is in my own Great White Whale that I drive into Las Vegas—not a white Cadillac Deville but a white Kia Optima with purple Arizona plates. And I arrive not in the afternoon with a trunkful of drugs, mind blown on counteracting uppers and downers, but in the early morning, an hour after sunrise, high on watery gas station coffee. There are no bats in the sky. The sky is infinitely empty, and the city's avenues feel spacious as the White Whale rolls slowly through the eastern part of town past palm trees and their stark shadows, scraggly vegetation, half-brown grass struggling to grow. I only see one or two motels, and no pawn shops, and the city seems like any other.

I settle on a skatepark in the corner of a large green field crisscrossed by winding paved walkways. It has the same modern plaza aesthetic as the one I skated in Tulsa. The park is an oval track comprised of mini-stair sets and ramps, mini handrails and big handrails, quarterpipes, a bank ramp, a wedge, boxes and ledges and drops linked together in a thoughtful way. The surface is smooth, pink cement just slippery enough for powerslides and under-rotated backside 180s. It is a street-oriented skatepark that opposes the expansive transition-oriented skateparks I saw in Phoenix. The more progressive design paradigm makes sense: skaters can amuse themselves endlessly on smaller features that are easier and less expensive to build, while large, brutalist gaps and stair-sets are costly and limiting in regards to who can use them.

It's not even eight in the morning, but there are already five other people skateboarding.

I start lapping the track without interrupting momentum to go back to the small ledge or ramp where my board flipped onto its top, instead just continuing forward, trying to flow, trying to skate the entire city, and when I come around again, I retry the ollie-manual or noseslide that eluded me before. In the few cases when I land something, I land looking at the next target like a tennis player preparing for his next shot. I stick a shove-it over the wedge, kickflips on and off the box, a backside kickflip on the steep bank ramp, a boardslide down the mini handrail above the mini stairs which makes me feel like I'm boardsliding a real handrail down a real set of stairs.

Two of the other skaters are friends who stick closely together, but the rest skate by themselves. One is a young man about my age with unkempt hair and patchy scruff on his cheeks. He arrives with a six-pack of Modelo and sits at the picnic table by the entrance drinking beer as he watches us skateboarding. After he polishes two bottles he grabs his skateboard and rolls out into the park, extroverted and interested in making friends. He says something when I almost land a noseslide down the ledge of the mini-stair set.

"Oh, man, that was close!"

"I wasn't expecting to lock onto it!"

I grab my board and jog back up the stairs. Several attempts later, I pop into a noseslide, scratch down the ledge, push off and stomp bolts.

"Yeah!" Scruff gives me taps. He seems like a beginner—he's trying to boardslide the mini handrail but not getting close—but he's still having fun. After each try he looks up expectantly and laughs.

"Haha! *Did you see that?*"

I had been unsure about skateboarding so early in the morning—it hadn't seemed right or natural to skateboard when there were long shadows on grass wet with dew—but as sweat breaks through skin I think of early morning soccer practices when the team was silent as we dressed, dumb with somnolence, but then began to yell back and forth and joke as we jogged through warm-ups. It turns out that skateboarding, too, can be morning exercise and that the morning is in fact perhaps the best time to skate if one lives in the middle of the desert.

Awake, loose, I'm beginning to see the weeks of skating pay off. I'm landing tricks I wouldn't have considered trying at the beginning of my trip. I'm in the flow zone—three baskets in a row and I'm on fire, can't miss, slip, or fall. I envision a trick then execute, and there's no gap between the visualizing and the realizing. After popping a kickflip over the steep wedge—a kickflip that in my mind is as lofty as anything the Great Brandini ever achieved, but in reality is barely off the ramp—I skate through the gate to the water fountain. Modelo is back sitting at his picnic table.

"Warming up a bit," I say.

"Yeah. Still cool enough to skate, though. Want a beer?"

It's 8:30 in the morning. I think for a moment.

"Yeah, man. Thanks."

He reaches into the plastic bag and hands me a cold Modelo. I borrow his lighter and pop the cap.

"Cheers."

Just as with the morning skateboarding, I'm again surprised that beer tastes so good so soon after sunrise. I think of Dr Thompson.

"This park is sick," I say.

"Yeah. I love this park, man. You haven't skated here before?"

"No, I'm just traveling, actually. First time in Vegas."

"Oh, yeah? What do you think about it?"

"Well, I've been here for an hour. But it seems more like an actual city than I thought it would."

"Yeah, man. People actually live here, too. There's the Strip, and you see that on TV and stuff. But most people who live in Vegas never even go over there."

"What do you do here?"

"Like, work?"

"Yeah."

"Uber and weed, man."

We laugh.

"Have you been skating long?" he asks.

"Since I was a kid. So, twenty years or so. But I stopped for a while and just started back up again."

"I just started, too. Wish I did it when I was younger though—I suck!"

"Looks like you're getting the hang of it."

We sit in the warm dry morning air and chat. Modelo introduces himself, and I immediately forget his name. We crack the remaining two beers and I sink into the buzz, the dry desert air, the comfortable shade under the pavilion, the calmness of enjoying where I am without wanting to be anywhere else. I sink into the soft song of a bird and the soft, plush buzz of the cold beer. I'm happy; the only pang of displeasure comes at the idea I don't live in Las Vegas and that I will have to leave its limits later that day.

"You want me to get a video of that noseslide?" Scruff asks.

My first reaction is to say no, because it would be embarrassing for two grown adults to be filming each other on iPhones in the skatepark.

"Sure," I say.

I give him my phone and we skate to the mini-staircase. It takes a few tries, then I land the noseslide. My friend does a moving follow-cam, holding my phone low for the angle, and when I land he says, "Yeaaahhhh" in a gravelly, excited voice. The voice is recorded on my phone, and when I listen to it later that day, and in the weeks and months afterwards, I recognize the voice as that of a person I once spoke to whose life takes place far away from mine, who I had no reason to meet except that I was skateboarding, but also traveling, that special act that allows you to pretend, for a moment, you live as someone else and in so doing become free.

TOMMY SAID THAT when he and Ashley were hanging out at her house, they tasted her father's wine.

"No!" I said. We were standing in our boxers on the bank of the river, adrift in the summer between middle school and high school.

"Yeah, we did." He chucked a rock at the rope hanging from a tall tree growing over the river. The rock missed and clattered on the cliff.

"Was her dad home?"

"No, he was out."

"And you guys didn't, ya know..."

"No. All in good time, Clint, all in good time. You can't rush these things."

"What did it taste like?"

"It didn't taste very good."

"Did you feel anything?"

"A little bit. I was feeling a little drunk."

"What did it feel like?"

"Eh, wasn't really a big deal, man."

"Well we should go back to her house and get some more!"

"You wanna?"

"Yes!"

"Haha, alright!"

We threw rocks at the rope until we were dry then jumped in again. I opened my eyes underwater and swam to the channel on the far bank where the water was deepest. There I could frog-swim against the current and stay in place. The sun refracted through the moving water and danced in lines over the rocks. I distinguished each individual rock of the riverbed and the flecks of twigs and leaves floating past. If I looked ahead, I couldn't see anything in the green translucence, which scared me because it was easy to imagine something rushing towards you out of the unknown.

When we climbed dripping onto the sandy, stony riverbank, the water began evaporating off our skin in the sun.

"OK, if I hit this one," I said, "Then I'm going to make out with Danielle later!"

"Ha!"

The rock missed.

"If I hit this one," Tommy said, "then I will absolutely stomp tre flip down Shaw's drop."

Miss.

"If I hit this one, Danielle and I are going to share a sleeping bag in the same tent!"

"When are we even going camping?"

"I don't know!"

The rock flipped through the air and made a soft noise when it hit the worn fabric of the rope.

"Yeah!"

"OK, if I hit this one then Ashley and I…"

We provoked our desires and exercised our imaginations until we crossed the river where it was narrow and fast and climbed the boulders to where our jeans, shirts, socks, shoes, and skateboards were scattered in a trampled circle at the edge of a field of tall grass.

"But isn't her dad going to notice the wine's gone?" I asked.

"I don't know! That's not for us to worry about, though. Ashley says they've just been sitting there forever, anyway, and her dad has completely forgotten about them."

"OK."

"Don't worry, Clint! It's going to be fine! You'll see."

We walked between the walls of grass. The grass grew over

our heads, green blades drooped from their stalks to tickle our necks and ears. We turned at the No Trespassing sign to traverse the well-manicured lawn. We hadn't stopped taking this route once the sign had appeared, it was simply too far to go up around the church then back along Main Street, so we walked quickly without talking, half-expecting the lady to come out of her house and start yelling at us.

When we got to the gas station, we went straight to the soda fountain.

"Say her dad's there tonight, though?"

"Then we'll wait for him to go take a dump, then grab the bottle!"

"What did you guys even do there?"

I put the 32 oz. jug under the Mountain Dew spigot. Pushed the PUSH button. Neon green concentrate came out between streams of clear soda water.

"We just hung out in her room and listened to music."

"No funny business?"

Switched the cup to the Pepsi spigot. Push.

"No man, I told you. Now we get to go hang out there tonight."

"Is Danielle coming?"

"Think so."

There was too much ice and soda in the cup and yellow-brown liquid spurted through the slits in the lid when I pressed down. The soda ran over the sides to puddle on the counter. I grabbed a hot-dog from beneath the heat lamp and we headed to the register.

The skinny redneck girl with glasses was working. She had a word in large cursive letters tattooed on her forearm.

Was it someone's name?

"Two seventy-eight."

I dug in my pocket. Pulled out two crumpled bills.

Oh, crap.

I had thought I had three dollars.

I dug in the other pockets. Only found a quarter in the little pocket for change.

"Oops."

"You don't have it?"

"Could you spot me a dollar?"

"C'mon Clint!"

"Or just fifty cents."

Tommy dug in his pocket and found two quarters. He handed them to me, I handed them to the cashier and took three pennies from the dish, uncrumpled the dollars and handed them over, too.

"Thanks, hon."

Tommy paid and we walked around the store to the stone wall out back. We sat on the high ledge with our feet dangling.

"So, are you gonna call her?" I asked.

"Yeah, I'll call her."

Tommy unwrapped the cheeseburger from its colorful aluminum wrapper. He unstuck the top bun, placed it on his lap, then began ripping ketchup and mustard packets and squeezing their contents out onto the brown patty dotted with patches of bread that had stuck to the melted cheese. He had a bite then placed the burger on the ledge next to him.

"OK, I'll call her," he said.

Ashley had a cellphone, too, which meant it would be easy—we wouldn't have to talk with anyone in her family if she didn't get to the phone first. This was never a problem with Ashley, though, as it was with some of the other girls—she only lived with her dad and always kept a house phone close to her bed. Tommy put his flip phone to his ear.

My heart started beating.

"Hey, Ashley, how's it going?"

He looked at me with big eyes and nodded. It was amazing he didn't have to tell her who was calling.

"Nice, nice. Yeah, I'm just hanging out with Clint in town,

skating a little bit. Would you want to hang out later? ...Yeah, that would be great... OK, sounds good, yeah we'll just be at the skatepark... OK, see you later."

"What did she say?"

"Her and Danielle are going to come meet us at the skatepark around four!"

We ate, dipping our food into little piles of ketchup and washing it down with soda that tasted different than the soda you got in bottles. When we finished we leaned over the ledge and let spit drip from our mouths in fat drops. The globs of bubbly saliva arced through the air to form two clusters of dark spots on the rocks below us.

We left the gas station with our half-filled cups of soda and skateboarded through town, turning at the hotel, skating through its busy parking lot, past the diner, up the street by the elementary school that was slightly uphill so you had to push hard. I was filled with an excitement born from uncertainty—so much was changing so fast, and I didn't know what to expect. We had never simply hung out with girls before, and now we had suddenly decided to try drinking, too!

Everyone had assumed Tommy would be the first to drink. He was the friend who knew people in the Older Crowd and hung out with them when he went snowboarding. He was also the most gregarious and the most charismatic, which meant he was the coolest, and there was an implicit notion that the cool kids were the first ones to try new things like drinking. To deny what everyone said, Tommy was vocal about being straight edge. He was adamant that he would never drink, and whenever someone from the Older Crowd joked that he was going to be a partier, he would ironically quote an anti-drinking slogan we had seen on TV or heard in health class. Because Tommy had this stance we would all speak critically if we ever heard of someone older than us getting drunk for the first time.

For some reason that changed swiftly and definitively that sunny summer day. Suddenly the reassurances we had been making to ourselves and to our parents revealed themselves to be false, and we admitted that, yes, we wanted to drink. The idea entered our heads and razed all assertions we would never drink like flames across a hillside.

So much was changing so fast.

The skatepark was empty. In the sun sat two plywood quarterpipes, one with unharmonious segments and coping that stuck out from the top and the other with a large hole that oozed splinters. A box, the down rail, the bank ramp. A cement parking block gray on the sides and black on the top from wax. That was all. On afternoons like this, summer afternoons when there was already a sense of torpor about town, the only noises at the skatepark were the cries of halfhearted cicadas and the sigh of traffic from across the swamp. When there was this calm, and the sun was baking the skatepark and all of its pebbles and loose nails, we sometimes lounged in the shade or the warmth of the sunny pavement, listening to the insects, the wind, and the traffic without saying anything.

Today, though, we were excited. Tommy and I started to skate.

Tommy pushed into the quarterpipe. He dodged the hole and ollied to the bank ramp. Landing, he pumped the transition, pointed for the rail and slid up the second half.

"Yoop," I said, tapping the nose of my board against the asphalt. I dropped, slid the down rail then ollie-to-fakie'd on the bank ramp. On the run out I tried cab-slide on the cement block but the board stuck and I jumped off.

The session began.

We took turns dropping, always starting and ending at the corner of the park near the road down to the courts, skating at the quarterpipes and bank ramp while perhaps hitting the rail or box en route or on the runout. When my flipping, spinning board stopped its gyrations suddenly under my feet and the wheels cracked on the pavement, Tommy *woop-wooped* in falsetto and charged at the quarterpipe, did my same backside flip as a quarterpipe-to-bank ramp transfer, stomped it, and stomped olllie-manual on the box afterwards. One of us landing something energized the other, our skating become more and more frantic and we started landing harder and harder tricks. I front-boarded the down rail; Tommy 5-0'd the box and nose-stalled the ledge above the bank ramp; I got kickflips and backside one's over the cement curb and back 5-0 on the quarterpipe, which was an easy trick but one I could never do so I was excited. If one of us saw the other do something cool he might try it, too, and this was fine because we were friends and skated at the same level, and always had—perhaps because we had progressed at the same rate from the same starting point, like plants in adjacent pots acquiring the same length and characteristics due to the similar nutrients in their soil and equal exposure to sunlight.

We were both dripping sweat when Ashley and Danielle crested the hill on their bikes.

"Hey!"

"'Sup guys!"

I became nervous, and the antidote to the nervousness was dumb, corporeal movement. So as the girls biked closer I kept skateboarding, pretending that what I was doing was very important and that I was very engaged in doing it. Perhaps Tommy was nervous, too, because he also kept skating. The girls put their bikes down and climbed up the bank ramp to the ledge at the top. We pretended we were oblivious to them, but in fact the opposite was true—every second we were aware of them and everything we did was for them, and we began acting and skating differently than we had when they weren't there. If one of them had been Nikki—who I kissed in the woods behind the skatepark and hadn't been able to talk to since—or Lauren, who I also liked and thought about throughout the school day, then I would have kept skateboarding until it was dark and I collapsed from dehydration.

"How are you guys doing?" I said, skating up the ramp and sitting next to Ashley.

"Good!"

"What have you been up to today?"

"We've just been biking around. It's so nice out!"

"I know!"

Tommy skated up the ramp and plopped down next to me.

"What's up, ladies!"

They laughed.

"Hi Tommy!"

"So, did your dad say anything, Ashley?"

"Haha. You didn't say anything to Clint, did you?"

"I'm afraid I did, Ms Ashley."

"Tommy!"

"It's OK! Your secret is safe with me."

"Speaking of which…"

"We were wondering…"

"Just an idea…"

"What if we…"

"The four of us…"

"Head to your house this evening?"

"Just an option."

The girls laughed.

"Tommy!"

"What!?"

"I would be up for that."

We were in no rush to leave, though. We sat on top of the bank ramp until the sweat had dried to salty paste and the dark ovals on the backs of our shirts had disappeared. Michaeliam showed up with Dan and Miles, then Noah was dropped off by his mom, and Sawyer drove up in his Jeep, and the girls, Tommy, and I watched everyone skating below us like uninterested spectators

227

at a one-sided baseball game.

We didn't say bye to anyone when we skated across the park and parking lot towards the hill. The girls pedaled next to us on bikes too tall for them, wobbling and turning the handlebars back and forth so they zig-zagged.

"Where are you guys going?" Mike yelled over the roar of our wheels on the worn pavement.

"What!?" we yelled.

"Where are you guys going!?"

"What? See you in a bit!"

Mike dismissed us with a wave, and we kept skating. We didn't want Mike to come because then Miles and Dan would come, too, and then we would be five guys and two girls, which would be less special, but would also mean that our mission to drink the wine would become more difficult.

The four of us weaved around one another down the road past the elementary school, down the sidewalk behind the library to the library's chewed-up front walkway, through town to the church and the hill to the bike path. We traversed the gravel parking lot and entered the tall reed grass on the dirt trail. I held out my hand to pluck a stalk from its sheath and chewed on the white, crunchy bottom.

The river was in shadow, now, and the light on the riverbank was a deeper hue of sunshine, though it still felt like the afternoon. Tommy and I ripped off our shoes, socks, shirts, and jeans like we had earlier in the day. The girls kicked off their sandals, unbuttoned their jean skirts, took off their tank-tops and then they, too, were in their underwear.

Don't look, don't look.

Ashley's panties were maroon, while Danielle's were striped.

Clint!

We clambered over the sharp boulders until we each stood on a rock and the river flowed at our feet. The water was clear and you could see rocks at the bottom. The surface undulated in a static shape, though the water passing through to form the troughs and peaks was constantly changing.

"Ready?" I asked.

"You guys gotta jump in here, and ride the current down to the rope."

"We will! But you guys have to jump in first!" Ashley said.

"I don't believe you!"

"We will! Just go in!"

"Alright, ready Clint?"

Then Tommy and I sang in unison: "One for the money, two for the show, three to get ready, and four to *go*!" We jumped. The current quickly swept us downstream to the deep pool where the river opened and the current became imperceptible. We climbed the cliff on the far side of the pool. Tommy held the rope by the fat knot at its bottom and brought it up with him. The girls swam through the pool to the flat rock at the foot of the cliff and began climbing out, too.

Oh, no.

Of all my boxer shorts, why today of all days did I have to wear the one pair that didn't have a button on the fly?

I twisted the elastic waist.

I tried not looking at the female bodies climbing up the rock, but then I was just thinking about it, which was worse: there were girls in their underwear just a few feet away from me. So I looked into the sun-dappled green canopy and did what I did in class when I tried to get rid of the boner I thought everyone could see.

I began listing the names of all the Red Sox players in order of their position: Kevin Millar, Mark Belhorn, Pokey Reese, Kevin Youkilis, Manny Ramirez, Johnny Damon…

Who played right field again?

Trot Nixon.

Then I started with the Yankees, who I knew from their games with the Red Sox.

Matsui, Jeter, Rodriguez, Posada, Bernie Williams...

Tommy jumped onto the fat knot of the rope and flew down just over the river surface. The frayed threads from the rope's bottom streaked through the water, and then he swung up, and up, until he was weightless high above the river, just below the bottom-most branches of the high trees. He leaned backwards and let momentum gently push him upside down.

The rope swung back to the cliff. Danielle grabbed it, and then it was her turn. She jumped and sat on the knot, swung down just over the water and let go high in the air, screaming and kicking her legs.

Afternoon gave way to evening as we made our way up the bike path. Shadows stretched, clouds colored, the blue of the sky deepened, birds changed shifts so that new ones started singing, or the same ones began anew with more sorrowful songs as the day ended. Tommy and I pushed hard to keep up with the girls on their bikes. We yelled back and forth, ollied storm drains and cracks and painted arrows saying to keep right.

We turned off onto the little trail through the woods that led to Ashley's house.

"Dad! Hello!" Ashley yelled as we walked in. "I don't think he's here. You guys can sit down." She nodded at the couch. Tommy and I sat next to each other with our skateboards propped between our legs. Ashley went into her bedroom and came out with a backpack. Danielle followed her into the kitchen. I studied the living room, examining the rug, the TV, the bookshelf, the coffee table. The unfamiliar smell and the curtains glowing with evening light.

When they came out, Ashley was wearing the backpack.

"OK, should we go back down to the river?" she asked.

"Sure."

The girls left their bikes and their sandals at the house and ran down the grassy slope in their bare feet. They ran fast on the little trail. We yelled and kept pulling our pants up as we tried to catch them. The sun came through in abstract shapes to paint the forest floor, the leaves, the bushes, the sticks, the frames and bouncing brown hair of the girls in golden light.

Oh, how angry our parents would have been!

Here the riverbank was covered in round stones, and the river was a gentle, shallow stream. People passing on the bike path were hidden by the foliage and the two bridges in either direction were out of sight. Ashley unzipped her backpack and pulled out the bottle. It was strawberry wine with a wire twisted around its cork. The colors of the label were faded, and there was a residue of dust which had long covered the curved slope of the glass.

Ashley began turning the wire circle like she was winding a clock. When it was off, she popped the cork without hesitating.

"Who wants to go first?" She asked.

We were all quiet. She handed the bottle to Tommy.

Tommy considered the full bottle in his hands. "Well, here goes nothing," he said, and started raising it to his mouth.

"Wait!" Danielle said. "You gotta make a toast first!"

"Oh, right." He was thoughtful for a moment. "To Tarzan, Topanga, and Timon and Pumba!" We laughed, and Tommy tipped back the bottle. He made no reaction after having a sip.

"Hmmh, it's good," he said.

"Really?"

"Yeah, it's good. Your turn, Clint."

He passed the bottle.

My heart was pounding, but it was imperative that I act like Tommy.

"To Ms Sullenberger!" I said, toasting the math teacher who had hated me all year.

"Haha. To Ms Sullenberger!"

"To Ms Sully!"

Back it went. Wine filled my mouth.

Agh!

I swallowed.

It was horrible.

Disgusting.

This is what people drank?

But my face remained indifferent.

"Yeah, it's OK."

"You don't like it!"

"No, no. I like it. It tastes good."

"You're lying!"

"No, I'm not! Here, watch." And I took another swig even bigger than the first.

"Woah!"

I passed the bottle to Danielle. She gulped, exhaled, and passed the bottle to Ashley who did the same. Then around the bottle went again.

The color of the sunlight, the blue sky, the clouds, and the leaves deepened, as if, as evening progressed, someone was slowly altering the hue in a photo application. The breeze tickled branches and there was the occasional sound of a pair of bicycles rolling past. The river continued over its bed of round rocks.

A sense of poignancy swelled within me: joy and wistfulness, a melancholy tied to beauty and the knowledge that the beauty would be brief. I had felt this sensation several times before, always in the evening during the summer and always when I had been alone. Now the presence of the others somehow soothed the sensation so that it was sweet instead of panicked. I was glad to be close to other human beings, friends who could hold me with their smiles, whose soft, regular respiration and quiet laughter could reassure me, who could save me with each sharp inhale and the unique scents coming off their skin.

Perhaps the alcohol was doing something.

We hobbled across the uneven stones in our bare feet to where the river turned and there was the stagnant pool underneath the third bridge. We took our clothes off and jumped into the water. The river bottom was now dark so that the girls' bodies were pale to fluorescence as they cut through the current. We acted silly and said silly things and laughed, pushed and splashed each other. We swam close, yearned to swim closer, yearned to touch each other longer, to succumb to the summer evening and the swarms of unfamiliar chemicals wreaking havoc in blooming bodies.

ONLY A WEEK later, Ashley convinced her dad to let her host a bonfire party. Of course he said yes—what's the worst a group of kids could get up to?

It was a similar day, the type of summer day marked by a sense of endlessness, especially for students on summer vacation whose days are undistinguishable unless something extraordinary occurs.

We skateboarded all afternoon, taking breaks to swim in the river and sit behind the gas station. We skateboarded up the bike path as the sun was setting and shadows filled the air between swathes of forest like water rising within a trough. When you went through a field you were draped in dramatic light and cast long shadows over the grass.

This time when we turned off the bike path and walked through the woods there were ten other students from our class waiting for us. There was a quiet, anticipatory air about the group. Ashley had made a circle of stones behind a copse of trees that blocked the bonfire from view from the house.

Nikki was sitting in the grass next to two of her friends. I sat down with them.

"Do you want some?" she asked, offering me a Dasani bottle.

"What is it?"

"Vodka. Have you ever had it before?"

"Once or twice."

"Oh, yeah?"

She handed me the bottle. I unscrewed the cap and took a big gulp, thinking about all the people I had seen drink liquor on TV.

The liquid singed every corner of my mouth. For a second I thought she had tricked me and filled the bottle with gasoline, or cyanide. Still, I swallowed. My eyes welled with tears.

Nikki laughed.

"Just like last time?" she asked.

"You bet."

Nate—who was from the grade above and was now at prep school—unzipped his duffel bag to show the red and white cardboard of a Budweiser thirty rack. Ashley wanted to wait until it was dark before we took out the beers. So as the first stars began to appear in the sky and sunset gave way to twilight, and twilight to dusk, we sat around in the grass and tended to the fire, collected wood and paced around looking up at the lights of the house seen through the trees.

The signal was given, the thirty rack came out, and each person was given a beer.

"OK, ready everyone…"

The can was cold.

"One, two, three!"

Aluminum tabs cracked and foam bubbled over the rims of the cans. We drank.

The beer was too carbonated and tasted bad. Each sip made me shudder, but I kept drinking.

I kept drinking and waited but didn't feel anything. The great anticipation was beginning to seem like a mistake because the negligible effects of the alcohol paled in comparison to what I had been imagining. After the sip of vodka, I drank two Budweisers, all the while asking and responding to the question being repeated around the campfire: "Do you feel anything?"

I left the group to walk into the dark woods. When I was far enough away, I unzipped and started peeing. From where I stood the flames of the fire made silhouettes of the trees between us. Dim orange light pulsated on bark and the forest floor. Voices were audible, but not their words. People talked and laughed and squealed and screamed around the fire, though I could only see the faces of Tommy and Ashley—their faces were lit softly, and orange burned in their eyes.

When I zipped up and turned to walk back to the fire, I tripped and collapsed on the dry leaves. When I stood someone tilted the earth, and I fell over again.

Was there an earthquake?

The earth continued to rock like the deck of a ship. Something was wrong—I couldn't stand up!

And then I realized (and the realization was an epiphany) that I was drunk. I was drunk and it was magnificent, and I suddenly understood why even the smallest towns had bars and why big cities were filled with them, why there was always wine at dinner parties and the Older Crowd sometimes drank beers in between runs at the skatepark. I realized all of these things in the instant I realized I was drunk and simultaneously realized that I loved it.

I stood slowly with wide, planted feet like drunk people have, and there in the forest a few yards from the light of the bonfire and the people talking I laughed because I felt so good. I went back to the fire and drank two more beers and had another sip of vodka and then, suddenly, Danielle was sitting on me, and we were kissing, and for some reason it didn't bother us that there were people around, which was strange and wonderful. We went away into the dark where no one could find us and lay on top of one another in the dewy grass, rolling around with our tongues in each other's mouths, drying the wetness in the grass with the clothes on our bodies.

I hadn't known humans could experience feelings like that.

Mike's mom came to pick us up at the end of the night. She played the classical station and chatted with Mike in the front while Tommy, Keith, and I were drunk but trying to act sober in the back, smiling and giggling and poking and tickling one another. When we got to Mike's we took sleeping bags and blankets out to the lawn. There was infinity above us, stars and a sky without clouds, the Milky Way a gash through the universe. We talked about the party in soft voices and listened to Mike's portable radio tuned to the classic rock station. Four songs played on loop with no commercials interrupting. Eventually we stopped talking. My friends fell asleep one by one without saying goodnight. I couldn't sleep, though, for I was too excited, and I stayed awake with the emotions and wide eyes, looking deep into millions of stars and the Milky Way. I was so, so excited—excited for the life ahead of me, excited for my life to get started. If the fundamental characteristic of adulthood is detachment, or apathy towards everything, then what I felt on Mike's lawn in my sleeping bag next to my sleeping friends, beneath the brilliant Milky Way—a bag of sugar cast upon a black floor—was attachment. Deep, strong attachment to life and my emotions and desires, to the earth and the people who inhabited it with me. I was sick and shaky with attachment to existence, and though I had no idea what the future would bring, I knew that it would be great and that life would be beautiful.

Venice Beach, California

THE CHILD OF THE COLONY OFTEN KNOWS LITTLE OF THE metropole where his language comes from. So it is with me and skateboarding. I know nothing but a disoriented whisper of a place named Dogtown. For me, skateboarding's founding fathers aren't California surfers but Chris Cole in baggy pants, Ali Boulala, PJ Ladd, Bastien Salibanzi. I never learned how to skateboard in pools or vert ramps; I can't slash backside turns like I'm surfing, because I don't surf. I know how to skateboard on flat cracked patches of pavement and basketball courts lit by floodlights on summer nights when it feels like Florida in Vermont. I know that skateboarding is the reason I had the friends I did and the reason we spent every day together. I know that when we stopped skateboarding we drifted apart, or that when we drifted apart we all stopped skateboarding.

My project isn't about the history of skateboarding. So it is perhaps odd that I end my trip in skateboarding's historic birthplace. As I travel from Vegas to Los Angeles, though, the idea grows on me. Perhaps deep below the surface of the activity that my friends and I cherished in the skatepark between the swamp and the hill was an essence that transcended time and place. And perhaps that essence could still be found, even for someone like me, at the beach where skateboarding began.

Every afternoon thousands of people visit the skatepark in Venice Beach, California. A few go to skateboard, and the rest go to watch. They come from Europe, Mexico, Japan, China, Nigeria, Australia. They are tourists on their first holiday in America, and this is a destination: the most famous skatepark in the world, half on the boardwalk and half on the beach, filled with real American skateboarders. This site is the Mecca of the global American export called skateboarding that they have all seen in their own countries, or at least on *The Simpsons*, which is good enough.

I stand with the hordes and feel like I'm in a zoo. Listless groups of vacationers stop to rest and gaze at the spectacle below, turning to their newlywed or cousin or recently reunited uncle to offer an asinine observation about the animals in the pit beneath them. I hide my skateboard between my legs so someone from Latvia won't ask me why I'm not down with the rest. It's four in the afternoon and the park is brimming with skaters, all of whom seem to be launching from transitions with tweaked grabs and lofty alley-oops, steezy kickflips and aggressive, powerful 5-0 grinds.

I can't skate here.

I'm not even a skateboarder—and everyone standing here will know it, too.

A Rocket Power kid with bleached blond hair under his helmet pumps around the track and boosts a 360 mute Japan over a guy holding a skateboard above his head. The kid stomps and a cameraman follows the runout.

Hasn't this whole trip been to prove that I'm actually a skateboarder?

I lean over the railing and watch the skaters in the vert pool.

Hasn't this whole trip been to prove myself at this moment, here, at Venice Beach?

I stand straight, and the people next to me watch as I walk away.

Teenagers sit on either side of the park entrance. "Watch out, here comes Tony Hawk," one of them yells. I stop and look at him, he looks away, snickering, and his friends snicker with him.

I push out into the park and enter the session.

The park is overflowing with skaters. Little packs jostle at drop-in spots, kids whizz by in opposite directions, dodging incoming bodies just after landing. I'm too intimidated and aware of the many eyes to lose myself in the skateboarding. The street section is small and there's no space or opportunity to session the little things I find interesting. The corners are congested and people are aggressive, not in terms of how they look or talk to you but in how they skate—if you're on a crash course they don't stop but keep skating, waiting for you to get out of the way. Every time I go back to the quarterpipe I have to stand in line and drop when no one else steps up.

Perhaps unsurprisingly, I can't land a single trick.

The people around me don't speak to one another. They're all too focused on the flow of the park, the whitewater river rushing with logs you have to anticipate to swim between.

Like a poker player losing chips, I realize I have to go all-in. There's one big drop in the street section. It's three ledges high, about five feet tall but longer across so that you need speed if you want to clear the whole thing. One guy keeps hitting it. He kickflips it, heelflips it, nollie backside flips it, frontside flips it, and, for good measure, does a massive backside 360 over the entire gap. I know that to just ollie the drop would now be glaringly inappropriate—I have to launch a kickflip, at least.

When my turn comes, there's no time for visualization or deep breaths, I just drop in. Ollie the euro gap and point my board at the yawning chasm.

I can do this.

Pop, flick with my front toes, the board drifts away, my legs flail with nothing beneath them until I crash on the cement. I roll, and roll, an incoming skater jumps off his board and swears. Somewhere from the entrance I hear a familiar voice.

"Tony Hawk!"

I get up and apologize. He makes eye contact—he's thirty and angry, skinny with scruff—and doesn't stop to chat.

I don't want to show the kid in the peanut gallery that he got under my skin, so I keep skating. But he had—I keep wondering if he's watching.

He won.

I skate for fifteen more minutes in an effort to save face but skate out of the park as soon as I feel enough time has passed. I keep skating to the bus stop and ride back to Culver City with my forehead pressed against the glass, back to my friend with whom I go to the local dive and drink enough beer to once again be in love with Los Angeles.

The next day we go to see a movie in West Hollywood. My friend goes directly from work while I spend the afternoon in the LA County Museum of Art then skateboard and walk up the long hill to the shopping center with the theater. My friend's on his bike, so after the movie he tells me to take an Uber home. I tell him I'll skateboard.

"Well, to be honest I don't really feel like going slow or waiting for you."

"Fine. I'll see you at the apartment."

I check Google Maps for directions. It's a four-mile skate straight down La Cienaga Boulevard. I repeat the name aloud as I carve back and forth on the wide sidewalk, and the elegant syllables give me pleasure each time they touch my tongue.

La Cienaga, La Cienaga, La Cienaga. La Cienaga Boulevard.

Skateboarding down La Cienaga Boulevard.

There's a steep hill and then the road flattens out. The sidewalk is wide and smooth and empty. The few pedestrians I pass don't move out of the way or look at me. I use them as slalom gates, carving back and forth over the cement squares of the sidewalk as my wheels clack over the cracks between each square, ticking with a regular pace like a sped-up metronome.

Clack, clack, clack, clack, clack.

The air is dry and cooler than it had been in the day. The drooped heads of streetlights float above one after one, and above them is the moon, yellow and nearly full. I push harder, carve, ollie on and off curbs, manual through crosswalks, zip between restaurant doors and their outside patios, hug turns around old men carrying plastic bags and young professionals talking into their cell phones. Joy and pleasure grow with the air and the speed, the easy fast movement through space, and with the moon and the brightness of the lights against the charcoal haze of the night sky. The joy comes from these things but more so from the name I keep repeating:

La Cienaga Boulevard.

And the knowledge and sound of the sentence: *Skateboarding down La Cienaga Boulevard.*

Skating down La Cienaga.

The revelry ends when I pass a Taco Gordo and enter back into the realm of the familiar. I'm no longer flying through the night but just skateboarding. I consider taking La Cienaga all the way to its end to try to recapture the sensation of dreaming, but quickly decide against it: La Cienaga leads directly to Venice Beach.

On another day in Los Angeles I skate from Silver Lake west across the city via other boulevards with famous names: Sunset, Santa Monica, Melrose. I skate with my backpack stuffed with my toothbrush, clothes, and books bouncing on my back. Workers come and go in their office clothes, old people wait at bus stops in their too-baggy pants, homeless people relax on benches. All my observations contrast with what I had been expecting, for the neighborhoods are unremarkable though the names of their streets are glamorous. The simple bodegas and graffitied buildings and steady flow of plain, everyday traffic—buses and moving trucks and sun-bleached Hondas—makes me happy that I'm in this city.

I cut down from Santa Monica to Melrose Boulevard on the lookout for the right coffee shop to hide in and read. Suddenly, coffee shops start popping up one after another, as do cocktail bars and clothing shops and stylish restaurants with alternative flair. Everything is becoming nice, and I realize: oh, yes, I'm back in

West Hollywood. I stop at a chain café and read for half an hour, then skateboard to the bar where my friend told me to meet him.

I haven't seen him in two years. When we used to be room-mates, though, we were close confidants with similar beliefs and dreams. Or, more accurately, he was my confidant, for I told him everything from my past while he never told me anything from his. That is very much how it goes now, too—he asks me countless questions about my trip, my life, my writing, all the time avoiding telling me about anything he does in California, his own writing, his work, or the situation with his forever coming-and-going girl-friend. As soon as we're past the first beer, though, none of these things matter anymore. We're on a sunny balcony overlooking the Sunset Strip, glamorous and beautiful people pass on the sidewalk, and it feels like we're roommates again. We both forget two years have passed and pretend nothing has changed since our happy days together. We quickly order another beer when the first dis-appears, and with it a shot of tequila.

We barhop from the afternoon to the early morning. We plun-der the Strip, getting drunk and drunker in tacky tourist bars, craft beer bars with outside patios, fancy hotel bars next to swimming pools. We eat dinner late at night in an empty Thai restaurant, wasted and yelling at the excited owner to bring us more Chang. The food is so spicy I feel the pressure inside my skull bubbling against my eardrums, and my friend asks me if I want to smoke a joint.

"Sure. But do you have one?"

"No, man. But this is LA. We can just go buy one."

He leaves the restaurant to find a dispensary. When I come out, he's waiting on the sidewalk with a gift bag. We find a ripped couch in an abandoned parking lot and light up.

With the first drag, intoxication suddenly asserts itself.

We smoke the entire joint and sit for a long time on the couch in the dimly lit parking lot, or perhaps it simply feels like a long time, as if we've landed on a planet where years pass in relative minutes to those back on Earth. We talk about abstract and personal things and silly things that make us laugh without being able to stop. We sit in cross-faded stupor until I see a chain stretched between two cement pillars at an entrance to the parking lot. I give my friend my phone and skate to the drooping chain. He stands next to the run-in and begins filming.

"OK, dude. Go for it!"

In the video, you see me drop my board and push at the chain. I ease my board forward underneath while lifting my feet up and over in a frantic hop. Both feet snag, the chain rattles, I am whipped forward to smash hard on my elbows.

I lie for a long time groaning and rolling while my friend films and laughs.

The adjacent street is freshly paved and slopes downhill. Without saying anything I jump back on my board and start skating. My friend yells something, but the asphalt is smooth, my board's wheels make little noise as I drift back and forth, and again there is the pleasant joy of easy, effortless movement as I bring myself to the left and then the right side of the road, flying an inch off the ground down the dark street between expensive homes with sophisticated combinations of shrubs and trees in their gardens, waiting for the pitch to mellow or to become too steep, but the perfect hill continues endlessly and I keep smiling and laughing. I tell myself to stop and go back but it feels too good, I can't stop, I'm flying, carving through powder. The warm fresh evening air slips around me and embraces me. I don't know how far I go but walking back up the hill takes a very long time, and when I make it to the parking lot with the chain between the pillars and the ripped couch in the darkness, my friend is gone.

My other friend—the one who lives in Culver City, with whom I saw the movie—wants to show me downtown. I take the train in and walk around while he's still working. When I stop in a small coffee shop I talk biscotti with the lackadaisical barista and another customer. The customer and I sit down together at the only table available. His name is William. William is originally from Los Angeles—"not a nice part", he says—but works as a chef in Indianapolis. My friend appreciates friendly and eccentric people, so I invite William to join us for drinks.

The three of us meet at the pub where Bukowski used to go. There's red leather and shiny brass lit by a dim, warm light. We sit at the bar and drink cocktails and beer and order the beef au jus sandwiches. We each catch a buzz and become happy and excited about everything we talk about. Eventually William asks if either of us has seen Skid Row before. We say no, and he takes us there.

Skid Row is unbelievable. At one point we walk past a tent and a strong smell I don't recognize. William tells me it's crack smoke. We go to a warehouse brewery in Little Tokyo, then William brings us to another bar. We walk inside and go to order. When the bartender comes over I notice that he's wearing only a speedo, and that all the other servers are likewise ripped men in thongs. The other customers are older and more overweight men sitting with their backs to the wall, and there are no women in the room.

"So, what do you think?" William asks.

"Um, it's nice."

"Can you tell it's a gay bar?"

"Yes."

"So you're gay, William?" my friend asks.

"Yeah I am. You couldn't tell?"

"The thought crossed my mind," I say.

"Are you guys gay?"

"Well, I'm not gay."

"I'm not gay either!"

The three of us laugh.

"You know, I thought you might have been gay," William says to me.

"Nope. Maybe we should have cleared this up earlier?"

"Ha. It doesn't matter either way."

"No, it doesn't."

I feel awkward and out of place in my dirty jeans and T-shirt and ripped skate shoes with my skateboard propped against the bar, for I have the impression that gay people are generally quite stylish and well put together, that they must be disgusted with my shabby appearance. That's why they keep staring, right?

We have two beers each and leave. My friend and I order an Uber. William stands waiting with us, and when the Uber comes and we drive off, I look back and see William still standing on the edge of the sidewalk where we left him, watching as we disappear down the empty Los Angeles street.

All the while that I'm putzing about Los Angeles drinking and sleeping on couches, I never stop thinking about the skatepark in Venice Beach. I skateboard everywhere I go because I know I have to go back and am therefore preparing like a boxer for a fight. I take the Surfer Express down to San Diego and bring my skateboard with me. My two friends who live there take me to a skatepark, and I skate with a special kind of motivation, trying tricks I've never tried before and landing a few of them. It feels good when my friends say they'd never seen me skate so well.

So my confidence has mostly been rebuilt by the time I return to Venice Beach, the day before I'm to leave Los Angeles.

It's half past eight in the morning when I step off the bus from Culver City. The sky is a low, gray ceiling, and the air over the roads and between the buildings is hazy with fog coming off the Pacific Ocean. The mist muffles all noise and the town and board-walk seem deserted—gone are the tourists and the crowds, the street performers and the vendors hawking T-shirts and fidget spinners. People are either alone or in pairs, walking their dogs or jogging in sweatpants, yoga pants and Lululemon thermals. These are the locals enjoying their own town before it's overrun for the day. I skateboard down the boardwalk and turn between cement beds of palm trees just beyond Muscle Beach.

The skatepark isn't empty, but it isn't crowded, either, and there aren't yet any tourists filling the peanut gallery. There are perhaps a dozen people scattered throughout the skatepark, four or five in the street section while the rest take turns in the bowls. I turn left at the entrance and go down a ramp, pop out of a quarterpipe, watch another skater drop in, wait—no one else?—drop in myself, ollie a gap I hadn't been able to hit before, ollie off a mini kicker, drop off a ledge. I turn around and go back to where I had come from, feeble stall the peak of the quarterpipe and drop back in and keep going, and something terrific happens—I start skating unconsciously as a child plays with his blocks, and the Venice Beach skatepark becomes like any other.

It becomes like any other park except when I look over its cement quarterpipes and see the beach, the sand and the waves, the people sitting on colorful canvas chairs with their toes in the surf. It's like a normal skatepark except that it's surrounded by palm trees. I can hear waves rolling and receding, smell the salt in the air, see surfers with their wetsuits peeled halfway down their bodies, their hair stuck in wet strands over their faces.

The street section isn't large, but it's complex and condensed. Ledges cascade in stair-sets, small slivers of ramps present themselves where you aren't expecting, angle-iron covers corners so that you can grind anything. I skate the euro gap, the kink ledge over the pyramid, the double ledge, the mini bank ramps on top of the plateau, the mini handrail over the stairs by the entrance, the two bowls and the snake run. I can only skate the bowls like mini-ramps—I go back and forth in a straight line, rock-to-fakie to tail-stall, 50-50 to feeble—and avoid the corners. I watch in between runs as other skaters pump around and grind the curves with fast backside 5-0s and smiths and drop back in with speed, traversing freely with power and spontaneity and aggression. I skate the bowl with impotent unoriginality, and when I skate the huge vert pool with ceramic tiles that jut out over the walls, it's all I can do to drop in and make a few turns before hauling myself out from the depths.

Most of the other skaters are thirty-something skate dudes in the bowls. Otherwise there's a pair of high schoolers filming each other trying to ollie a ten-stair without getting close, and a couple of guys my age who are there early to avoid the crowds. One of them looks homeless—his long curly hair is unwashed, as are his clothes, and the scruff on his face is long but only grows in patches. He's wearing a Baja hoodie with nothing underneath.

Baja isn't a very good skateboarder. He mostly sticks to flat-ground tricks, popping little shove-its or kickflips or ollies and rarely landing anything. Sometimes he builds up speed and rides over the ramps to drop off the ledges without ollieing. He gives me taps when I backside 50-50 the kink ledge, grinding over the top with just enough speed to make it over the kink.

"Yeah!" he yells, and smacks the tail of his board against cement.

He gives me taps perhaps because we're on the same energy level and not far off in terms of skill. Though other skaters skate a line and then wait, both Baja and I are skating hard even though we're bad. And so if one of us lands something, we're both excited.

He's sitting nearby when I try to noseslide a curved ledge. I slip out, and my board shoots to him.

"Shit, not bad, man," he says, holding out my board.

"Yeah, not great." I sit down. "You got a couple tricks, too, man."

"Ha. No, I suck. I'm getting better though."

"That's what it's all about."

"For sure. You skate here very much?"

"No, man, I'm just visiting."

"Oh."

"How about you?"

"Yeah, dude. I used to surf every day but I fucked my shoulder up and can't paddle anymore. It sucks. So now I skate."

"That's sick."

"Yeah. I skate here every morning. Kind of my morning routine. See that pier over there? I get my coffee and a breakfast sandwich and skate to the end of that pier. Then I sit down and look out over the ocean and smoke a spliff, and just chill man. Enjoy my breakfast and think about things."

"That sounds like a great way to start your day."

"Haha! Yeah, man, it is! It's my little Zen ritual, ya know? And then I'm really in the right headspace to come and skate. I'm focused."

"I know what you mean."

We become quiet sitting next to each other on the ledge. There's the sound of seagulls and sighing waves.

"I saw you drop that ledge," I say, nodding to the second stair you can skate onto and drop off, clearing the ledge below it. "Thought about trying the next one up?" I mean the three-ledge gap I had seen the guy destroying on my first visit.

"Not yet, that's fucking scary, man."

"I've been thinking about kickflipping it."

"Do it, dude!"

"I don't know."

"I think you got it."

"If I try then you gotta ollie that thing."

"Haha, ohhhhh, shit!"

"If I kickflip it, then you can definitely ollie it."

Baja is quiet for a moment.

"Aha, alright, man!"

"Let's do it."

"Now?"

"Now's as good a time as any."

We skate to the deck of the quarterpipe facing the euro gap.

"You gotta ollie the euro first," I say, "Then just point it fucking straight at that gap, man. You don't need to go too fast, just ollie a little bit."

I drop in, ollie the euro gap. Approach the drop and ollie. The board sticks to my feet, I land hard five feet below and five feet forward.

Baja slams his board into the coping and howls.

"Now your turn, dude!" I yell across the park. Baja drops in, but he doesn't make it over the euro.

"Damn, dude!"

"You were close!"

I skate back over. "I think you're gonna stomp this, man. It's gonna be sick!" Baja says. I take a deep breath and visualize flicking the right side of the board between the bolts and the nose, just in the little concave indent, catching the board and falling through the air, stomping. I visualize stomping and imagine how good it will feel.

I drop in and ollie onto the plateau. The waves crash on Venice Beach. When I reach the edge I pop and flick, the board rotates correctly but drifts away, spinning and wobbling several feet in front of me. I land on my feet and roll over the cement.

Baja is waiting for me back at the quarterpipe.

"Not bad, man. You need a couple tries to figure it out."

He drops in and fails again, I drop in and fail again, too, and the session begins.

We loop the high ledge, clearing the euro, skating the dips of the plateau, sending the drop, fetching our boards and skating back to the quarterpipe. We try five times each, and then ten. Our tries get closer and then further from success and then closer and further while the energy grows. We both want desperately to land our tricks but just as desperately want the other to land his. The outcome is uncertain—maybe we'll land it, maybe we won't—but we both know that stomping the drop is within the realm of pos-sibility, albeit requiring the best versions of ourselves. Failing to land the trick becomes tantamount to acquiescing to the universe and letting reality smother that most precious of flames: subjec-tive hope. Hope that you are something, that you are good. Hope that *they* are wrong and *you* are right, that they are wrong for not believing in you and that you are right for believing in yourself.

I *can* do this.

Was she right to stop seeing me?

I *can* land this.

Why was I not good enough?

I *can* do this.

Why do I suck?

And landing the trick becomes the most personal of inner struggles of the greatest consequence. If you don't land it—if you kickflip, catch the board high in the air and come down with it under your feet, but your back foot slips off and your front foot shoots forward and you do a split—you scream from the pain but more from the frustration that you were close but not quite good enough and that this will always be the case.

"AAAAAAHH!"

And that you were always that way before.

"AHHHHHH!""

The knowledge hurts.

"Fuck!"

And each impact on the cement hurts.

"Shit!"

But if you're lucky, your friend is there. He senses your pain, and feels his own, too.

"Ah, man! Come on, you were so close!"

"Come on, man. You're right there. This is the try. Just focus. Slow it down."

You're motivated to land it because giving up is easier when you don't have someone to let down. And suddenly I think of all the people I met in skateparks across the country. I think of the chubby dad in Morgantown, of the scooter guy in Hannibal, the crack-smoking dad in Tulsa, the priest in Farmington, the graffiti artist in Lubbock, my friends in El Paso, my co-conspirator in Apache Junction, my drinking buddy in Las Vegas.

What would they say if they were here right now?

They would say: Stomp this shit, Clint!

And I know that this is the culmination of my trip. Practically, it's the culmination of my progression as a skateboarder. But, romantically, it's the culmination of a quixotic, drunken dream, a goal that was ambiguous to myself and even more so to those I explained it to when I met them in their skateparks, though the ambiguity did little to reduce their enthusiasm or encouragement. The moment has arrived to prove that everything I have done was either meaningful or hollow.

I drop in. Ollie the euro gap.

The mist from the sea, breeze that tastes of salt.

It *had* happened. I had felt it.

I pop, flip, and the cement drops away. My board rotates beneath me. The grip tape disappears, I continue upwards and outwards. The wheels keep spinning on their trucks. The grip tape comes around—I put my feet down and stop my board at the apex of trajectory. When I do, there is no hesitation, only resolution.

I fall back to the skatepark with the board beneath my feet. When I land there is the same sensation I felt in the fourth grade when I was with Tommy and my brother at the skatepark: it was so much easier than it had been in my worried mind.

"Wooooo-hoooo!!!" Baja yells.

But I say nothing. Just turn my board and look back at Baja. He's smiling and clapping his hands.

Several tries later, Baja ollies, flies through the air, and lands back on his board below the double ledge. He rides away craning his neck to see me. And when he skates over, he doesn't even bother with a high five—he jumps off his board and gives me a hug.

About the Author

CLINT CARRICK is a writer, house painter, and skateboarder. He lives in Burlington, Vermont.